BODY WORK

The teenager's corpse lay on the floor, on its right side, facing away from the door and toward the bunkbeds against the opposite wall. Her arms were stretched out in front of her, and her legs were bent, her knees drawn up. She had short, dark curly hair. She was nude except for a pink t-shirt and white bra, which were bunched up above her small breasts, and her white gym shoes and socks. An irregular red stain pooled out on the carpet under and behind her, with a black, plate-size patch at its center.

The deputy took two careful steps into the small room and leaned forward, then involuntarily jerked his head back. The girl had been eviscerated, her intestines spilling out in front of her in a red, tangled jumble on the gold carpet.

CHILLING ACCOUNTS OF
TRUE CRIME CASES

BORN BAD   (0-7860-0274-3, $5.99)
by Bill G. Cox
Excerpts from author's personal "death diaries"!
On a lonely backroad in Waxahachie, Texas, the body of 13-year-old
Christina Benjamin is discovered, head and hands missing. She had
been mutilated, disemboweled . . . and then raped. Just a few feet away
was the badly decomposed corpse of 14-year-old James King who had
been shot to death and dumped in a ditch. All his life, good-looking
Jason Massey had a craving he needed to satisfy. His heroes were Henry
Lee Lucas and Ted Bundy and he fantasized about eating the flesh of
his classmates. One sweltering summer night in 1993, Jason became
the country's most celebrated serial killer.

SAVAGE VENGEANCE   (0-7860-0251-4, $5.99)
by Gary C. King and Don Lasseter
12 pages of shocking, never-before-published, photos!
On a sunny day in December, 1974, Charles Campbell came to rural
Clearview, Washington. He attacked Renae Ahlers Wicklund, brutally
raping her in her own home in front of her two-month-old daughter.
Sentenced to 30 years for the crime, Campbell was out on the streets
only eight years later. He'd been set free by an incompetent criminal
justice system that failed to inform Renae of his early release. Now,
she would pay the ultimate price . . .

THE EYEBALL KILLER   (0-7860-0242-5, $5.99)
by John Matthews and Christine Wickers
12 pages of never-before-published photos!
In this chilling true crime, investigative cop John Matthews exposes
the private demons that turned one man's sick fantasies into one of the
most apalling murder sprees in the annals of Texas crime. In December
1990, prostitute Mary Lou Pratt was found brutally murdered—with
her eyes cut out. And in the ensuing months, more prostitutes became
the victims of this twisted killer. The murderer was Charles Albright,
a 57-year-old devoted husband, teacher, and football coach from Dallas.
But beneath Albright's charming demeanor was a savage mutilator obsessed with the eyes of beautiful women.

*Available wherever paperbacks are sold, or order direct from the
Publisher. Send cover price plus 50¢ per copy for mailing and handling to Penguin USA, P.O. Box 999, c/o Dept. 17109, Bergenfield, NJ 07621. Residents of New York and Tennessee must
include sales tax. DO NOT SEND CASH.*

A PERFECT GENTLEMAN

Jaye Slade Fletcher

PINNACLE BOOKS

KENSINGTON PUBLISHING CORP.

Some names have been changed to protect the privacy of individuals connected to this story.

PINNACLE BOOKS are published by

Kensington Publishing Corp.
850 Third Avenue
New York, NY 10022

Pinnacle and the P logo Reg. U.S. Pat. & TM Off.

First Printing: May, 1996
10 9 8 7 6 5 4 3 2 1

Printed in the United States of America

For Margo,
my inspiration, my friend, my fan, my mentor,
my sister . . .

Part I

INDIANA

* * *

WINDY PATRICIA GALLAGHER
BORN: DECEMBER 7, 1970
MURDERED: OCTOBER 13, 1987

One

It was 7:30 A.M, October 13, 1987. Det. Lt. John Mowery of Griffith, Indiana, woke up and started what he thought would be a day like any other. He woke his twelve-year-old daughter for school. They had their regular morning routine and they went about it quietly so as not to disturb his sleeping wife. While his daughter was in the bathroom getting ready, Mowery brought in the morning *Griffith News* and leafed through the paper as he did every day, checking to see what had gone on in his town overnight.

Griffith, Indiana, just outside Gary and about forty-five minutes from Chicago, was a little town, but tucked as it was between the two sprawling city giants, Griffith had known its share of action.

All kinds of things tend to spill over from big cities into the little satellite towns that surround them—good things, sometimes, like fringe businesses. Griffith had Packaging Corporation of America, a factory that produced corrugated containers—egg cartons and the like. PCA kept a few hundred area people working. It wasn't glamorous work, but the factory provided a living wage, and that meant something, especially after the late 1970s, when the big Midwest steel mills, like Inland and U.S. Steel, and the huge refineries, like Atlantic Richfield and Amoco, in nearby Whiting, announced drastic production cuts.

Tens of thousands of blue-collar union workers, clustered

in dozens of little midwestern towns like Griffith, suffered economic disaster as the steel industries collapsed like so many dominoes and America moved away from heavy industry and toward service-oriented business instead. Some of the displaced blue-collar workers moved; some just went under and stayed under. Others found work in the small surrounding factories and got along the best they could. Their houses were small, their budgets were tight, but they made do with what they had.

Overall, Griffith was somewhat better off economically than some of its neighboring towns, where many residents lived at or below the national poverty level.

Sometimes, the big-city spillover brought bad things, like narcotics and street gangs and the mindless kind of violence that had motivated people to seek small-town life in the first place. In the late 1970s and early 1980s, Griffith, population 30,000, was a dumping ground for victims of a South Chicago auto-theft war whose rival factions took to shooting at each other during high-speed chases through town. The south end of Griffith was still undeveloped farmland at the time, and in early 1980 a South Chicago auto dealer with an unsavory reputation was found shot to death and summarily tossed into the Griffith town dump. And, as with other small towns all across the country, Griffith's cozy isolationism ended when the interstate highway system came into being in the 1950s. Little towns across America could no longer hide out as no-name dots on a map; they became instead, like Griffith, easy exits off the freeway.

Now, John Mowery lit a cigarette and sat scanning the morning *Griffith News,* skipping, as always, to the local crime round-up. A square-statured man, Mowery has a controlled military bearing belied by kind, melancholy gray eyes that see the world as it is and wish it was a better place.

His daughter was already on her way to school when Mowery left for work just before 9 A.M. The station was only minutes away, and Mowery was soon at his desk, sipping black coffee and stubbing out one cigarette after another as he attended to paperwork.

The town police station is a modern, one-story tan brick building attached to the larger Griffith City Hall next door. The station is at the same time pleasantly functional and rather stiffly security conscious. Townspeople coming through the front door into the small lobby can either ring the bell or pick up a house telephone before being buzzed through one of two steel doors into the rear offices where police business is conducted. The squad room at the rear of the station has police officers' gray lockers lining two walls. Atop each locker, like so many blue basketballs, hang the officers' riot helmets. Above them and all around are framed photos and testimonials to the department's participation in the Boy Scouts, local softball tournaments, and other civic activities. A sparkling stainless-steel sink stands against the third wall, with more than three dozen assorted coffee cups resting upside-down on the drainboard. Coffee is as much a part of a cop's daily life as are pens and notebooks, and Griffith, like police stations everywhere, had even more cups than cops.

John Mowery, as chief of Griffith's five-man detective division, had to review all his subordinates' reports as well as work his own cases, and he spent the morning buried in paperwork. It was early afternoon before he was able to step out into the rear parking lot, get into his midnight-blue unmarked squad car, and make his daily tour of the town.

School hadn't let out for the day yet, and Mowery didn't see any truants hanging around Franklin Park at the town center, their usual congregating spot. He cruised up and down a few residential side streets and then turned onto Broad Street, into Griffith's central business district. Two young women in jeans and sweaters walked along the sidewalk, one of them pushing a stroller. Mowery knew they were headed toward the Griffith grade school, where they would meet their youngsters and walk them home. He double-checked that a Griffith marked car was in its proper place at the corner, ready to cross the little kids as soon as the bell rang and they came pouring out the door.

Satisfied that everything in town was as it should be, Mowery stopped at Herb's Barber Shop in the strip mall at the corner of Elmer and 45th Street for a haircut and a chat.

Herb's son was a young police officer in a neighboring town, and Herb and Mowery were friends. The barber shop was a friendly little one-chair operation, and Griffith officers would stop by now and again, have coffee, and talk. Herb's still boasted an old-fashioned chest-type soda dispenser, and Mowery lifted the lid, deposited his thirty cents, and pulled up a bottle of his favorite drink, Kayo chocolate soda.

As Herb trimmed his hair, John and he chatted about nothing in particular: how Herb's son was doing in his new police career, what plans the town had to entertain kids for the upcoming Halloween festivities. Mowery looked idly through the plate glass window onto Elmer Street, watching the passing traffic.

A tall, dark blond, strikingly handsome young man walked past the shop. Mowery watched him walk out of sight and then thought no more about him.

His steel-gray hair neatly trimmed, Lt. Mowery left Herb's just before 3:30 and decided to drive around the rear of the strip mall and through the side streets back to the station. He cruised past the Crestview apartment complex, a long row of neat, two-story brick buildings that front on Elmer Street. Bright autumn leaves skittered, but the October sun was still warm, the lawns healthy green, the air crystal fresh.

At home that evening, Mowery changed out of his business suit into well-worn jeans and a T-shirt. He stood around in the kitchen, chatting with his family as his wife made roast chicken and mashed potatoes for dinner. Mowery tossed the salad and listened as his daughter sat at the table, telling her parents about the day's events at school and getting ready to do her homework.

Mowery had been home for about half an hour when the telephone rang. His wife answered, and with a tired sigh at the interruption, handed the phone to him. "The office," she said. "Again."

It was hard holding onto any meaningful private family time when your husband was always on call, and the Mowery marriage was in deep trouble over this issue. John couldn't give any less than his full heart and soul to his job, and his wife, understandably, wanted more of his time and attention at home with his family.

Mowery took the phone with a "What-can-I-do?" shrug. Cradling the receiver against his shoulder, he reached into a kitchen drawer and pulled out a notepad and pen. The department wouldn't call him at home unless it was important. He noted the time on the kitchen wall clock: 7:40 P.M. Then he answered, "Mowery here."

"Lieutenant Mowery?" It was Johnson, the night dispatcher. "There's been a homicide over at the Crestview apartments, Lieutenant. On North Elmer Street, apartment B-7. It looks like a young girl."

As he pulled out of his driveway, his dinner still untouched, Mowery couldn't know that for the next three months, he wouldn't spend more than five hours at a time, awake or asleep, at home with his family. By then, just in time for Christmas, his marriage would be over.

Two

An unmarked detective car and a patrol sergeant's marked squad car were already angled in front of the apartment building when Mowery pulled up thirteen minutes later. Sgt. Ken LaBuda was waiting at the top of the raised first-floor landing. The door to the apartment on the right, B-7, stood open.

"What've we got, Ken?" Mowery asked.

Sgt. LaBuda took a deep breath and closed his eyes a moment, exhaling. "It's a young girl. In the bedroom, and John, it's real bad."

LaBuda told Mowery that the two detectives, Steve Markovich and Karl Grimmer, had looked around inside, but that all of them had been careful to touch nothing. The detectives were out now, said LaBuda, "knocking on doors," checking to see who else was in the building, and whether anyone knew or had heard anything.

Steve Markovich had been with the Griffith detective division for nearly seven years. He was an accountant and something of a math wizard who went about his job in an orderly, methodical fashion. Karl Grimmer, his young partner, had just been appointed a detective six months earlier, but he was a sharp young man and Mowery knew Grimmer would watch and learn, following his more experienced partner's lead in whatever they came across.

Mowery went into the apartment, Sgt. LaBuda just behind him.

The lieutenant's first impression was that the place was very neat and very small. Schoolbooks lay on the floor near the couch, mail was stacked on the television set, and a single half-filled water glass stood on the octagonal oak end table next to the couch.

Mowery took a quick glance into the tiny kitchen. There was a pizza on the table with two slices missing. Also on the table was a small brown leather purse with a long shoulder strap. A man's faded blue denim jacket was draped over the back of a kitchen chair.

Mowery stepped to the bedroom door and looked in. Then he drew in his breath. "Oh, no," he whispered. "Dear God, no."

It was obviously a young girl's room. In fact, it was set up to accommodate two girls. Twin mattresses lay at right angles on opposite sides of the room, a matching dresser next to each bed.

Beige drapes closed off the double window facing onto Elmer Street. On the white walls were taped posters of the latest batch of handsome young movie stars, and a big Garfield poster. Two red-and-white crêpe-paper pom-poms lay on the floor, and a heart-shaped green satin pillow was propped against the wall. A curling iron lay on one dresser among scattered hair combs, brushes, and a few pieces of plastic costume jewelry.

She lay on her back, her body half-sprawled on the mattress, her blue eyes open, staring up at nothing. Her arms were stretched back behind her head. Pooled blood haloed the sheets around her body. Her bra and her yellow-and-white-striped shirt were bunched up around her neck. Strips of cloth bound her wrists and were tied together in a knot. Another strip of cloth garroted her neck and the lower part of her chin like a gag that had fallen down. Her lower body was nude, except for the white socks on her feet. Jeans, yellow underpants, and a pair of white boots lay near her. She had been stabbed many times in the throat and chest.

One long vertical gash had opened the right side of her abdomen, and thick coils of her intestines protruded. She appeared to have been disemboweled.

Mowery and LaBuda stood framed in the doorway. "Why?" Mowery groaned. "Jesus Christ, Ken, she's just a kid!"

"I know." LaBuda nodded. "I know."

The two men backed out of the bedroom and out of the apartment. In the hall, LaBuda explained that he had called the crime lab and they were on the way. A small town like Griffith couldn't support a full-service crime lab, and as in many other Northwest Indiana towns, Griffith called on the sheriff's county lab at Crown Point, six miles to the southeast. While they waited for the lab technicians, Mowery radioed for his detectives to return to the hallway outside B-7.

Markovich and Grimmer came into the lobby a few moments later and filled him in on what they had so far.

The dead girl's name was Windy Patricia Gallagher, and she was sixteen years old. Her fifteen-year-old sister, Christine, known as "Chrissy," had found her at about 7:15 P.M. Chrissy had run out of the apartment and gone screaming upstairs to a female neighbor in apartment C-7.

"My sister! My sister!" Chrissy screamed over and over. "Help me!"

"Chrissy, calm down!" the woman said, holding on to the girl's flailing arms. "What about your sister? What happened?"

"My sister's cold," Chrissy moaned. "She's so cold."

The woman yelled to her husband to call the police, and then she went downstairs and saw Windy for herself. Chrissy, upstairs, called her father, Patrick. The girls' parents had recently separated; they lived in apartment B-7 with their mother, April, who was still at work.

Patrick Gallagher could make no sense of what Chrissy was saying. She kept telling him, in a robotic voice, that

"Windy was cold," and "Windy was asleep." Finally, he told Chrissy just to stay where she was, that he'd be right there. He called April at work, and both parents rushed home.

After he listened to his detectives' account, Mowery left instructions with them that no one was to enter the apartment again until the crime lab arrived. He went out to his squad to get a steno pad, then climbed the stairs to talk to Chrissy Gallagher. The layout in C-7 was identical to that of the apartment below. Chrissy was hunched forward on the couch, the neighbors supporting her from either side. Mowery was immediately struck by how closely the fifteen-year-old resembled her murdered sister. He introduced himself to the neighbors and motioned for them to let him sit next to Chrissy. Then he sat down and explained to the distraught girl who he was and that he was going to have to ask her some questions.

Chrissy nodded, but she was so convulsed with gulping sobs that her entire body was shaking. Mowery held her hand awhile and spoke softly, hushing and calming her until she could bring herself under control and make her thoughts and voice work again. Her fingernails bit sharply into his palms. Slowly, little by little, Mowery was able to piece together the day's sequence of events.

April Gallagher and her daughters, Windy and Chrissy, had gotten up about 6 that morning, April getting ready for work and Windy and Chrissy getting dressed for school. April had left the apartment about 6:40 to head for the first of her two jobs, as a deli clerk at Banner's, a grocery store. She would leave there around 1:30 in the afternoon and head right to her second job, as a factory worker at Owens-Illinois. The girls had left the apartment together about five minutes after their mother.

Chrissy said that when she and Windy had left the apartment, she'd locked both the doorknob lock and the deadbolt above it. Then both girls had walked together to Calumet

High School, about twenty minutes away. Each went about
her own schedule, and they saw each other in the halls between classes. Chrissy said that she was the manager of the
Calumet High girls' swim team, and she'd stayed after
school for swimming practice.

Windy left school as usual at 2, according to her sister,
but then, when she got home, she realized that her keys
wouldn't open the deadbolt lock. Chrissy said that Windy
had had trouble with that key before, but that the girls
hadn't thought about it when they'd left the apartment that
morning. Windy had gone back to the school and exchanged
keys with Chrissy and then walked home again. Chrissy
told Mowery she thought it had been about 2:40 when
Windy had left Calumet High the second time, headed for
home.

Chrissy told Mowery that she'd called home around 4,
wanting to remind Windy that if she went out, she shouldn't
lock the deadbolt. No one answered the phone and Chrissy
tried again around 6. Still no answer.

After the swim meet, Chrissy's father had picked her up
at school and driven her home. They'd sat in his car in front
of the building for maybe twenty minutes, talking about
Chrissy's various school activities. Then, she'd gone upstairs
into the apartment and turned on the lights and the television. No one was around and Chrissy assumed her sister
had gone out somewhere. She thought it was odd, though,
that the drapes in the living room were closed. Whoever
got home first usually opened the drapes and watched for
the other sister. They usually didn't close the drapes until
everybody was home and it started to get dark outside.

Chrissy went back downstairs for the mail and then put
a frozen pizza in the oven and sat down to watch *Who's
the Boss?* She watched TV for a while and then had a couple of pieces of pizza. She was beginning to wonder where
her sister was and whether Windy had, in fact, come home

after school, changed clothes, and gone out again. She got up and wandered into the bedroom to check.

As she got to this point in her story, Chrissy started to hyperventilate again. "It's okay, Chrissy," Mowery said, his voice low and soothing. "Take your time, there's no need to hurry."

Downstairs, Dets. Markovich and Grimmer were in the hallway, guarding the open door to B-7. Off-duty Griffith police officers who'd heard about the murder wandered into the apartment building one after another, asking what they could do to help. Markovich sent them out to scour the neighborhood and to start taking down the license plate numbers of every car in the Crestview complex's rear lot. Just behind the rear parking lot the Elgin, Joliet & Eastern Railroad tracks ran along a raised embankment, and Markovich told one patrol officer to take his flashlight and walk the tracks a mile in each direction.

"If you come across anything, anything at all that looks out of place," Markovich told him, "don't touch it. Just stay there, radio back here, and we'll get the crime lab guys out there."

Just then, a young couple came into the building and stopped, looking up at the detectives. They said they lived in the apartment just across the hall and asked what was going on, why were there police cars all over the place? What had happened in apartment B-7? Karl Grimmer looked to his partner, but Markovich wouldn't answer their questions. Instead, he asked some questions of his own. What were their names? How long had they lived there, and what time did they leave home today? The guy answered for both of them, and Karl Grimmer, as he listened and watched, figured out why his more experienced partner wasn't giving anything away.

Both of these neighbors were obviously drugged on something. The young woman glanced around listlessly and looked like she was listening to some kind of mystical mu-

sic inside her head. The guy's pupils were huge, and he
jiggled and twitched strangely. Grimmer glanced over at his
partner. Markovich's dark expression said volumes about
his opinion of these two, who claimed not to have been
home all day. Markovich took down their information,
pointedly ignoring the guy's repeated questions, and then
suggested they go into their own apartment. They did.

Upstairs, Mowery was going over his notes, confirming
with Chrissy that he had his times and facts accurate.

Suddenly, high-pitched shrieking could be heard downstairs,
and Mowery asked the neighbors to stay with Chrissy. He
went downstairs and did his best, along with Grimmer and
Markovich, to comfort April Gallagher, who had just come
running into the building. The distraught mother kept trying
to get past the detectives, insisting she had to go into the
apartment; she had to see Windy. But the detectives knew she
didn't need to see what they'd seen in her daughters' bedroom.
They stood talking with her, convincing her that she should
stay out in the hall for just a bit.

Chrissy, upstairs, heard her mother and went running out
into the hall. The two met halfway up the stairs and held
each other. The detectives stood helplessly by, thinking of
their own families and knowing nothing they could say
could ease these terrible moments. Patrick Gallagher arrived
along with his brother, Robert, and April's mother. Then the
crime lab van pulled up out in front. Mowery told Grimmer
and Markovich to take the Gallaghers upstairs and start taking statements. He would stay with the lab technicians while
they went through the apartment.

The lab techs were Ron Lach, whom Mowery knew from
many previous cases together, and a young technician who
introduced himself as Bud Matthews. The three men walked
into apartment B-7 and stood at the doorway to the girls'
bedroom, looking at what had until a few hours ago been
a beautiful blue-eyed teenage girl. Lach studied the crime
scene for a few long moments. Then he turned to his young

partner. "No offense, Bud," he said, "but for this one, I need Mike Reilly here."

Matthews agreed, and they radioed their dispatch center to page lab technician Reilly on his beeper and ask him to report to the scene, even though it was his day off. Mowery didn't say anything—this was the technicians' territory, after all—but he was secretly relieved. Lach and Reilly had worked together on hundreds of Mowery's cases and he knew the two to be an absolutely seamless team.

While they waited for Reilly, Ron Lach told his young partner to go out to the van and bring in the cameras, as well as his bag of evidence-collecting paraphernalia. Lach carried his gear around in a white canvas newsboy's delivery bag. His job often took him into strange places: junkyards, overgrown fields, flooded basements, railroad yards, and the like. He had worked out his own methodology years before, and he found it most efficient and convenient to sling his canvas bag over his shoulder and then head in to the job.

Lach took out his spiral notebook and began making pre-liminary notes. One of the things he needed from Mowery was a list of the names of everybody who had been inside B-7 since the murder had been discovered. The technicians would have to take fingerprints of everyone, as well as of all the family and any friends they could name who had ever been in the apartment. That way, they would be able to identify, by process of elimination, any fingerprints in the apartment that couldn't be accounted for.

Mike Reilly pulled up in his car a few minutes later, and Lach filled him in on the type of crime scene they had. The technicians put on Latex surgical gloves and went in to start their examination.

First, they had Matthews photograph the entire apartment, just as it was, before they touched anything. Then Matthews took dozens of photos of Windy's body from every angle, while Mike Reilly pointed out items of possible evidence and Ron Lach kept running audio notes and commentary on what they were doing. A dozen times or more, one man would say to the others: "What do you think? What about this here? What do you think?"

At one point, Ron Lach stood back a bit next to Mowery while they watched Matthews photographing Windy's body.

"You know, John," Lach said, "she looks almost . . . well, *posed*. Like maybe the guy was putting together a stage show, or something. A stage show from hell."

Three

Each of the detectives who stood staring down at Windy Gallagher's body was struck by the same inescapable conclusion: the murderer had concentrated his attack on Windy's stomach. Why? This had all the characteristics of a psychosexual attack, from her unclothed body to the fact that a killer would likely have no other motive to make his way into an apartment in broad daylight and murder a sixteen-year-old schoolgirl; the victim herself spoke of her own innocence. She wasn't a rich old aunt, she wasn't anybody's cutthroat business partner threatening to bring in the IRS—she was just a sweet sixteen-year-old schoolgirl. Usually, a psychosexual murderer will wreak destruction on his victim's sexual organs, but that wasn't the case here.

True, there were a number of shallow, tentative puncture wounds in the area of Windy's throat. But her breasts and genitals were unmarked, and the obvious focus of the killer's insane rage had been the girl's abdomen. *Why?*

The police officers threw ideas back and forth quietly among themselves as they worked. It had always been a joke between the technicians and John Mowery that whenever the lieutenant would ask their opinion about something on a case, they would reply: "You're supposed to be the detective, you figure it out." But none of the men brought up their little joke now.

Lake County coroner Malamatos arrived and made the official pronouncement of the death of Windy Patricia Gal-

lagher at 8:07 P.M. The office of coroner is an appointed
position in Lake County, and the duties are largely sym-
bolic. The pathologists who actually do the autopsies work
out of the Lake County crime lab. The autopsy itself would
be done at a local funeral home.

There was blood all around Windy's body, and the technicians had Matthews make a careful photographic record
of the stain patterns. He also took close-up photos of the
green satin pillow, which had blood spatters on it, and of
the drapes, which had small smears of what appeared to be
blood in the lower right corner.

"We've got medium-velocity spatters here, and over
here," Lach said, pointing, as his partner moved in closer
to take photos.

"And? What does that mean?" Mowery asked from the
doorway.

"Blood spatters are loosely grouped into three catego-
ries." Lach talked as he continued to stoop and inspect every
aspect of the crime scene. " 'Low velocity' means the blood
was just dripped, like if you cut your finger and you just
stand there and let the blood fall. You get medium velocity
when you move in a fast, flinging motion."

"So there's a 'high velocity,' too?" Mowery asked.

The evidence technician nodded. "That's what happens
when a bullet passes through you and the blood hits the
wall at tremendous speed. There're no high-velocity spatters
here. No gunshots."

Mowery watched from the doorway as the techs got down
on their hands and knees and examined the floor in a grid
pattern, using tweezers and small coin envelopes to collect
hairs and fibers. On the carpet near Windy's body they
found a small earring. It was a tiny gold ball with a hanging
letter "F" dangling from it. The techs recorded and collected the earring in an evidence envelope. They also collected a small piece of what looked like a broken-off human

fingernail and a crumpled piece of a blue Extra sugar-free gum wrapper.

As they were going over the bedroom, the technicians pointed out to Mowery that the strip of cloth around Windy's neck had obviously been torn from her comforter, which lay bunched on the floor, partially covering her left leg. The material was white, with a pattern of tiny blue flowers and green leaves. The material binding her hands together was different, white with no pattern, and looked like cotton sheeting. Bloodstains splotched the part of the fitted sheet near Windy's body, including a stain in the exact shape of a wide, curved knife blade.

The small area of what looked like blood on the lower right-hand corner of the bedroom drape bothered Ron Lach. "This isn't a spatter like the others," he said, peering only inches from the stain but careful not to touch it. "This is a smear."

"What does that mean exactly?" Mowery asked.

"A spatter would have been flung against the wall. This is a smear—somebody with blood on himself brushed up against this drape."

He and Mowery stood looking at it, speculating between themselves, and trying to reenact the killer's movements in the room, the sequence of events. What did he do first? What was his next movement? That corner of the drape was maybe eight feet in a straight line from where Windy's body lay sprawled on her mattress. And the apparent bloodstain was about two feet up from the floor.

"Maybe he was still on his hands and knees," Mowery speculated. "I mean, after he killed her."

"Could be," said Ron Lach, "and then he crawled over to the window, pushed the drapes aside with his hand, and looked out to see if anybody was watching."

The lab techs continued working their way through the apartment for nearly two hours, collecting samples and photographing and sketching everything before they actually

touched Windy's body. Then they took a clean light green
sheet and spread it out on the bedroom floor. They carefully
lifted Windy's body and placed it on the sheet, wrapping it
tightly around her to preserve any trace evidence or foreign
fibers on her body.

Mowery walked through the apartment with the lab techs
as they dusted everything for fingerprints. In the living
room, they photographed the half-full water glass on the
end table. Mowery had gone upstairs and checked with
April and Chrissy, who both said they didn't remember the
glass being there that morning when they'd left the apartment. Mike Reilly put all five fingers into the glass, lifted
it up, and poured out the water without touching the outside
of the glass. With his fingers still inside the glass, he dusted
the outside with black fingerprint powder. Mowery was
standing next to him, watching the process.

"Ho, ho," murmured Reilly, "what have we here?"

They looked at each other when six clear prints, in two
sets of three each, appeared on the smooth surface of the
glass. It was collected along with everything else. Whatever
evidence the technicians garnered that might have bloodstains on it they wrapped carefully in paper. They never put
blood samples in plastic, since blood wrapped in plastic
would immediately begin to heat up and decompose.

People from Burns-Kish Funeral Home arrived and removed Windy's body at 10:17 P.M. Mowery checked first
to make sure the family was still behind closed doors upstairs, so they wouldn't have to watch her being carried out.
Her remains would be kept at the funeral home awaiting
the next day's autopsy. The lab techs collected the fitted
bedroom sheet with the bloody knife imprint. Then they cut
out a large square of the bedroom carpet where Windy's
body had lain and took that, too, out to their evidence van.

On Windy's dresser, along with her hair combs and ribbons, the technicians found a small datebook, which they
dusted for fingerprints and then turned over to Lt. Mowery.

Mowery put on a pair of the Latex surgical gloves and sat in the kitchen to read.

It was obvious that Windy had used the notebook as a combination scheduler and diary. She was a pom-pom dancer for the Calumet High Warriors football and basketball teams. Her team called itself the "Warriorettes." Windy also worked after school several afternoons a week at a nearby McDonald's, so her calendar was pretty full. She kept a daily running total of how much money she was earning at McDonald's, and on certain pages she had penned in little remarks about her feelings or whether that day at school had been particularly good or bad. Mowery turned to the October 13 page. Windy did not have cheerleader practice scheduled, and she wasn't working after school at McDonald's.

From the hall, Mike Reilly heard Mowery swear under his breath.

"Something, Lieutenant?" Reilly asked.

Mowery shook his head and raised the diary so the evidence tech could see what Windy's entry was for today. She had written in, in her round, neat schoolgirl handwriting, "Tuesday! My no stress day!"

As they were processing the kitchen, Mike Reilly reached into the pocket of the faded blue denim jacket and pulled out an Indiana driver's license. It belonged to one Danny Jeffries. Mowery took the license upstairs, where April and Chrissy told them that Danny was Windy's boyfriend. Chrissy remembered that Windy had been wearing Danny's jacket when she'd left Calumet High that afternoon. Mowery told Grimmer and Markovich to send a car to find Jeffries and have him picked up and taken into the station. Mowery would meet them there as soon as the lab techs were finished.

Chrissy had told the detectives that the brown purse on the kitchen table was hers. Windy, she said, always carried a small gray clutch purse with her school ID, a few dollars, and some pictures in it. The detectives searched the entire apartment, but Windy's purse wasn't there, and this seemed particularly significant to both Mowery and Reilly. Both had teenage daughters, and in their experience, wherever a teenage girl was, her purse was going to be right there with her. It seemed highly unlikely that Windy had simply forgotten her purse at school, or left it somewhere on her way home. Where was it?

The lab techs went over the kitchen next, dusting for prints and collecting samples of anything that might later prove to be evidentiary. There were a few dishes and utensils in the kitchen sink, which April Gallagher, from the hallway, said were the family's breakfast dishes. On the kitchen counter next to the sink, the lab techs printed and then sealed and collected a brown-handled kitchen knife. They noted traces of a reddish-brown stain on the knife blade, which they would later test at the lab. They would also match it against the bloody imprint of a knife blade on Windy's bedsheet.

Everyone was exhausted by now, and the technicians had collected more than enough to get started on. Mowery wanted to get back to the station and sit down with his detectives to compare notes and see what everybody had so far. He needed to coordinate everybody's efforts to make sure that one area of investigation was not being duplicated while another was being missed altogether.

He went upstairs to talk with the Gallaghers for a few minutes and to make sure the family had somewhere to stay. They decided to move in temporarily with one of Patrick's relatives in Hammond, and everyone gave Mowery his or her keys to apartment B-7.

"I can't go out there," Chrissy said from the window, meaning the street. "I'm not going out there." The others joined her and looked down. Hundreds of people had gathered along the parkway in front of the building. Across the street, whole families were standing together, the little kids skipping around, their parents looking up toward the apartment. Cars were jammed every which way up and down the block, and the whole front of the building was lit by portable spotlights. A dozen or more reporters milled around. Heavy black electrical cables snaked out from the television vans to loudly humming generator trucks parked haphazardly on sidewalks and lawns.

Mowery told the Gallaghers to wait until all the police officers and lab techs went outside and pulled away. He knew the reporters would follow them to the police station, hoping to get more information. The gawking crowds would also begin to drift away when they saw all the squad cars leave. The Gallaghers could then get out quietly without being accosted.

Downstairs, Mowery made sure all his men and their equipment were out. Then he locked the door to B-7, including the deadbolt, with April Gallagher's keys. He sealed the door with bright yellow crime-scene tape, and then, after everybody else was outside, he put tiny pieces of clear cellophane tape in the corners of the door. It was a quirk, he knew, but he thought of it as extra insurance. When he returned to open the door the next day, as long as his hidden tape was still in place, there could be no question of contamination of the crime scene.

Danny Jeffries was already at the Griffith police station when Mowery got there, and the teenager was obviously scared and upset. Word had spread from phone to phone across the town that the "Gallagher girl" had been killed. Danny had heard about it even before the Lake County police had come by his house to pick him up.

Mowery and Markovich took Danny Jeffries from the squad room, where he was being guarded by a Lake County police officer, into their office. At seventeen years old, Jeffries was technically an adult, but still the detectives allowed his parents to accompany him to the station. The Jeffries family now waited in the lobby. Young detective Karl Grimmer stood at the doorway, both to guard against Jeffries's escape and to watch Mowery and Markovich at work. Mowery read the terrified teenager his rights, and Markovich repeated them. Then they sat down to ask questions and to talk.

Within ten minutes, Mowery and Markovich looked at each other, the same knowledge in both men's eyes: this boy hadn't killed anybody. Danny had left school with a group of friends, who'd then seen him walking into his house. He'd been home with his family ever since. When Mowery asked about his relationship with Windy, Danny's shocked face told them what they'd already guessed. The boy had assumed the murdered "Gallagher girl" was Chrissy—not Windy, his girlfriend. He broke into tears, and as soon as the detectives finished getting his formal statement, they walked the grieving teenager out to the lobby and released him to his family.

Mowery gathered all his investigators around the long rectangular table in the station's conference room. He appointed Det. Mike Teeling to begin a running file of all movements on the case. Then, each man around the table spoke in turn, laying out who he'd interviewed, what addresses he'd been to, and where he needed to go back for follow-up the next day.

Markovich said he definitely wanted to talk some more with the drugged-up young couple who lived across the hall from B-7. Maybe by tomorrow they'd have slept it off. The lab techs would be working all the next day, Wednesday, at their lab in Crown Point. But they promised to stay in touch with Mowery throughout the day, keeping him up to date on test results as they became available.

It took some time to put everyone's activities in context. When it was done, an air of gloom settled around the long table as each man came to the same realization: so far, they had absolutely nothing.

* * *

It was nearly 4 A.M. when Mowery finally headed home. The streets were deserted, the businesses were closed up tight, the homes of Griffith were dark. He was exhausted, but many emotions were churning around inside him. John Mowery the husband and father felt for the grief that April, Patrick, and Chrissy Gallagher were experiencing and would continue to experience for a long time, maybe forever. The human being in him recoiled in horror at what had been done to Windy Gallagher. That first sight of her sprawled, violated body had burned a toxic picture in his mind that he couldn't erase.

But John Mowery was also a police officer. It was what he knew, what he did, what he was very good at, and now, driving home alone in the dark, he struggled to put the grief and the horror aside, to make himself think and feel and react as a police officer. Griffith was his town, Windy Gallagher was one of his people, and it had been his job to keep her and everybody else in Griffith safe. Whoever had done this terrible thing to Windy had violated all that Mowery worked for and believed in, and he was enraged. "Who could do something so . . . savage?" he kept asking himself. "And, for God's sake, *why?*" He let the cold rage wash over him, and it was almost a relief.

Later, unable to sleep, Mowery sat in the dark on the edge of his bed, smoking one cigarette after another and trying to put a name to the queasy fear he was feeling.

Next to him, his wife stirred. "John, what is it?"

"What if I never get this guy?" Mowery whispered. "What if I never even find out who did this? I couldn't stand it. It would destroy me."

Four

Det. Karl Grimmer leaped out of bed when the alarm clock went off at dawn on Wednesday morning. His wife, Becky, was still asleep next to him, and he went into the bathroom quietly so as not to wake her or their three young children in the next bedroom.

As he showered, Grimmer shook the sleep from his mind and tried to get his thoughts in order for what he figured was going to be a godawful day.

Becky had been waiting up for him when he'd gotten home at 3:30 A.M., and they'd sat at the kitchen table, talking. Actually, he'd talked and Becky had listened. As he told her about the Windy Gallagher homicide, he'd tried to put into words, for Becky and for himself, just how terrible had been the scene in the bedroom of apartment B-7. Karl and Becky Grimmer were not only husband and wife, they were best friends, and he had never felt more grateful for that. Windy Gallagher's was only the second homicide Karl Grimmer had worked since becoming a Griffith detective in March. The first had been the shooting of a woman's new boyfriend by her ex-boyfriend just a month before. But neither that case, nor anything he had ever imagined, could have prepared the sincere and good-hearted young detective for what he'd seen that night.

On top of facing the most important day yet of his new career as a detective, Karl Grimmer found himself in the middle of a personal business crisis, too. He had started a lawn service business, Perfection-Cut Lawn Service, a couple of years before, and he now had fourteen people working for him, including a number of teenagers. The teens had been slacking off over the summer, not showing up for jobs and doing sloppy, half-hearted work even when they did report to a job site. Grimmer was up to his neck in complaining customers.

When he'd come in at 3:30 A.M., Becky had told him that one of his trucks had a broken part and he was going to have to fix it in the morning before he went in to the station; otherwise, his crews wouldn't be able to go out that day at all and what was already an impossibly bad business situation was going to get even worse.

No one was around when he got to the service garage around 7 A.M., and he figured he'd just have time to fix the truck, clean himself up a bit, and get over to the police station by 9 A.M., when he knew Lt. Mowery and probably everyone else on the force would be there, waiting. Mowery, in the early morning hours, had told his exhausted detectives to try and get at least a few hours of sleep and then be in no later than 9 A.M. But Karl Grimmer knew that the lieutenant would be at the station long before that, already at work on the Gallagher case, and would appreciate his detectives showing enough initiative and concern to report early, too.

Grimmer idolized Mowery and thought him the most single-minded, implacably thorough police officer he knew. He hated having to waste time fixing his stupid truck at a critical time like this.

Grimmer rushed around the service garage, but he was so tired and so stressed, he couldn't make his hands work right. He kept dropping his tools and scraping his knuckles. He realized he was going to have to use a drill to unscrew a fractured bolt, and he hurriedly fixed a new bit on the hand drill and started to work. Suddenly, the drill bit, which he hadn't tightened properly, flew off with the speed of a bullet and hit him right in the eye.

Grimmer screamed with pain and staggered back, holding

his hands over his eye, nearly faint with the pain. His eye immediately began weeping clear, sticky fluid, and the lid was quickly swelling shut. He knew he had to get to the hospital fast.

At St. Margaret's Hospital, the emergency room doctor told the young detective that he had scratched his cornea, but luckily, the drill bit hadn't actually pierced the eye's protective membrane. Grimmer was to apply antiseptic salve every few hours, and then follow up in a few days with his own doctor.

It was nearly 11 A.M. when Grimmer finally pulled up in front of the police station, almost two hours late. He was glad the damage to his eye hadn't been any worse, but it hurt like fire and the inside of his eyelid felt like it was sprinkled with broken glass. He dreaded having to walk into the station, and he was right.

Mowery was smoldering. He stood in the detective room doorway staring at him, waiting for an explanation. It was one of those dreadful moments when anything you can say in your own defense would just come off sounding lame. It was only the evidence of Grimmer's puffy, weepy eye that saved him from the dressing-down he knew Mowery had waiting for him. As it was, Mowery just nodded at Grimmer's apologies and asked shortly if he was going to be okay to work that day. When he said he was, Mowery motioned him into the conference room.

Every detective on the force, and every uniformed officer who was on duty, who had voluntarily come in, or who could be reached and called in, had been put to work on the Gallagher case. Rumors had been flying around town that Windy Gallagher had been killed as a sacrifice in some sort of Satanic ritual, and the telephones at the Griffith police station were going berserk. Mothers wanted to know if their daughters were safe on the streets, or if there was some kind of underground Satanic cult at work in Griffith. Someone had phoned in early that morning to point out that the murder had happened on the thirteenth, a significant date for Satanists. Someone else wanted to be sure the police knew that Halloween, just two weeks away, was the most high holy day of the year for Satanists. Maybe Windy had been murdered as some sort of "practice session," and maybe somebody in town was going to be killed every day until Halloween. The *Griffith News* had rushed a small article about the murder into print. In the article, the coroner said that Windy's body was a "horrible sight," and that the murder was "the worst I've ever seen."

The rumors were flying fast and heavy, and so far, the Griffith police had no answers to give. They couldn't just discount the Satanist theory, wild as it sounded, because they didn't have any idea yet who had killed Windy, or why. Mowery had the department's civilian administrative staff answering every call and logging every tip, every suspicion that came in. Every phone line in the station was tied up, and as soon as the operators hung up with one call, the phone immediately rang with another.

Mowery assigned Grimmer to go to Calumet High to interview Windy's school friends and work with school administrators to put together any information that could be helpful. Special counselors were already at the school to help students deal with the crisis of one of their own having been brutally murdered.

As Grimmer waited in the school's administrative offices, he could feel the level of barely controlled hysteria among the huddling teenagers like an electrical current that zinged from one group to another. "Did you hear she was . . . ?" "No! What I heard was that . . ." No one was talking about anything else, and as rumors were spread up and down the halls, they grew and began to gain an air of legitimacy among students in the way that something repeated often enough will begin to take on the authority of fact. The kids were saying that Windy's living heart had been cut out of her body and eaten, and it seemed everyone now knew "for a fact" at least one other student who was into the occult and who had been acting weird lately. Grimmer knew that just his presence alone was enough to turn up the tension at the school, that he was physical proof that the murder had really happened. He determined to keep his voice and demeanor matter-of-fact as he set about interviewing Windy's friends and acquaintances one at a time.

Windy's classmates had a lot to say about her, but nothing that might help find her killer. She was popular, smart, and artistically gifted, and wonderfully, outrageously funny. The kids told Det. Grimmer dozens of anecdotes about Windy's doings in and around school, and one after another, they tried to get Grimmer to let slip with some piece of factual information about her murder—something, *anything,* that they could then take back out into the halls as an inside scoop. Grimmer, like any experienced police officer, asked everything but gave nothing.

As the day wore on, different detectives were tracking down information in different directions. Steve Markovich headed back to the Crestview apartments to see if the Gallaghers' next-door neighbors, having slept off their recreational chemicals, would make any more sense today than they had the night before. They did.

The young woman was looking ragged and ill-used this morning, but she had apparently turned off her mystical head-music of the night before. Clothes and cats and overflowing ashtrays littered every flat surface in the apartment. When the young woman offered Markovich a seat, he said he'd prefer to stand, thank you.

She said that she and her boyfriend were into the occult and liked to hang around with a few other like-minded friends. But, she said, that didn't mean they were Satanists or went around killing little girls. It was more, she explained to the skeptical detective, like "communing with unseen universal forces. Getting in touch with the powerful spiritual vibrations that surround us all. Stuff like that."

"Uh-huh, right," said Det. Markovich. "So, where were you and your friends yesterday afternoon and evening?"

She and her boyfriend gave Markovich a detailed summary of their movements up to the time Windy was found murdered. They had left their Crestview apartment with a couple of friends in the late morning.

And those friends? Who were they?

She named Jerry Moffat and Stan Bridges, two local Griffith men who were well known to the police. Bridges was a hardscrabble, no-account biker type. He lived in a little trailer out at the edge of town and eked out a living of sorts as a two-bit dope dealer. He favored thunderous Harley-Davidson motorcycles, beer by the case, a wardrobe of black leather and silver chains, and a major bad-ass attitude.

Moffat, the other member of this communal group, liked to stride up and down the streets of Griffith deliberately decked out to scare the townsfolk. He was tall and skinny as a wraith, with long, filthy strings of mouse-brown hair framing his skeletal face—a twentieth-century midwestern Rasputin. Jerry was never seen without his trenchcoat flapping around him. He didn't work but lived off his elderly grandmother. Police presumed it was from her that he'd gotten what little money he ever had to buy his dope with. Moffat never seemed too securely anchored to reality in the best of times. He could sometimes be found standing in the middle of the street, waving his arms, exhorting the heavens about one divine injustice or another, his trenchcoat flapping around him, his eyes glittering with otherworldly zeal.

Markovich concluded his interview with the Gallaghers' neighbors and headed back to the police station with two pretty solid suspects in mind.

Meanwhile, crime lab technician Mike Reilly phoned in from Crown Point. He told Mowery that of the six fingerprints he'd lifted from the water glass in the Gallaghers' living room, three were Windy's. The other three did not match any of the family's or officers' prints.

It was the first promising lead in the case. The men theorized that Windy had gotten a glass of water for somebody, which accounted for her fingerprints. She'd handed the glass to that person, who'd taken the glass, leaving his prints on it, and then set it on the end table. This imaginary scene, as they talked it through, "read" well—that is, it offered a logical sequence of events that explained the physical evidence. It also offered a first possible glimpse into the method used by the murderer to entice his way into the apartment: he'd simply asked for a glass of water. Could he have been feigning illness?

It was all still rudimentary speculation on the detectives' part, but it was a first tiny step in the all-important reconstruction of events.

Reilly also said that they had pretty much eliminated the kitchen knife with the reddish-brown stains as the murder weapon. The stains proved to be tomato sauce, probably from Chrissy's pizza. No blood was found on the knife, and it did not match the distinctive, wide-bladed knife imprint on Windy's bedsheet.

After Reilly finished telling Mowery what he had so far, he said that Ron Lach was waiting to talk next. Lach got on the phone. It still bothered him that what looked like bloodstains had been found on the lower right corner of Windy's bedroom drapes, and he talked to Mowery about getting back into the apartment and dusting the entire bedroom for prints. If the killer had crawled on his hands and knees to the window to look outside, Lach speculated, he might well have stood up there and touched the wall to brace himself. The technicians hadn't seen any visible prints on the white walls, but Lach wasn't about to accept defeat so easily. He gave Mowery a rough outline of some rather complicated techniques he wanted to apply to the walls of the Gallagher apartment. Mowery listened, afraid to hope, but ready to try anything. He agreed to meet the technician at the apartment on Thursday morning.

Five

Evidence tech Ron Lach was waiting in front of the Gallaghers' Crestview building when Mowery pulled up. The look on Mowery's face spoke of more than just weariness.

"What's wrong, John?" Ron Lach asked, as they cut across the lawn. "You look like you could chew nails."

"Have you seen this?" Mowery glowered.

"This" was an article about Windy Gallagher's murder in the *Post-Tribune,* the largest newspaper in Northwest Indiana. Lach read the eleven short paragraphs setting out the time the body was found and by whom, a statement from Mowery that there were no signs of forced entry, and a few brief comments by Calumet High School counselors and students.

"Okay," Lach said. "I read it. What's wrong with it?"

"The headline is what's wrong with it," Mowery said. "The reporter asked me if we thought somebody broke into the Gallagher apartment while Windy was inside, and I told him there were no signs of forced entry. So now, here's this big headline that says, 'POLICE SAY IT'S LIKELY GIRL KNEW HER KILLER.' These reporters can drive you crazy. You say one thing and they stretch it to mean something else."

Lach wisely didn't comment, but stood by, his canvas newsboy's sack slung over his shoulder, watching as Mowery checked for the bits of scotch tape he'd stuck into the corners of the Gallaghers' front door. The tape was still intact, and Mowery removed it and the official yellow crime-scene tape sealing the door. He unlocked the door with April Gallagher's keys, and both men went inside.

The Gallagher apartment carried the embarrassed, ashamed air of a private place that had been violated, first by the killer and then by the police. Black desiccant fingerprint powder formed sooty blotches around the living room and kitchen, and in the girls' bedroom, big pieces of the carpet were gone and the bare flooring showed through. Blots of Windy's blood still stained what the evidence techs had left of her bedding, and then there was that mysterious little stain at the bottom of the drape.

Mowery stood watch as Lach went out to his mobile crime lab van and began carrying in what looked like floodlights on tripods. They were actually high-intensity photo lights, and he set them up facing the walls in Windy Gallagher's bedroom. He worked quietly, steadily, saying little as he went back and forth to the van and stacked bottles and boxes of equipment in the hallway outside the bedroom. Lach plugged heavy-duty extension cords into the photo lights, and Mowery had to step to one side as the bedroom doorway became littered with thick black cables.

Lach was the senior officer at the Lake County sheriff's crime lab, having been an evidence technician for nearly ten years. He loved his craft, and in all seventeen Indiana towns serviced by the lab, no one had ever disputed Lach's expertise. Police officers, including Mowery, marveled at his artistic way of making inanimate objects give up their tales of murder. Tall and skinny, Lach had the rangy walk and slow-talking speech pattern of a small-town New England farmer, but the wizardry he produced with his bottles and tweezers and envelopes often left defense lawyers with nothing to argue.

"What're you doing now?" Mowery asked. The two men were in the hallway outside Windy's bedroom.

"Luminol," Lach said, holding up a small glass vial and

pouring several drops of liquid into it. He shook the vial and then opened another small bottle and eye-droppered another liquid into it.

Mowery shrugged and waited.

After a few minutes, Lach seemed satisfied with his vial of liquid. He broke a new plastic spray bottle out of its wrapper and poured the liquid into it. Then he went into the kitchen. Mowery followed.

Lach sprayed the liquid all around and into the Gallaghers' kitchen drain. Then he turned off the kitchen light and stood back, camera around his neck, and watched. Mowery watched, too.

"Well?" Mowery asked finally.

"Nothing," Lach answered, and headed into the bathroom, where he repeated the procedure with the washbasin drain.

Luminol, the chemical concoction Lach was using, has been around for about sixty years. It is a simple mixture of sodium perborate, sodium carbonate, distilled water, and a microscopic 0.5g of luminol. Its seemingly magic property is that it glows with a ghostly green phosphorescence in the presence of blood. Even old blood that has been stored for fifteen years at room temperature will assume a bright luminescent glow when sprayed with Luminol. Obviously, if Windy Gallagher's killer had used one of the sinks to clean himself up, he had let the water run long enough to wash away any traces of her blood.

Back in the hallway outside Windy's bedroom, Lach again reached into his canvas sack and took out packets of material. Mowery kept asking questions, and finally Lach explained what he was doing now.

The evidence tech was mixing a potion of silver nitrate crystals with ether alcohol, which produced a film-developing compound. He would spray it on the walls one small patch at a time, and turn on the high-intensity light and the chemicals would "develop" whatever hidden markings, including fingerprints, were on a wall's surface. He could

only do about a two-by-four-foot area at one time, and each
would take ten or fifteen minutes to develop. If a "picture"
began to develop on the wall, Lach would move in quickly
and photograph it with his high-speed 35mm camera before
it overdeveloped and became unreadable. The developing
solution would bring out latent prints that even fingerprint
powder would be unable to show.

"Whew!" Mowery exclaimed, as soon as Lach sprayed
the first section of the wall. Eye-watering fumes, like stale
beer mixed with ammonia, clouded the air.

"I know," Lach said. "This is ether alcohol. Just like they
used to use for surgery. Stay back by the window or out in
the hall, and try to breathe in the fumes as little as possible."

Lach had begun his spray-sectioning of the room with
the wall just inside the bedroom door. He did a section
about four feet wide and two feet up from the baseboard.
Then, he and Mowery went out and stood in the hall to get
away from the intoxicating fumes. But Lach kept stepping
back in the bedroom to look every minute or two, watching
to see what might come up. After about fifteen minutes, he
mixed a new bottle of the solution and sprayed another two
feet higher on the wall. So far, nothing was showing, no
picture was developing. The walls were newly painted and
clean.

Out in the hall, the two talked quietly about the case.
Mowery told the evidence tech about Markovich's conversation with the next-door neighbors and said his men were
out right now looking for Jerry Moffat and Stan Bridges,
neither of whom had been seen in town since the day before.

"Some goofy, tripped-out girl called the Lake County
sheriff's police," Lach said. "She claimed her ex-boyfriend
is some kind of apostle of Satan, talks to the Evil One
personally, I guess. She says that she's seen the boyfriend
chant some hocus-pocus spell and then the sun darkens, the
winds blow—you get the idea. Then, she says, the guy can
reach out and lift up another person with one finger. Can

hold them suspended up in the air like that, with just his little finger. Says he's done it to her, even."

Lach said that Lake County was going out to talk to the ex-boyfriend, among others they'd gotten calls on. This case seemed to be attracting Satan wannabes like roaches coming out of the woodwork.

The day passed slowly as Lach patiently painted Windy's bedroom walls one section at a time. It was mid-afternoon before he reached the section next to the window drape with the tiny mysterious smudge on it. Lach painted the two-foot-high section above the baseboard and then stepped quickly out into the hall with Mowery. Both men had raging headaches from the fumes and felt a little giddy, as though they'd downed a couple quick shots of Jack Daniels.

Lach made another trip into the bedroom to check on progress. Suddenly Mowery, still out in the hall, heard the evidence tech yelling from the bedroom. Mowery rushed in to find Lach on his knees, clicking away with his camera.

"Look at that, will you!" Lach shouted. "Isn't that just *beautiful?* Look at it!"

"I'm looking at it, I'm looking at it! *What* am I looking at?" Mowery shouted back. Lach's excitement was contagious. As they watched, a vague pattern began to take shape on the wall, just two feet above the floor and a couple inches to the right of the window frame.

At first, it looked like several long stalks branching out from two wide splotches. Then, as the men watched and Ron Lach clicked away with his camera, the shapes on the wall gained clear outlines. They were the prints of a human's right and left hands. Large hands. A man's hands.

Probably, the killer's hands.

Six

Lt. Mowery headed back to the Griffith police station in good spirits. His headache from the ether fumes was still pinching at his temples, but he hardly felt it. It was a minor annoyance, of no consequence whatsoever, compared to his elation at seeing those palmprints come up like magic on Windy's bedroom wall.

Lach had hurriedly turned off the high-intensity lights to stop the developing process, then cut out the sections of plasterboard and wrapped them in dark paper to take to the lab. Lach said he'd have to double-check, of course, but he felt pretty certain that the man who had left three finger-prints on the water glass in the Gallaghers' living room was the same man who'd left his entire palmprints, with all the fingers clearly defined, on the bedroom wall.

Bridges was already at the station when Mowery came in. The "Biker Dude," as he called himself, was attired in his customary leather and chains, but his usual "F———you, Copper!" attitude was nowhere to be seen. Bridges was being questioned in the detectives' conference room at the rear of the station. He had already been fingerprinted and palmprinted, and the prints were on their way to the crime lab to be checked against those found in the Gallagher apartment.

Mowery conferred with his detectives before going in to talk with Bridges. The biker vehemently denied knowing anything about Windy's murder, but he was clearly very afraid. He gave a long, complex alibi which involved, like most of his days, tooling around on his motorcycle, hanging out with the guys, partying with friends, and finally crashing for the night at his house trailer.

Mowery went into the conference room. "How you doing, Stanley?"

"Lieutenant Mowery! Jeez, am I glad to see you, buddy!" Bridges greeted Mowery—to whom he had never before spoken a civil sentence—as if the two of them were now the world's closest friends. "I mean, Jeez, what's going on here, Lieutenant? All this hassle and crap, you know?"

Mowery sat at the conference table and motioned Bridges to sit, too.

"Here's the deal, Stanley," Mowery said in his most bored, casual voice. "We got ourselves a little problem. We've got a murdered girl, we've got you being in the apartment across the hall from her on the morning she was killed, and now we've got you sitting here. And between us, Stanley, man to man? Your alibi sucks."

"Well, Jeez! How'd I know I was going to need a alibi at all, let alone a *good* one, you get me? But Lieutenant, you known me for years, right? I mean, around town and all? You know I didn't off no little girl. I mean, Jeez!"

"I don't know anything, Stanley," Mowery said, "except this: I know we need to get into your house trailer and take a look around. What do you think about that?"

Bridges jumped up. "Shit, no, man! I mean, that's my pad, you know? My place!"

Mowery stood up and turned to leave the room. "No problem, Stanley. We'll just go find a judge and get a search warrant."

"No, wait." Bridges stepped in front of Mowery, cutting him off from the door. "Come on now, Lieutenant. No need being a dickhead about this, right? I mean, sure, your guys can go through my place. You don't need no warrant. I mean, us being friends and all."

Mowery's "friend" Stanley Bridges signed a consent-to-search form and told Mowery the trailer was unlocked, that they could just go right in and look around. Mowery gave the biker a cup of coffee and told him to relax.

Back in his office, Mowery called the Lake County crime lab and made arrangements for Ron Lach, Mike Reilly, and Bud Matthews to meet Det. Mike Teeling at Stan Bridges's trailer.

The trailer park was a depressing, weedy clutter of tin-roofed shoebox homes-on-wheels. Bridges's trailer was locked. Teeling went to the manager's office and got a pass-key. Then, he and the evidence technicians went inside.

The interior of the trailer looked just like its owner—messy, unwashed, and uncared for. Teeling stood at the door while the lab techs went over the place. They found a knuckle-knife under the tweedy green plaid sofa. A knuckle-knife is constructed of a ridged steel band that fits around the knuckles of a man's fist, with a short, thick blade protruding from the end. It makes a wicked weapon.

Under Stanley's disheveled twin-sized bed was a black-handled hunting knife, tucked carefully into the corner within easy reach of someone lying on the bed. Obviously, Stanley Bridges wanted to have a knife close at hand whether he was sitting on the sofa or lying in bed.

In the bedroom, hanging on a hook, was a filthy denim jacket with a bloodstained tissue in the pocket. The evidence techs also collected a pair of jeans, a pink terrycloth towel, and a dirty bed pillow, all with unidentifiable dark stains on them.

Back at the station, Mowery asked Bridges to submit to a blood test, as well as have some of his head and pubic hairs clipped by Lach, who would then take all this new evidence back to the lab for comparison with standards they'd taken from Windy Gallagher's bedroom.

At first, Bridges put up a macho fuss about the pubic hair-clipping procedure, declaring loudly that he wasn't about to have "some dude with scissors poking around in his privates."

Finally, Stan decided to cooperate, but he would do it his way, the man's way. He pulled out his own pubic hairs by the roots and handed them over to the lab techs. Stanley Bridges was released then, pending the outcome of lab tests. He was warned not to leave town without notifying the detectives.

While these procedures were being carried out in the rear conference room, Mowery was called to the dispatcher switchboard.

An obviously elderly caller said, in a creaky, terrified voice, that she was Jerry Moffat's grandmother. She said that detectives had been at the house earlier looking for Jerry, but that she'd told them he hadn't been home all night.

"Jerry just came home a little while ago," the old woman said. "He kept after me and after me to give him some money, but I didn't have any more. I gave him all my money when my Social Security check came in last week—$475.06. But Jerry wouldn't believe me that I didn't have any more to give him." She was crying now.

"Did he threaten you, ma'am?" Mowery asked.

"He said he was going to have me and his grandfather killed, just like him and his friends killed that little Gallagher girl."

"Those were his exact words?" Mowery asked, scribbling on a notepad and motioning the dispatcher to go bring his detectives up front.

The woman's voice quavered. "Jerry said they gutted her like a hog. He said they were going to cut her heart out and eat it while it was still beating."

Mowery sent a team of detectives to the grandmother's house, while another team was dispatched, with a uniformed back-up team, to pick up Jerry Moffat at a friend's house where the grandmother said he was hiding out.

Twenty minutes later, the front door of the police station opened and Jerry Moffat, his filthy trenchcoat swirling around him, strode in and told the dispatcher "the cops are looking for me." He asked for "the detective in charge of the Gallagher case."

"So tell me, Jerry," Mowery asked, "do you practice Satanism?"

They were in the rear conference room, where Stan Bridges, the "Biker Dude," had been until half an hour ago.

"I've studied theology," Jerry answered. "And I read the Satanic Bible sometimes. Stuff like that."

"I see," Mowery said, noncommittally. "And were you bragging around recently that you and your friends killed Windy Gallagher, and you were going to cut her heart out?"

"Aw, that's just my grandparents talking." Jerry shrugged.

Mowery asked why Jerry thought it was his grandparents who had passed on the comment. Jerry said that they were senile and very religious.

"They're always calling me a demon," he smirked. "For some reason, they think I'm possessed. So I just let them keep thinking it. It keeps them on the level, you know?"

Mowery had to take a moment to step away and light a cigarette. That someone like Jerry Moffat should be able to keep his elderly grandparents in a constant state of fear was appalling.

Jerry said he couldn't remember where he'd been on the afternoon of Windy's death, but he thought he might have been at the Dunkin' Donuts on Ridge Road, since that's where he usually hung out in the afternoon, waiting around for his friends.

When Mowery asked if Jerry owned any knives, he said that he had once had two—a big, wide-bladed hunting knife, and a yellow-handled scissor knife—but that he hadn't seen them around for more than a month and didn't know what had happened to them.

Jerry said he knew the couple in the apartment across from the Gallaghers, but he didn't think he'd been there recently. He couldn't quite remember. The only thing he did seem sure about was what he'd been wearing on Tuesday, the day of Windy's murder. Jerry said he'd been wearing a black T-shirt, blue jeans, and—a trenchcoat.

Jerry Moffat signed a consent-to-search form for his bedroom at his grandparents' house, and Mowery radioed his detective team, already at the house, that they could now go through Jerry's room. Moffat also submitted to blood and hair samples, though he chose the usual clipping procedure rather than doing it Stan Bridges's way. Like Bridges, Moffat was released pending the outcome of the lab tests and was warned to keep himself available. Mowery detested having to set Jerry free—enabling him to return to terrorizing his elderly grandparents—but legally he had no choice.

Late that night, before going home, Mowery, Grimmer, and all the other Griffith detectives met for coffee and sandwiches at the all-night Jedi's Garden Restaurant. This was a habit they had fallen into every night since the Gallagher murder. It served two purposes: they were able to catch each other up on the day's progress and brainstorm ideas for furthering the investigation; and most of them, Mowery included, were so inundated during the day with the hundreds of calls and details of the Gallagher case that they rarely stopped to eat, and now they could relax a little.

Tonight, the topic of discussion was whether Stan Bridges and/or Jerry Moffat had had any part in Windy Gallagher's death. The men tossed opinions back and forth; neither of the suspects was likely to win the town's outstanding citizen award, but the answer would have to wait for the lab tests.

Dr. Young Kim, the Lake County pathologist, had that afternoon delivered the autopsy results, and the detectives fell quiet now and passed around the report. The actual autopsy protocol comprised many pages, but the relevant findings took only four short sentences: Windy Gallagher had died from laceration of the liver, multiple stab wounds of the abdomen with evisceration of the intestines, laceration of the trachea, and stab wounds to the neck.

Seven

Mowery stood smoking a cigarette and looking out at the bleak, incessant drizzle. Sighing, he turned and slumped tiredly into his well-worn fake-leather chair. He mashed out the cigarette. Closing his eyes, he rocked his head from side to side, trying to loosen his aching neck muscles. His mouth tasted of stale tobacco, bitter coffee, and not enough sleep. Mowery wondered if a man could feel worse, physically or emotionally, than he did at this moment. It was early morning on Saturday, October 17, and looking out, he knew the sun would not shine today. It seemed appropriate.

Lach had just called with the bad news that neither Moffat nor Bridges matched the prints found in the Gallagher apartment. Neither, for that matter, did any of the dozens of other local ne'er-do-wells Mowery had ordered picked up and printed. Back to square one.

Windy Patricia Gallagher, who'd forever remain just sixteen years old, would be buried today. As the town's chief of detectives, Mowery would be there, of course, along with most of the Griffith police force. They would make themselves unobtrusive, but they would be watching, looking out for anyone or anything out of place. Up on the hill that swept back from Windy's gravesite, a police photographer with a long-distance lens would capture the faces of everyone attending the service.

The Griffith police had been called to Windy's wake the

night before, when a young man had suddenly begun acting crazy, screaming and pushing his way through shocked mourners who were gathered around Windy's white coffin. The teenager had pulled out a pocketknife and begun stabbing it into the wall of flowers next to the bier. Several men wrested the knife away from him, and the boy, still crying and screaming, ran out into the street and collapsed just as the first squad car pulled up. He was taken to the station and questioned, but it turned out he was a friend of Windy's from school who'd gotten intoxicated and simply lost control in his grief. Mowery was going to make damn sure nothing like that happened at the cemetery today.

But, Mowery thought now, driving slowly through the gray rain, he would have attended the child's final earthly ceremony in any case. Over these last days, he had spent a great deal of time with the Gallagher family, and the more he got to know them, the more he liked them. Even in these worst hours of their lives, the Gallaghers gave him their instant faith and trust, letting him know they believed he was doing his best. They didn't question his investigation, make demands, or accuse the police of not doing enough, as many grieving families do. And that made Windy's murder and Mowery's own frustration all the more rankling to him.

April and Chrissy, Windy's mother and sister, usually sat side by side, holding hands and wiping away each other's tears, when they talked with Mowery. He asked them about Windy's friends, her habits, her hopes—anything he could think of that might give him some kind of lead on where to look next for her killer.

As they talked about Windy, first April and then Chrissy would start telling some little family story that would set them both to smiling and laughing in remembrance—until the fact of her death hit them again. Mowery could see it happening, the sudden look of shock on their faces, the quick glance at him, this policeman sitting here in their living room to investigate Windy's death. It must be real, then. Mother and daughter would break down then, and Mowery would rage inside all over again that he was having to put them through this, that he'd been unable to step right in and bring down Windy's killer the way a professional detective is supposed to do.

April Gallagher talked about what an honest, open-hearted child Windy had been. The three of them, "the girls," as they called themselves, liked to jump in the car on any impulse and just go places. They might all be sitting around, watching TV, or whatever, when Windy or Chrissy or April would suddenly say, "Hey, let's get some ice cream!" or, "Let's go check out that sale at Venture." All three would jump up and run for the car, and they were off and running together again. Whenever one had an errand to run, anything from picking up the cleaning to going to the dentist, all three would go together. These excursions were usually planned out every morning by April and Chrissy. Windy wasn't a morning person, usually the last to get out of bed, the slowest of the three to get showered and dressed.

Slow morning starter or not, once her day got going, Windy was irrepressibly bubbly and optimistic. Chrissy tended to be sensitive and would cry if one of the girls at school said something mean to her or if she thought a teacher was being unfair. But Windy was always able to tease her out of it. "Hey, don't cry," she'd say, putting her arm around her younger sister. "It'll make your eyes puffy and your make-up will run and you'll be all ugly. And what good will that be?" Chrissy would laugh then, unable to stay sad in the face of Windy's cajoling humor.

Patrick Gallagher, Windy and Chrissy's father, was also suffering terribly following his oldest daughter's death. He had been talking with his Windy about getting the money together to fix up April's old Chevy for her to use, once she passed her driver's course. Windy and her father figured it would cost about $150 to get the car in working order, and Windy, like all teenagers eager to drive, wanted to help pitch in earning the money. Patrick had said no, he was going to get the parts and fix up the car as his gift to Windy. But now Windy was gone.

Everyone in Griffith was talking about the murder. A drunk in one of the local bars had stood up and announced, with alcohol-fueled certainty, that in his opinion, Patrick Gallagher had killed his own daughter, maybe for insurance money, or maybe because of something even uglier going on between father and daughter. There wasn't a whit of truth or evidence to justify the dirty little innuendo, but it spread anyway, whispered from ear to scandalized ear. People usually started the story with, "I don't believe a word of it, of course, but I heard . . ." Patrick learned of it from an outraged friend, and in the middle of his grief over his daughter's murder and rage at her killer, he now had yet another burden.

Well, Mowery thought, crushing out another cigarette and shrugging into his tan raincoat, the only way to get this over with is to do it.

The Burns-Kish Funeral Home in Munster was filled to overflowing. The Warriorettes, Windy's cheerleading teammates, were there in their red-and-white outfits, along with hundreds of students, teachers, family friends, and Griffith townspeople who'd come to pay their last respects. The Gallagher family was up in front, and Mowery stopped to say a few words, as did all the Griffith police and detectives.

In the background, they could hear the soft strains of the 1960s Association song "Windy."

The soft rain continued to fall as the four-block procession left the funeral parlor and wound its way past Calumet Township High School to St. Mary's Church, where the Rev. Tony Valtierra delivered the eulogy. "It doesn't make any sense at all," the reverend said. "Why did it happen?" Then he exhorted the mourners: "The smile on her face will be missing, but remember the joy Windy brought to us."

At Mount Mercy Cemetery, the Warriorettes stood huddled in a group next to the Gallagher family. Then, one by one, each girl stepped forward in the rain and placed a red or white carnation on Windy's white satin-lined coffin. Someone else stepped forward and put a single yellow rose among the red and white flowers.

As the Rev. Valtierra said, "The service has ended," Chrissy Gallagher doubled over and fell forward in her chair. Her parents propped her up and walked her to the waiting black limousine.

The next morning, the *Sunday Times* headline read: "TRIBUTE FOR SLAIN TEEN: 400 ATTEND FUNERAL." The *Post-Tribune*'s banner was: "GALLAGHER CASE EVOKES PRESSURE FOR POLICE, ANXIETY IN COMMUNITY." The whole town seemed subdued this Sunday morning, as though the initial shock of the terrible crime was beginning to wear off, but the fear that everyday life would now be changed forever was just settling in.

John Mowery and the entire Griffith detective division, all of whom had worked until 1 A.M. the night before, were back in the station at 9 A.M., facing a new stack of telephone tips, mostly anonymous, that had come in through the night. The rain had stopped. The grinding casework went on.

Eight

"Hey, Lieutenant? I think you got a nibble on that piece you put in the paper about the Gallagher girl's purse."

The dispatcher handed Mowery a message slip and he juggled his coffee as he buzzed himself in and walked down the hall to his office. He flipped his coat and briefcase on a chair and sat down behind his desk, lighting a cigarette and staring at the message slip. He didn't care much for reporters, but they could be useful to the police at times, and some of the local guys were pretty good about helping out. On Monday, two days after Windy's funeral, Mowery had called the *Times* and talked to Thomas Inkley, one of the staff writers. This morning, when Mowery woke up and stepped outside to get his paper, there was the front-page headline: "PROBE FOCUSING ON VICTIM'S PURSE." The article described Windy's small gray clutch purse and quoted Det. Lt. John Mowery as saying the girl's purse appeared to be the only thing missing from the apartment.

Mowery looked at the message slip again. Then he buzzed the front desk.

"Is this the only call that came in about the purse?"

"Sure is," the dispatcher answered. "The only one since I been here, anyway, and I been here all night."

"This message shows a 312 area code—that's Chicago. You sure you got this number right? And what's the caller's name?"

"Oh, I got it right. And her name's Wilson, like the balls,

you know? She says she got grabbed and got her purse snatched way up to hell and gone on Chicago's far North Side, and then she got a call her purse was recovered way down on the South Side. Some guy found it in a burning trash barrel and wanted money to give it back to her. She drove to the South Side and picked it up, and when she got home, she found Windy's purse, too, right there with her own."

"The guy handed her *two* purses back?"

The dispatcher sighed. "Okay, okay," Mowery said. "I'll make the call. It just seemed odd, that's all. A call from Chicago about Windy's purse."

"Seemed odd to me, too," the dispatcher said. "But what do I know? I just answer the phones and write down what they tell me."

Mowery dialed the number and asked for Joyce Wilson. He listened for a few moments, then grabbed his pen and began to ask questions. "Ms. Wilson," Mowery said, trying not to sound as excited as he felt, "can you hold on just a moment?" He put the line on hold and intercommed the front desk. "Get ahold of the crime lab, right now. See if Ron Lach's working and tell him to get over here on the double and bring all his stuff with him. And call Karl Grimmer in off the street."

"What if Lach's not working?"

"I don't care!" Mowery nearly yelled. "Get him in here anyway. He's going to Chicago with me."

It was just past noon when they pulled up in front of the brown brick multi-unit building on West Touhy. Joyce Wilson had given them directions as best she could, but even so, Griffith, Indiana, is forty-five minutes southeast of the southern tip of Chicago, and this address was as far north as one could go in Chicago before crossing into Evanston. It had been a harrowing hour-and-a-half drive from I-94 into the Loop, north on Lake Shore Drive, and from there, north on Sheridan Road. Sheridan, which stretches along Lake Michigan from the north side of Chicago all the way to the Wisconsin border, is a city street that poses as an expressway. It is six lanes wide, and traffic careens along at fifty-five or sixty miles an hour between sky-scratching highrises, even while cars are making left turns, pulling out of driveways, and stopping every few blocks for red lights.

"Hi, come on in. I'm Joyce Wilson." The three detectives stepped into the apartment, suddenly feeling huge and awkward. Joyce Wilson was a perky, elfin sprite of a young woman, barely five feet tall and well under a hundred pounds. Her oversized tortoiseshell glasses dwarfed a tiny face. Ron Lach, from his bulky 6 3¢ height, thought she looked like Tinkerbell with glasses on.

"How old are you, Ms. Wilson?" Karl Grimmer asked, as the men seated themselves in the living room.

"Call me Joyce, please," she said, smiling. "I'm twenty-one, but I know, I look younger, right?"

"Sure do. About twelve, if you don't mind my saying so."

Joyce laughed, nodding. "I hear it all the time. Even though I work in a nightclub downtown, every time I go out to a bar, I get carded! Isn't that great?" She offered coffee all around, but Lt. Mowery refused for all of them. He was so intent on hearing the details of her story that he couldn't stand the thought of any further delay.

"Please just run through for us what happened to you, and how you came to have Windy Gallagher's purse," he said, motioning for Det. Grimmer to take notes. "We'll go back over it all again when you're through. This happened on Monday, right? Columbus Day?"

"Yes." She nodded. "Monday afternoon. It was about ten after four, and I was walking to school. I'm a student at Northwestern University. I was walking in the alley along the El tracks between Estes and Sherwin. This car, a blue car, turned into the alley coming toward me, but I didn't think anything of it. When it pulled up alongside me, it stopped and I could see the driver. He was a good-looking, clean-cut guy. I thought he was stopping to go up the back way into one of the buildings, so I just kept walking."

Joyce hesitated then, looking down at her hands.

"I realize this is hard for you," Det. Grimmer said. "It must have been really terrifying."

The three men were surprised when Joyce Wilson looked up again. It wasn't terror in her eyes; it was fury.

"The next thing I knew, he was behind me and he grabbed me by the waist. With his right arm. He put his left hand over my mouth and just lifted me right off the ground and dragged me into a corridor that opens into the alley."

Joyce described how she'd struggled and kept trying to scream against the hand pressed to her mouth.

"Then he put a knife against my throat and threatened to kill me."

"What were his exact words?" Mowery asked. "Do you remember?"

"I'll never forget. He said, 'If you don't stop screaming, I'll kill you.' He said it real calm, real cold, like he meant it. I kept saying, 'I'll stop. I'll stop.' He said did I promise, and I nodded. He took his hand away then and asked if I had any money."

Joyce said she told her attacker her money was in her purse, but then she looked around and realized she had dropped her purse in the struggle. It was lying halfway down the corridor. She pointed to it and told the man her money was it.

"I wasn't even thinking what I was doing, I guess," she said. "I reached into my pocket where I keep my Mace and pulled it out. I didn't even notice that I had it in my hand, but he saw it and put the knife against my throat again. He told me to drop it, and I did."

Joyce said the man stood there with the knife against her throat for a few seconds, and then he backed up a step or two.

"He started to turn away to look for my purse," she said. "But then, all of a sudden, he crouched and whipped around real fast, like, to see if I had moved or something, and pointed the knife at me again. I knew if I moved a muscle, he'd kill me. I just stood there, frozen like a statue."

Joyce said the man suddenly lunged at her and began ripping at her skirt, ordering her to pull it down.

"Then I heard a noise, like a car coming. He heard it, too, because he stepped into the alley and looked back and forth. Then he just snatched up my purse and jumped in his car and took off. A Franco's pizza delivery truck drove by just then. That was what we had heard."

The same unspoken question was on all their minds: would Joyce Wilson be sitting here today if that pizza delivery truck hadn't turned into the alley just when it had?

Joyce told the detectives she had made an armed robbery police report; the evening after the attack, Chicago's Area 6 detectives had called her at work to say they had some mug shot photos for her to look at. They wanted her to come in to Area 6. At the detective headquarters, Joyce said, she went through book after book, and finally she came across a photo of a man who looked very much like her attacker. She told the Chicago detectives he "looked close" to the guy, but she couldn't be sure.

"The Chicago detectives kept at me," Joyce said now, "like they wanted me to say for sure this man was the one who'd attacked me. They said this guy, his name's Joseph Rinazzi, had been arrested not far from here a couple of months ago. They said he drove up to a girl in an alley and, uh, you know, exposed himself. They said if I didn't identify the guy, that he'd be free to just walk out of there. I just wasn't sure, do you know what I mean? He looked like the guy, but it seemed like there was something different, even so."

Finally, Joyce said, she'd identified the man, even though she'd still had doubts about whether he was the right one or not. "I was sure in my own mind after the attack that I'd know the guy anywhere. And this guy in the mug shot looked so, so close; slim, nice looking dark blond hair parted in the middle. The Chicago people kept saying over and over how he was going to go free to hurt other women if I didn't identify him. So I did. They picked him up and charged him with armed robbery. They've got him in jail now."

Joyce looked unhappy when she finished talking. After a few moments, Karl Grimmer said: "Do you still think he's the one?"

She looked at all three men in turn. "After the attack, I was positive, I mean positive, in my own mind that I'd know that guy anywhere if I saw him again. Then, I saw that mug shot and it *looks* like him, but I'm not a hundred percent certain. All I can say is, if it's not him, it's his almost identical twin. That's the best I can do."

Mowery nodded, content for the moment to leave the identification question alone. If Chicago had the guy in custody, he wasn't going anywhere for now and Mowery would work together with Chicago to go over the guy's alibis and movements with a microscope. If he was the one who'd attacked Joyce Wilson, they'd prove it one way or another. If not, they'd prove that, too. Meanwhile, he wanted to know about Joyce having come into possession of Windy Gallagher's purse.

Joyce said that on Saturday, October 17, her mother got a call from a black man who said he'd come across her telephone number when he'd found a purse in a burning trash barrel in an alley. He was willing to give the purse back, he told Joyce's mother, but he wanted a reward for it. On Saturday, while Windy Gallagher was being buried in Indiana, Joyce Wilson and her boyfriend drove the sixteen miles to Chicago's South Side and retrieved her purse, for a small reward.

"I knew as soon as I opened it that someone else's stuff was in my purse," she told Mowery and the other detectives. "There was this little gray clutch purse inside my purse, and then all kinds of other little stuff mixed up with mine— cosmetics and things. There was a little calendar book in the gray purse with the name 'Gallagher' inside the front cover. I called Information and got ahold of a Gallagher in Griffith, Indiana. The woman said it wasn't hers, but she told me about the murder and that's when I called you at the police station."

Joyce took the detectives into her kitchen, where her purse and the little gray clutch purse were laid out on the table with all their contents. With a nod from Mowery, Ron Lach set about dusting and printing both purses, along with as many of the cosmetics and other items as would hold a smooth surface. Then Joyce walked with the detectives downstairs and out into the alley where she'd been attacked. She reenacted exactly where she had been at each point throughout her ordeal and Mowery thought to himself that if the opportunity ever came, Joyce Wilson was going to make an excellent court witness. And that made her uncertainty about identifying Joseph Rinazzi all the more troubling. She was a very sharp young woman, and if she felt ambivalent about the ID, Mowery was worried about it, too.

Grimmer stayed in the alley with the lab technician while he set out all his equipment and prepared to dust and photograph the entire crime scene. John Mowery and Joyce went back up to her apartment to go through every single item recovered from the two purses.

"It looks like all Windy's stuff is here," Mowery said a few minutes later. "Except for the money, of course, which you'd expect. And except for her school ID photo. That's missing, too."

He was talking more or less to himself, but Joyce leaned forward at his words. She pulled her wallet out of her recovered purse, and flipped through it.

"Well, can you beat that? My picture is gone, too! I didn't even realize it until you said that about the Gallagher girl's photo. Now, why would anybody do that? I mean, I have all these other pictures in my purse, but the only one missing is the picture of me."

Joyce was still looking down, so she didn't see John Mowery, across the table from her, suddenly look up at her with an awful knowledge in his eyes. *Trophy.* The word, and all its implications for the Gallagher murder case, clicked on in his mind like the flip of a switch. Mowery, like every other homicide detective, recognized the signs of that peculiarly elusive human predator who stalks his prey, brings it down with the savage joy of a starving tiger, and then leaves the bloody scene with a trophy, the better to reminisce, the better to relive the euphoria of the kill. *A serial killer.*

Could a serial killer have murdered Windy Gallagher? And could they possibly be lucky enough to have brought him down with the arrest of Joseph Rinazzi?

Nine

"I say it's Rinazzi," said Det. Markovich. "It's got to be. It all fits together. Like the pieces of a jigsaw puzzle."

Lt. Mowery and Det. Grimmer, listening, pondering the possibilities, looked at him across the table. Det. Teeling, sitting next to Markovich, put down his coffee cup and snorted. "Pieces of a jigsaw puzzle? What're you, Sherlock Holmes all of a sudden?"

It was midnight and the Griffith detective squad was assembled in a booth at Jedi's for their nightly debriefing on the developments in the Gallagher case. As was their usual routine, they had finished sharing and comparing each man's efforts thus far and had now wandered into speculations, "what ifs." Each had thrown all his reasoning power into the case, endlessly rehashing every moment, every known fact surrounding Windy's life and death, looking, looking for that missing key. The process was mentally exhausting and, so far, fruitless.

"No, listen up," Markovich said. He pushed aside their plates and coffee cups, clearing a space in the center of the table. Then he looked around and picked up a salt shaker.

"Say this is the site of the Joyce Wilson attack." He set the shaker down to his left. "We know the guy was here, on the far North Side of Chicago, Monday afternoon, October 12. What was it? Four o'clock?" The others nodded.

"Okay, then." Markovich set the matching pepper shaker to his far right. "Twenty-four hours later, he's all the way down here in Griffith, right? He kills Windy Gallagher, takes her purse. But then what does he do?"

"Okay," Mowery said, "keep going. Let's hear it out."

Markovich traced a route with his finger from the pepper shaker on his right toward the salt shaker on his left. "He heads straight back *north,* back into Chicago, back to where he came from. And Rinazzi, who just happens to be a sex offender, lives in North Side Chicago, right?"

The men sat in silence a few moments, sipping at their coffee, working through Markovich's scenario.

"The problem is," said Grimmer, "what's he doing at South Creiger, where the purses were found? He'd have to get off the expressway halfway between Griffith and Chicago's North Side, drive around through residential neighborhoods, find that alley, dump the purses, and then get back on the expressway to head up north."

"Which is maybe exactly what he did," Markovich said. "I mean, if it *is* Rinazzi, you wouldn't expect him to wait until he was back up in his own neighborhood to dump the purses, right? He'd want to dump the evidence far from his home base, and yet far enough away from Griffith so we wouldn't stumble into it right off the bat."

"It's a good speculation, Steve," Mowery said, "but that's all it is right now. Speculation. It could just as easily have gone the other way around. The guy could be from around here, maybe he even lives in Griffith, but he likes to wander around up in Chicago for some reason. A girlfriend, maybe, or drugs, or whatever. While he's up there, he attacks Wilson. Then he jumps in his car and heads home, here to Griffith. The next day, he kills Windy. He wants to get out of town fast, maybe because he knew Windy or maybe somebody saw him leaving her building, so he heads right back into Chicago, but to the South Side this time. Maybe he figured that's a high-crime, high-drug neighborhood and somebody would come along and snatch those purses right out of the garbage can. Hell, maybe he lives on the South Side. Maybe this, maybe that, maybe anything."

Mowery toyed with his fork, pushing cake crumbs around on his plate. "But the one thing there's no 'maybe' about is that we *are* going to prove one way or another whether Mr. Rinazzi is our guy. Ron Lach is working on a print comparison over at the lab to see if it was Rinazzi's prints on the water glass and on Windy's bedroom wall. We should have an answer tomorrow morning. I'm not hopeful; I mean, I want to be hopeful, but it all just seems too easy, too pat, somehow." Mowery shrugged, massaging his thumb and forefinger against his temples. "Who knows? But if it *is* him, if it *is* Rinazzi, we're going to nail his ass to the wall, and that's a fact."

The detectives were beginning to yawn by this point. It was past midnight and they had all been putting in fifteen-hour days for a week. Mowery signaled the waitress for the check. While they waited for their change, Mowery went over their next-day schedules. He and Grimmer would be at Chicago's Area 6 headquarters at 9 in the morning to begin digging into Joseph Rinazzi's life. The other detectives would continue following up on a couple of promising local tips. The whole town still seemed frozen with horror, and it seemed that every other person in Griffith knew somebody who'd been acting suspiciously since Windy Gallagher's murder.

The group of detectives stood up, and shrugging into their overcoats, threw several dollar bills on the table. They were just heading for the front of the restaurant when three teen-aged girls came through the door. One of them was Chrissy Gallagher.

Chrissy saw the men and immediately made eye contact with Lt. Mowery. She smiled her sweet, sad smile and Mowery could see the question in her eyes. No one in the Gallagher family had ever asked him the question outright, but they couldn't hide that hopeful reaction whenever he saw them, which was nearly every day.

"Chrissy," Mowery said, taking her hand, "what are you doing out so late?"

"My mother said I should get out of the house for a little while. I haven't been out at all since . . . well, anyway, my mom thought some fresh air would do me good, so my friends and I just came by for a Coke."

Mowery stood holding her hand and wondering whether to say anything. He had kept the Gallaghers briefed, in general terms, about various interviews and lab results as they came in, but he wanted to be careful not to offer hope where there might not be any.

"We're working on something, Chrissy," Mowery said carefully. "It's not definite yet, we've still got a lot of checking to do. It's just a lead, you understand, and I don't want you and your family to get your hopes up too much. We'll know more tomorrow, okay? And the minute I know, I'll give your mom a call one way or the other. Will you tell her that for me?"

Chrissy nodded, courteous and nondemanding as always, but Mowery noticed that her shoulders seemed to sag. The child looked drained—pale and hollow-eyed to the point of illness.

"I understand, Lieutenant. I'm not even going to mention it to Mom tonight . . . you know how she gets. She'll be up all night, pacing back and forth. I'll just let you call her tomorrow and talk to her about whatever it is, if that's all right with you."

"I'll call her." Mowery said. "And hopefully by then I'll have some good news for all of us."

Ten

"April, I'm sorry to have to tell you this," Mowery said into the phone the next afternoon. "But no, I *don't* have any good news for you."

Windy's mother had called and left several messages for Mowery, which he'd picked up when he'd returned from a morning-long session in Chicago.

"I'm not trying to bother you or put any pressure on you guys," Windy's mother said quickly when Mowery returned her call. "But I just can't help myself. Chrissy came home last night with this look on her face like something was up, but all she would tell me was that you might have good news for us . . . ?"

Mowery felt his chest tighten at the hope, the trust, in her voice. He told her then about the Chicago connection to Windy's case, and about the sex offender that the CPD had taken into custody for the attack on Joyce Wilson.

"But it's not him," Mowery said now. "Believe me, we had our fingers crossed on this one, but we've checked this out every which way, and it's just not him. Rinazzi was at work, thirty miles north of Chicago, which would put him over a hundred miles away from here when Windy was killed."

"Could he have left work and then gone back with nobody noticing?" April asked. Mowery could hear the desperation and the beginnings of a quiver in her voice, and he knew what she was feeling. Now that she was having to accept that her daughter was gone for all time, the only thing she had left to cling to was finding Windy's killer and seeing him punished.

"We thought of that, of course," Mowery said, as gently as he could. "He works with a construction crew, and there's a dozen guys to swear he was never out of their sight. We talked to his foreman, too. None of the men left the site all day. I'm so sorry."

"Oh, no," April said, "I'm the one who's sorry, for constantly bothering you like this. I know you and your men are doing everything you can to catch him. I mean, we *will* catch him, won't we? In time? We'll know who did this to my girl?"

Mowery cleared his throat and put on his most confident voice. "We'll catch him, I promise you, because I'll never stop until I've got him. *Never.*"

But the weeks dragged on, and then the months. Mowery and his four detectives pulled in and tracked down first a dozen, then two dozen, then finally over fifty tall young men with dark blond hair worn parted in the middle. As always seems to be the case when one's focus is suddenly narrowed, the hairstyle was one none of them had even noticed before, and now every other young man in creation seemed to be walking around with his hair parted in the middle.

Joyce Wilson called to say that she remembered one other detail about the blue car—it was a small detail, but an important one. She said that as the car drove slowly past her, she saw a little sticker, a decal, on the windshield. It had the words "Delta Airlines" and some numbers printed on it. The Griffith detectives set up a meeting with the local Delta personnel director, who verified that the sticker gave airline employees access to special parking facilities at O'Hare and Midway. Weeks of paperwork turned up many airline employees who drove Datsuns, and many more who drove late model silver-blue cars, but none who drove a late model silver-blue Datsun *and* who could not account for his whereabouts on the afternoon Windy Gallagher was murdered.

"You're now sure it was a Datsun?" Mowery asked Wilson again and again.

"Positive." They had gone to a local car dealer and spread out glossy brochures now for their only witness.

"All right, then," Mowery said, "it's a Datsun. We're going to pull every single State vehicle registration for every single 1986 or 1987 blue Datsun on file in Indiana and Illinois."

And they did. By New Year's Day, 1988, every desk in the detective room was stacked with vehicle registrations, driver's license photos, and rap sheet printouts. By Valentine's Day, cardboard boxes sat alongside each man's desk. But as St. Patrick's Day approached, the trail was wafer-thin and as cold as the fear in Mowery's heart. A chilly cloud of despair hung over the men's daily grinding paperwork, and the detectives were no longer able even to pretend any confidence when they talked to Windy Gallagher's family.

When the call came, finally, it wasn't from Delta Airlines, and it wasn't from the Secretary of State. It was on March 16, 1988, and it was long-distance. From New Port Richey, Florida.

Part II

FLORIDA

* * *

JENNIFER LYNN COLHOUER
BORN: JULY 24, 1973
MURDERED: JANUARY 20, 1988

Eleven

The young man leaned into his Cougar's engine. The old car's hood was up and he was balanced against the left fender, probing so far down into the engine, looking for what he hoped was going to be only a leaky hose, that his Reeboks barely touched the pavement.

"Shit!" he swore, as he cracked the knuckles of his left hand against the radiator fan. He shook his hand and then, without thinking, pressed his bruised knuckles against his mouth. At the chemical taste of engine grease, he reared back, banging his head against the opened hood.

"Hey, Joey, get a load of what's coming up the street."

Joey straightened up, his knuckles throbbing, his face smeared with grease, ready to tell his buddy he didn't give a large rat's ass *what* was coming up the street, and besides . . .

It was a red Corvette. A sleek, glistening, lipstick-red 'Vette. Joey and his buddy watched, raw with envy, as the answer to every young man's dream purred closer, sparks of January Florida sunshine glittering off the 'Vette's black glass t-tops.

As the Corvette eased to a stop in front of them, both boys stood up straighter, and Joey unconsciously wiped the back of his arm across his face. The smoky-tinted driver's window slid down and the 'Vette's driver, himself a young man, smiled out.

"Hey, guys," he said. "What's going on?"

"Uh, not much, actually," Joey said, suddenly conscious of his sweaty T-shirt and raggedy cut-offs. This guy looked cool and clean with his perfectly feathered blond hair and white teeth. A rich playboy, or even a movie star, maybe.

"Having car trouble?"

"Uh, yeah. This old piece of shit clunker, you know how it is." Joey bit back the words even as he spoke them. For sure, *this* guy never had to bust his ass working minimum wage and pasting worn-out old junks together.

"Doesn't look like a bad car," the cool dude said. "How's it run? I mean," he said with a gentle laugh, "when it's running."

"Okay, actually," Joey's buddy said, and there was a sudden edge to his voice. "It gets us around just fine, thanks." Joey might be impressed with all the attention, but he didn't appreciate this movie star stud cruising along through the subdivision in his awesome 'Vette and stopping to chit-chat with the peasants.

The driver looked up at the defensive tone, his brilliant blue eyes full of understanding. "Well," he said, nodding a little and glancing at the gold watch on his tanned wrist. "It's getting late. I better take off. But I might be looking for a good second car. I think I could see my way to letting you guys have . . . say, $5,000 for the Cougar, once it's running. How's that sound? Give me a call if you guys decide to sell."

Smiling, he flicked a business card between his first two fingers and handed it to Joey. The smoked-glass window slid up and the Corvette eased back into the street with a whispery growl of controlled power.

Both young men watched in silence as the 'Vette rolled quietly to the corner and right-turned onto another side street. Joey looked down at the business card in his hand. "Terrell & Associates," it read, with a post office box address in nearby Zephyrhills. Joey turned the card over. There was a column of numbers scribbled on the back; "$150 dep.", and then, "$340 rent." Then a line, and the notation "$490 total."

"Shit," he said, slamming down the hood of his car and wiping his palms against the front of his shirt. He stuck the card in the rear pocket of his jeans. "Do you believe that dude? $5,000 he wants to give me for this piece of junk? I mean, what's the scam, man?"

"Hey, you should have grabbed it while you had the chance," his buddy said. "What does $5,000 mean to a guy like that? Chump change, that's what."

"Still and all . . ." Joey said, "something funny there. Rich people don't stay rich throwing money around on stupid shit like $5,000 for a junker. And why's a rich dude with a boss red 'Vette want something like this shitbox, anyway?"

"Probably so's he can keep the 'Vette inside during bad weather and just drive the junker. Makes perfect sense to me. Hey!" his buddy added, "maybe you should've asked if he wanted to *trade* the 'Vette for your Cougar! Straight up, I mean. Even Steven."

"Right," Joey laughed. "You smoking dope, or what?"

The boys walked toward the house to start cleaning up. Joey's parents wouldn't be home until late, and the boys had plans to meet a couple of girls and see a movie in Tampa. Joey had been hoping to get the Cougar running in time, but that didn't look likely now, since it was already after four o'clock. They would have to either bum a ride from friends, or hop on a bus.

"Besides," Joey said now, "who'd want a 'Vette, anyway? Everything'd cost a fortune with a car like that. It probably sucks gas like a pig."

"Yeah," his buddy agreed. " 'Specially, who'd want a *red* one? Jeez, you'd be fighting the broads off with a whip and a chair. It'd get to be a real drag, you know?"

Both young men whooped with laughter and disappeared into the house.

* * *

An hour later and just down the block, Adam Santiago was playing with his four-year-old son and puttering around on his front lawn. His house, too, was a roomy new split-level, as were all the homes in East Lake Padgett, a relatively new subdivision of upscale Land O'Lakes, Florida. Just north of Tampa and fifteen minutes east of the Gulf of Mexico, the subdivision was laid out as a series of cul-de-sacs and short, winding blocks that were designed to discourage thru-traffic. Teenagers sunned themselves on chaise longues and gossiped on portable phones, while in the big backyards their parents fired up brick barbecue grills next to crystal-blue swimming pools. Royal date palms swayed in their tropical majesty for miles around, and the steady Gulf breezes tanged the air with the bite of ocean salt.

Santiago stood on his grassed parkway and laughed as he watched his son. The little boy was intently playing with his miniature yellow-and-blue plastic lawnmower, stopping every few feet to mumble and lean down as though to pluck out an imaginary weed. The boy shook his head and sighed with apparent disgust at every stop, in perfect imitation of his father's weekly ritual.

At the sudden roar of an engine from down at the corner, Santiago instinctively stepped closer to his son and held out his arms, ready to grab him should the boy dart toward the street. Father and son watched as a red car sped toward them and then flashed past like a bullet.

"Idiot!" Santiago yelled, but the car was already gone. He told his son it was time to go in for supper and began to gather up the little lawnmower and other scattered toys. Suddenly, he heard the same engine roar from the opposite direction. The red car again thundered past him in a blur.

"You damned idiot!" Santiago yelled after it. "Slow down, for Christ's sake!"

"Adam? What's going on?" his wife called from their front door.

"Ah, just some idiot zooming around in a red Corvette."

As Santiago and his family were sitting down to dinner, his neighbor from across the way, Tom Colhouer, pulled into his own driveway. Tom's eight-year-old son, Jeremy, unbuckled himself from the seatbelt, and Tom freed his three-year-old daughter, Megan, from her restraints in the back seat.

Tom Colhouer worked at a construction company in Tampa. His wife, Cheryl, worked at Physicians' Laboratory of Tampa. Every day, on his way home from work, Tom would stop at Megan's daycare center and pick up both youngsters. Jeremy would wait each day with his little sister at the daycare center before his own classes began, and then again after school. The Colhouers' oldest daughter, fourteen-year-old Jennifer, was a freshman at nearby Land O'Lakes High School. Jennifer would be home now, setting the table for dinner.

"Jen?" Tom Colhouer called from the living room. Then, louder, "Jennifer?" No answer. He looked into her bedroom, which was just to the left of the front door. No Jennifer.

"Jennifer?" Tom called up the stairs. Again there was no response, and no sound of voices or radio noises anywhere in the house. In the kitchen, Tom saw Jennifer's key ring on the kitchen counter. He opened the refrigerator and took out a light beer. Popping the top, he sipped at the cold brew and stood looking out the rear kitchen window. In the back yard, near the deck, stood Jennifer's wire mesh rabbit cage. The cage was empty, its wood slat-and-wire top twisted awry and hanging open. They'd found it that way the week before, and Jennifer had been brokenhearted that some unknown animal, a fox, maybe, or a bobcat, had gotten her gentle pet. Tom reminded himself to set aside time this coming weekend to take her to a pet shop for another rabbit.

The Colhouers' next-door neighbor, Bill Moses, was just coming in off Lake Myrtle in his little fishing boat. Other neighbors up and down the shoreline were out, puttering around with their back lawns, or sitting and dangling their feet from the little residential docks that checkered the lakeside subdivision. It was a warm, golden Florida evening.

Tom dialed his wife's number at work, and they spoke for a moment.

"Jeremy," Tom said, hanging up the phone, "run upstairs and get your soccer gear together. We have to leave for the game in a few minutes. Hopefully, your sister will be back in by then, and she's going to hear it from me. She knows she has no business going anywhere without letting us know first."

Tom finished his beer and tossed the can into the kitchen wastebasket. "Megan, come on, sweetie," he said to his three-year-old, "let's get you a glass of milk. Daddy and Jeremy have to go to his soccer game, but Jennifer will stay with you 'til Mommy gets home."

"Okeydokey!" Jeremy said, already bounding up the stairs. "Jen? Hey, Jen, guess what happened in school today? Hey, Jen, where are 'ya?"

Tom Colhouer had just set the milk carton on the counter when the screaming started.

It was coming from upstairs. Jeremy!

"Megan, stay here, sweetie! Don't move!"

Tom rushed from the kitchen. Just as he reached the stairway, Jeremy, still screaming incoherently, came falling, headfirst, down the stairs.

Tom grabbed the boy to him. "Jeremy, what's wrong? Are you all right? Hey, buddy, I'm here, I'm here."

"Jennifer!" shrieked the boy, pointing up the stairs. "Jennifer needs your help!"

Tom took the stairs two at a time, then ran to the left and through Jeremy's bedroom door.

And then he saw Jennifer.

Twelve

On January 20, 1988, Pasco County road deputy Bobby Lightfoot, was working with a brand-new rookie. And not even a *he* rookie, but a *she* rookie, probationary deputy Ethell Bradshaw. Lightfoot was an FTO, a field training officer, for the sheriff's department, and as such, he was given a rookie fresh from the training academy as each new class graduated. The FTO principle was put into effect in police departments around the country during the late 1970s and early 1980s as a means of providing rookie officers with positive role models as they made the transition from the classroom to the street.

Prior to the FTO concept, rookies would be handed around from one veteran cop to another, which tended to result in confusing signals for the rookie and, in some cases, later lawsuits for the police department. Police officers develop their own particularities (and peculiarities!) over the years, based on the sum total of their own experiences, sometimes skewed by one bad personal incident. One old-timer might say, "Kid, forget everything they taught you in the academy about spread-eagling a suspect across the car hood. I did that once, just like they taught me, and the son-of-a-bitch turned on me and fractured my left kneecap. That cost me ten years' worth of surgery, and I'll never be able to play softball with my kids or work out in the gym again. Now, I make 'em all eat dirt—facedown on the ground the second I take them out of the car." The rookie wants to be accepted, to be street smart, to do the right thing in the eyes of his fellow officers. What should he do here?

FTOs are veteran street cops, too. They're usually chosen on an informal basis, designated by the watch commander or nominated by majority vote of their field supervisors, for their "sharpness." To be "sharp" in police language means having the ability to walk an indefinable line between the law enforcement concepts you learned in school and the harsh, practical truths you learned on the street. Throw into that mixture pride in your uniform and a continuing respect for your fellow human beings in the face of all evidence to the contrary, and you have a "sharp" cop. He (or she) is trusted by his partners because he's not a rigid, by-the-book clown, and yet his supervisors don't have to break into a sweat if he occasionally makes an unorthodox decision. They know it will be based on reason and common sense, not on bitterness and hatred.

FTOs are chosen from the sharp cops.

Now, Wednesday, January 20, at 6 P.M., FTO deputy Bobby Lightfoot and probationary deputy Ethell Bradshaw cruised their beat in South Central Pasco County, Florida. They were in a marked sheriff's car, white with a wide, brilliant green stripe along the sides and the big gold Pasco County sheriff's emblem on the doors. The chromed-steel Mars lightbar on the roof contained a red globe over the driver's side and blue over the passenger's—what squad car drivers refer to as "red overhead and blue on you." The deputies wore matching uniforms, short-sleeved, military-creased light green shirts and dark green pants with a gray stripe down the leg, though the uniform looked vastly different, of course, on the 6&2¢Lightfoot and his tiny female partner. They'd been on duty for three hours, and it was looking to be a slow day. Other than minor rush-hour traffic problems, nothing was going on, and rookie Bradshaw was eager to see some action. "Relax, maybe we'll get lucky and pull a signal 7," Lightfoot joked. Signal 7 was the code for a death investigation, something probationary deputy Bradshaw had not handled yet. Until she had confronted and come through this worst of all police assignments, she could not be properly judged by her peers and would not be accepted as one of them.

Lightfoot was telling his new partner the origins of his unusual name. The Lightfoot Lee family has a long, proud American heritage dating back to 1664, when Richard Lee emigrated from England and became a wealthy Virginia plantation owner and the founder of an extraordinary line of men, men who helped shape the future of their new nation. Richard Lee's grandson, Francis Lightfoot Lee, served in the Continental Congress and was one of the signers of the Declaration of Independence. His cousin, Harry Lightfoot Lee, affectionately known as "Lighthorse Harry" for his dazzling prowess on horseback, was a commander during the American Revolutionary War, and Harry's son was perhaps the most famous Lightfoot Lee of all—Robert E. Lee, commander-in-chief of the Confederate Army during what was then called the War between the States. Now, Dep. Bobby Lightfoot kept a framed parchment reproduction of the Declaration of Independence on his office wall.

At 6:17 P.M., the squad car radio sparked to life with a burst of static. "Unit D-3, signal 7," droned the police dispatcher. "Unit D-3, repeat, you have a signal 7. Proceed to Wayne Way. See Mr. Colhouer. Use caution." Police dispatchers everywhere have to be extremely circumspect about what they say on the air, because private citizens, reporters, and even many professional criminals listen to police-band scanners. It seems strange to career police officers, who are eager to shut off the "squawkbox" as soon as their shift is over, but they know that many people turn on their scanners with their morning coffee and shut them off only when they go to bed at night. So now, the dispatcher's inclusion of the words "use caution" was her way of telling Lightfoot that the "signal 7" on Wayne Way appeared to be bona fide.

"Deputy Bradshaw handled herself real well," Bobby Lightfoot would say later. "This was the most terrible thing even I'd ever seen, and this was her first day on the street, but she handled herself like a pro. She turned out to be pretty sharp."

EMS was already on the scene, the big white-and-red modular emergency-medical services truck parked in the Colhouers' driveway, its huge red globe lights splashing surrealistic red beacons across the houses and trees, and across the shocked faces of people standing in huddled little clumps up and down the sidewalk. Dusk was just falling; it was that time of day that happens just before sunrise and again before sunset, when, peculiarly, all colors seem to fade into shades of gray—except for hot, moving red light, which never loses its intensity, its message of urgency and alarm. The word "ECNALUBMA" was printed in big red letters across the hood of the EMS truck so that drivers out on the highways hearing a siren behind them and looking into their rearview mirrors would see "AMBULANCE" and pull over to let it pass. The big lights flung themselves like a metronome back and forth, back and forth, and up close, the mechanism's gears ground out a hypnotic background tune familiar to all cops and emergency personnel. *Whirr*-stop. *Whirr*-stop. *Whirr*-stop. The Mars Signal Corporation of Naples, Florida, makes the emergency bar lights used around the country. Their slogan is, "The Light from Mars," and even years after the other details of a crime scene have faded from a cop's mind, that endless *whirr*-stop, *whirr*-stop death song of the Light from Mars can bring it all flooding back again.

Dep. Lightfoot met the emergency services tech at the front door of the Colhouer house.

"What've we got?" Lightfoot asked.

"Looks like a homicide," the tech said. "A girl. Upstairs, first bedroom on the left."

As he opened the front door, Lightfoot turned to his partner. "Stand right here in front of the door," he said. "Nobody else in, and nobody else out, I don't care *who* it is."

Other squad cars were pulling into the cul-de-sac now—another marked green-and-white, a deputy's car, and still another, their sergeant's.

"Start a crime-scene log," Lightfoot told Ethell Bradshaw. "Get the names, badge numbers, and units of assignment of everybody who pulls in. No matter what rank they are, they identify themselves."

Then he went up the stairs. Whatever the medical tech or anybody else had said, this would not officially be classified a homicide until a police officer saw for himself and verified the sight. Bobby Lightfoot, as the first officer on the scene, had that responsibility.

She lay on the floor on her right side, facing away from the door toward wood-framed bunkbeds against the opposite wall. Her arms were stretched out in front of her and her legs were bent, knees drawn up as though in sleep. She had short, dark curly hair. She was wearing only a bright pink T-shirt and a white bra, which were bunched up above her little-girl breasts. Her back, buttocks, and legs were nude, but she still had on white gym shoes and white socks. An irregular red stain pooled out on the beige carpet under and behind her, with a black, plate-sized patch at its center. It was blood, of course, darkest where it had pooled the thickest.

Bobby Lightfoot carefully took two steps into the small room so that he could look at her face and verify what he already knew—that she was dead. He leaned forward and then involuntarily jerked his head back. The little girl had been eviscerated. Her intestines spilled out in front of her in a tangled red jumble on the gold carpet.

"God Almighty," Lightfoot whispered, stepping carefully back to the doorway.

"Look at this," the emergency tech said, pointing to an area of the floor just in front of them, about two feet from the corpse's head. Lightfoot looked down at a clutter of toys. This was obviously a little boy's room: toy cars, tractors, trucks, and other vehicles of every description were stacked on the three-shelf cabinet next to the bed, and lay scattered here and there—they ranged from bright-painted steel Tonka trucks to plastic high-tech futuristic-looking remote-controlled racecars. A well-used child-sized baseball bat lay half off the bottom shelf, next to a scuffed baseball and a smiling black stuffed monkey ready to clang little cymbals together at the touch of his control button. A big black-and-white stuffed dalmation with a happy smile and a red felt tongue stood on end next to the toy shelf.

Lightfoot looked down at the toys near his feet. Halfway under a red-and-yellow racecar with huge outsized back tires was a knife. It had a black handle and a nine-inch tapered stainless-steel blade clotted with blood.

As they backed out into the hall, the emergency tech tapped Lightfoot's shoulder and pointed. The doorjamb was pulled away from the wall, as though tremendous force had been used to push open the bedroom door.

Outside again, Bobby Lightfoot told his partner to get on their radio and have the dispatcher order up the crime lab and the detectives—they had a homicide. Then he approached the man who'd been pointed out as the girl's father. He introduced himself to Tom Colhouer, who was standing in the front yard, off to the side of the driveway. Mr. Colhouer was gray-faced, and Bobby Lightfoot knew from the man's glassy stare and jerky, disjointed head movements that he was in deep traumatic shock. Colhouer told the deputy that after seeing his daughter's body, he had grabbed both his younger children and rushed them next door to his neighbor's where they were now.

"Come on over here, sir," Lightfoot said, taking Tom Colhouer by the arm. He led the distraught father to his gray pick-up truck in the driveway and had him sit on the rear bumper.

"He looked like he was going to fall down any minute," Lightfoot said later, "and I couldn't let him go into the house to sit down, of course. We didn't know at that point what had happened inside that house, or who had killed the little girl upstairs. We wanted to be as gentle and caring as possible to this poor man, while at the same time we kept him in full sight until we were sure we could rule him out in the murder."

Lightfoot filled in his supervisor, Sgt. Howard Douglass, on what little they knew so far. Then, with the other deputy who had pulled up, he set about "taping the outer perimeter" with the ubiquitous yellow plastic tape with the words in black: "Police Crime Scene: Do Not Cross" repeated many times along its length. The deputies went out into the street and tied one end of the tape around a tree in the neighbor's driveway. Then they made their way, unrolling the big spool, across the front of the Colhouer property, along Bill's yard on the one side, along the vacant property next door on the other side, and then around the back of the house, almost down to the shore of Lake Myrtle, winding the tape around trees and bushes as they went. When they were done, the entire Colhouer property was enclosed in a huge rectangle of yellow plastic tape that fluttered and snapped in the evening breeze.

Now that the outer perimeter was secured, only police and emergency personnel would be allowed inside the tape, and only then with a good reason and *only* after probationary deputy Ethell Bradshaw had taken down their names and badge numbers.

Police work will never be an exact science, but it is more professionally administered now than it once was. Police officers learn from day one in the academy about mistakes made by their predecessors—mistakes involving oversight, thoughtlessness, or just pure stupidity on the part of cops who got so caught up in the excitement and fear of a moment that they lost sight of their ultimate goal. One of the lessons hammered into even a rookie cop's head is the immediate securing of a crime scene, particularly a homicide scene. Too many cases have been lost in court because evidence at the scene was contaminated, often by the very police officers who were supposed to be protecting the evidence. No one wants to have *his* crime scene destroyed because another cop carelessly left his fingerprints all over the place, or stubbed out a cigarette, or walked through a room, his shoes picking up fibers and trace evidence that could otherwise have been used to put a killer away.

Within minutes, the crime lab van pulled up, and then three detectives' cars. The detectives had all been at their monthly Fraternal Order of Police meeting less than three miles away. Their local FOP lodge had recently bought an abandoned boys' club on a nice but rundown piece of property fronting Bell Lake, and the men had been meeting to discuss their renovation plans. Suddenly, around 7 P.M., everybody's pagers had started going off. They all knew what this meant. Their jovial conversations came to an immediate halt. Det. Fay Wilber called in for all of them; then, they closed up the clubhouse and headed for the Colhouer home. Nightfall was now coming on.

The ID tech who got the call was Bill Ferguson, a huge bear of a man, and one of only two commissioned police officers in the Pasco County sheriff's office to hold the ID tech rank; all the other techs were civilians. Ferguson had been hosting his father's sixty-fifth birthday party at his home in Dade City when the sheriff's department dispatcher had called and assigned him to the Land O'Lakes homicide. "It's your case," the dispatcher'd said, "so get over there ASAP." That meant that he would not be assisting other ID techs, or helping out on the case, but would carry the full forensic technician's responsibility himself.

The words "your case" carry a heavy load of pride and responsibility in the police world. Decisions and courses of action have to be taken every step of the way, decisions no supervisor or oversight committee will second-guess at the scene, but that you'll have to defend and justify during criminal, and maybe civil, court actions for years to come.

The other cops on the scene at the Colhouer home were happy to see Bill Ferguson pull up. He was not only tremendously well liked by everybody; he was the best they had.

Det. Fay Wilber and the others stood in a group near the front of the house, waiting for the ID tech. It is standard procedure in Pasco County that once the crime has been established, which Bobby Lightfoot had already done, nobody else goes into the "inner perimeter" until the ID tech is finished with his initial processing. *Any* entry into a crime scene by a human being will leave some minute trace contamination, even if it is only a few flaked-off skin cells, or dust particles on the floor disturbed and rearranged by the air currents of a person's movements.

Outside, Cheryl Colhouer's car had just pulled into the cul-de-sac. All the police personnel stood by, as helpless now as the civilian neighbors to help a mother absorb that first second of knowledge that her daughter has just been murdered. It is a blinding, crushing moment. No matter how many people are around you, if you're a parent, you take that particular blow to the heart all alone.

Maj. Kim Bogart, the ranking officer on the scene, had been earnestly talking with Det. Sgt. Ron Carpenter. Bogart nodded and then walked over to Fay Wilber, who was standing talking with another detective, Gary Fairbanks.

"As soon as Ferguson and the lab boys are through up there, Wilber, you take over," Bogart said. "It's your case."

Thirteen

"Mom, can you take me to the store when you get home? I need hairspray."

Jennifer Colhouer had been making her 4 P.M. afterschool "check-in" telephone call to her mother at work. It was a rule in their household that each child had specific instructions about when and how often to check in. Jennifer, when she got home from school each day, was first to check the front and back doors of the house to make sure neither was suspiciously open before she put her key in the lock and went in. Then she was to call her mother at work to say that she was home and all right.

"Jennifer," said Cheryl Colhouer, sighing, "you use three cans of hairspray for my every one." While she talked with her daughter, Cheryl cradled the phone on her shoulder and fiddled with her computer. She was an administrative manager at Physicians' Laboratory, and they'd been experiencing computer glitches all day.

"Maybe we should just have your father shellac your hair," Cheryl teased. "That'd hold it once and for all. It'd be cheaper, too."

Cheryl's husband and Jennifer's adoptive father, Tom, was a construction contractor and experienced cabinetmaker who'd built much of their beautiful new home with his own hands. He'd also built a deck and playhouse in the back for the kids, the deck especially for Jennifer, who loved to lie on a chaise longue in the Florida sun, tanning herself and gabbing on the phone with her friends.

Now, Jennifer's response was that universal plaint of all teenagers when they're teased about their looks—"M-o-m . . . !"

"Okay, okay." Cheryl laughed. "We'll see when I get home. But I may have to work a little late. The computers are acting up, and I'm behind on some reports."

The mother and daughter exchanged a few more comments, and then Cheryl hung up and went back to work.

At 5:45, the phone on her desk rang again. This time it was her husband.

"Where's Jennifer?" Tom asked. "I've got to leave to coach Jeremy's soccer game, and she knows she's supposed to be here to watch Megan."

"Maybe she just ran across to the neighbors', or something," Cheryl said. "I'm sure she'll be right back." Neither parent was really worried. Jennifer was a freckle-faced, giggly fourteen-year-old, but she was as smart as a whip, and she never, ever went anywhere without checking first with one of her parents. The Colhouers were a close family, and the kids were happy to follow their parents' few simple rules.

Cheryl hung up with Tom and went back to work. About fifteen minutes later, she was able to take a break, and she called home, expecting to talk to her daughter. Tom and Jeremy would already have left for the little boy's soccer game.

The telephone at her home rang and rang; no one answered.

Cheryl went back to her reports for a few minutes, and then tried home again.

No answer.

Finally, a little worried now, a little angry, she put the phone on redial. Over and over she called. Over and over the phone rang, unanswered.

"I'm going to head on home," she said to her co-workers at 6:45. "Something's going on."

It was a forty-minute drive from Tampa to the Land O'Lakes cul-de-sac where her home backed onto Myrtle Lake.

A squad car blocked the entrance to the cul-de-sac. The Colhouers' neighbor, Bill Moses, was leaning down, talking to the officers in the squad car, but when he saw Cheryl's car pull up, he straightened up and walked over to her.

Bill opened Cheryl's driver's door. "Slide over, Cheryl," he said, an odd look on his face. "I'll drive in from here."

Cheryl just looked up at him. "What are you talking about? What's going on?"

She looked toward her house now and saw the ambulance with its flashing red beacons, the squad cars, the police officers and neighbors milling around her house.

"Bill, get away from me!" she said. "It's Tom, isn't it? Or Jeremy. Something's happened to Tom or Jeremy!"

Bill was trying to push Cheryl over so he could get into the driver's seat, and Cheryl was flailing against him. Suddenly, she grabbed him by the collar.

"What's happened to Tom and Jeremy? Tell me!"

The two police officers, one a young woman, came up now and stood next to Bill.

"Cheryl, Cheryl—they're fine," Bill said, grasping at Cheryl's waving arms. He held both her hands tightly in his own. "Cheryl, hold on, now . . . it's Jennifer. Jennifer's dead."

Relief flooded through her. "Bill," she said, *"whoever* it is, it's *not* Jennifer. I just talked to her a little while ago. Jennifer's fine. Whatever's happened, it's one of her friends or something. I have to get in there and see who it is. Oh, that poor mother. Will you *please* let go of me?"

The young female officer helped Cheryl, still protesting, out of her car and guided her over to the squad car. "Mrs.

Colhouer, would you like a sedative or something? Do you have a family doctor we can call for you?"

Cheryl pushed her away. Why wouldn't any of them listen? She had to get into her house, talk to Tom, and find out which of Jennifer's friends had had some horrible accident. As soon as she knew who it was, she'd be able to get right over there and offer her support to the poor child's mother.

She started to walk toward her house, and people began to turn toward her and then move back a step as she walked closer.

Tom came running out of Bill's front door when he saw her. He was sobbing and staggering as he walked, and he held out his arms toward her. "Oh, God," he wept. "Oh, God, Cheryl, baby, I'm sorry . . ."

Cheryl Colhouer started screaming.

Fourteen

Jennifer Lynn Jacobs had been born at St. Joseph's Hospital in Tampa, Florida, on July 24, 1973. "I threw up for five months when I was pregnant with Jennifer," Cheryl Colhouer would later laugh. "Then, once the throwing up was over, I was always so hungry that I gained fifty pounds before she was finally born."

From the first, Jennifer was a sweet-natured, untroubled feminine child, a very "girlie-girl," as her mother called her. Jennifer loved frilly dresses and lacy ribbons and all things feminine, but she had her own opinions, too, and she was clear about what she did and didn't like.

Once, when Jennifer was about four, her mother was trying to get her to eat her broccoli. "I tried everything," Cheryl said. "I disguised it in other food, I put cheese on it, but—no use, she wasn't going for it."

"Eat your broccoli, Jennifer," Cheryl said for the umpteenth time.

"I can't," the little girl replied, folding her arms and sticking out her lower lip.

"You mean you *won't*," Cheryl said.

"No, I *can't.*"

"Oh, and why *can't* you?"

"Because," little Jennifer said, "my taste bugs don't like it!"

At about this age, Jennifer Lynn invented an imaginary friend, "Cathy." Sometimes "Cathy" was Jennifer's best friend and sometimes she was her sister, but for the next three or four years, "Cathy" was here to stay. Jennifer didn't use "Cathy" as a scapegoat for her own little misdeeds, since Jennifer was a gentle little girl and rarely got into trouble; "Cathy" was quite simply her very own companion. "Cathy" became so much a part of Jennifer's existence that Cheryl, a little worried, asked her pediatrician about it. "Perfectly normal," the doctor said. " 'Cathy' will go away when Jennifer is ready to let her go." And she did.

Jennifer was a born mimic. She loved to play-act being a waitress. "Would you folks like a hamburger?" she would say to her family at the dinner table, an imaginary pen and notepad in her hand. "How about a refill on that coffee? Or some pie for dessert, maybe?"

Of all the famous people Jennifer liked to mimic, the singer/actress Cher was her favorite, and Jennifer would hold her imaginary microphone close to her mouth and belt out, in her best throaty voice, "I Got You, Babe," over and over. She had Cher's distinctive head movements down pat—her way of swaying her head to one side before flinging her head back to toss back her long black hair. On the little, curly-headed Jennifer, the star's sultry, exaggerated mannerisms were hysterically funny, and she happily played it to the hilt. When she walked out of a room, she would pause, one hand on the doorway, and look back over her shoulder, her expression heavy with movie-star angst. Then she'd toss her head back to one side and *sweep* out of the room in a grand Hollywood exit.

Jennifer's love of mime continued, and when they moved into the Land O'Lakes house and she had her own bedroom, she decorated her walls with brilliantly painted ceramic mime masks, each wearing a different expression and each with bright multicolored satin ribbons hanging down from bows on the sides of the painted faces. Then she hung a white sheet on the wall and drew it back, draped into a corner. She sprayed the sheet with red glitter paint, and the bright, speckled drape provided the perfect artistic backdrop for her mask collection. She also tied a number of soda cans, Coca-Cola and Seven-Up and such, to long colored ribbons and hung them from the ceiling.

"What's with the soda cans?" her mother asked.

Jennifer shrugged, looking up at them with satisfaction. "They just look *neat!*"

Cheryl Bishoff's first marriage had ended, and she was living in a trailer with her two kids and her friend Marcia in the summer of 1981, when she met Tom Colhouer, the man her family would always later refer to as "Tom Terrific."

Cheryl was working as a medical transcriber at St. Joseph's Hospital in Tampa. She came home one day to find Marcia standing around chatting with a man outside their trailer. Cheryl didn't pay much attention to him. But Marcia kept after her—"You should get together with this guy. He's great! He's single and good-looking, he's got a great job in construction, and he's nice as can be. *And,* he remembers you from high school. What more could you want?"

"Well, I don't remember him," Cheryl said. Marcia said Tom had told her that when they were all kids at H. B. Plant High School, he would come over to the Bishoff house and hang around with Cheryl's brother, Gary, trying at the same time to flirt with Gary's younger sister. Cheryl didn't remember him at all.

But Tom Colhouer kept coming around. One day he telephoned for Marcia and Cheryl answered the phone.

"Are you going to the reunion?" he asked her. Their high school reunion was coming up, and this now became Tom's refrain, his excuse to make conversation with Cheryl. He talked the reunion, he discussed the reunion, he did anything he could to keep up this mutual-interest dialogue with Cheryl.

Finally, on June 28, 1981, Cheryl agreed to go out for a drink with Tom Colhouer. They drove off for the evening in his El Camino and were never apart again. Toward the end of that summer, while Tom was at the trailer, waiting for Cheryl to finish getting ready, eight-year-old Jennifer marched up to him as he sat at the kitchen table. "When are you going to marry my mother?" Jennifer asked, with all the bald-faced, embarrassing honesty of little children.

Cheryl and "Tom Terrific" were married on November 28, 1981, five months to the day after their first date. Tom adopted Cheryl's kids, Jennifer and Jeremy, and together they adopted baby Megan. The family lived in Tom's house in Tampa while Tom, acting as general contractor, builder, and construction engineer all at the same time, built what was to be the family's permanent dream home in Land O'Lakes, Florida.

"Tom Colhouer turned out to be the best thing that ever happened to me and the kids," Cheryl Colhouer still says. " 'Tom Terrific' he surely was then and has always been since."

Fifteen

Det. Fay Wilber talked with Dep. Bobby Lightfoot, getting a briefing on what few facts were known so far. He nodded approval that Lightfoot had secured the outer perimeter, and that Ethell Bradshaw had been immediately assigned to begin a crime-scene log, and told her to continue with that as the night progressed.

The crime-scene log provides an accurate record of what would otherwise be a confused jumble of police activity around a major crime. That record then become a permanent part of the case file and usually proves invaluable to the investigating officers even years later, when defense attorneys try their best to make it sound like the police didn't know what they were doing at the scene. None of it has much to do with who actually committed the crime or why, but making the investigators sound like bumbling, confused goofs is a favorite defense tactic.

So now, the crime-scene log was being faithfully maintained. Det. Wilber told Dep. Lightfoot and several other "uniforms" to begin the canvass of the neighborhood. Always a good tactician, Wilber knew that it wouldn't be a smart move to have plainclothes officers wandering into people's homes and yards in the dark immediately following such a terrifying crime. No one had any idea who the killer was yet, or where he might still be hiding. The neighbors would, understandably, be on guard about strange men wandering around. The presence of uniformed officers provided reassurance at the same time they were gathering information.

"Get everybody's name," Wilber said now. "Not only of whoever you actually talk to, but the names of everybody else who lives in that house with them, and the names and addresses of anyone visiting anyone on this block anytime today. Ask about repairmen, garbagemen, delivery people, strangers, weirdos, cuckoo nephews—everybody. Find out who the mailman is and what time he comes by. Was it their regular carrier today, or was another mailman filling in? Ask if anybody heard anything, suspects anything, saw anything, *knows* anything.

"By the time you all get back here," Wilber concluded, "I want to know everything that everybody in this neighborhood knows."

Lightfoot and the others divided the block into a grid and assigned themselves sections. Then they set off, flashlights and notebooks in hand.

Many people in the neighborhood were still out on the sidewalks in front of their houses, huddled together in groups, clutching their small children to their sides, many of them with their hands pressed against their mouths.

Even though night had fallen, the Colhouer house, powder-blue with white trim and as neat and pretty as a model home, was lit up like high noon. For all the activity, the neighborhood was eerily quiet. All the police officers on the scene were tuned to the same radio frequency, so all their radios would simultaneously squawk into babbling noise, and then simultaneously, fall silent again. During those intervals, only the rattling of dry palm fronds far overhead and the soft *lap-lap* of nearby Lake Myrtle could be heard. Overlaying the whole scene, the Lights from Mars continued their *whirr*-stop, *whirr*-stop announcement of violent, unexpected death.

"How was Jennifer killed?" "What happened in there?" "Is it true poor little Jeremy found her body?" "How are her parents holding up?" The neighbors were desperate for information, but Lightfoot and the others could not, would not, tell them anything. The officers simply shook their heads in answer to the questions and then started asking questions of their own: What time did you come home? Did you see anything out of the ordinary? Who else lives here with you?

The single question most on the minds of everyone was: "Who killed Jennifer?"

A fourteen-year-old boy down the block told the canvassing police officers he was a classmate of Jennifer's at Land O'Lakes High School. "It's not fair!" the boy nearly shouted. "She just got her braces off two weeks ago, and she looked great!"

Two "suspicious" cars seemed to have been loitering around the neighborhood that afternoon—suspicious only because they didn't belong to any of the neighbors or any of their regular visitors. Oddly, both cars were red. One was a late-model red Ford, and neighbors described seeing the car at about 5 P.M., slowing down here and there along the block while the driver, a young white male, seemed to be peering at the fronts of the houses on Wayne Way. The Ford would slow down, crawl along, and then speed up again. It was seen by various people, traveling back and forth first in one direction, then the other.

The other "suspicious" red car was, unmistakably, a Corvette. The distinctive lines, the elongated, low-slung, sharklike shape of the Chevrolet Corvette, make it arguably the world's most identifiable car.

Several residents on streets surrounding the Colhouer place remembered seeing the 'Vette at differing times during the late afternoon hours. Dep. Bobby Lightfoot interviewed, among many other people, Adam Santiago, who told him about the "idiot Corvette driver" racing around the neighborhood right around 5 P.M. Santiago remembered the time because he and his little boy were just going into the house for dinner.

The house just down the way from Mr. Santiago's was empty, although an old blue Cougar was parked out in front. The deputies made a note to return to the address at a later time.

Satisfied that the neighborhood canvass was well under way and in good hands, Det. Fay Wilber met up with ID tech Bill Ferguson, who had done his initial walk-through of the scene. Now Wilber and Ferguson walked the house together, one room at a time. They looked, and pointed, and leaned forward to peer closer at this and that throughout the house.

They had no way to know what they were looking for, but both knew the killer had entered the house either through the front door or through the garage, gone into the family room and up the stairs, turned left, and entered Jeremy's bedroom. Then, when he'd finished his monstrous deed, he'd had to travel a path down the stairs, through the other rooms, and back out of the house. Somewhere, amid all the layers, the years, of Colhouer existence in this home, the stranger had left something of himself behind. They always do.

In the big, modern Colhouer kitchen, the men noted breakfast dishes in the sink and some silverware on the drainboard, including several sharp kitchen knives. The beige living room carpet had obviously been freshly vacuumed; foot-wide vacuum cleaner wheel tracks crisscrossed the room, undisturbed by any footprints. This was one room they would not have to process. Jennifer's own room was on the first floor, immediately to the left of the front door. A tiled hallway led back to the kitchen and family room. To the right of the front door was a powder room and then the living room, and directly ahead lay the stairway to the second floor.

Upstairs, Jeremy's bedroom door opened into the room.

Ferguson was chilled as he realized that the entire frame was smashed in, the screws that had held the door in place pulled loose from the wall. A quiet, gentle-speaking man, Ferguson's thought as he looked up and around the shattered doorframe was: "Boy . . . somebody powerful. Somebody in good physical shape."

"I was just stunned when I stood in the doorway of that bedroom and looked at that little girl," Ferguson would say later. "I had a six-year-old daughter of my own, and in my mind's eye, that might have been her. I've processed well over a thousand crime scenes, and it never really affected me like that before—I mean, personally, you know? It was just my job . . . until then. Until Jennifer Colhouer. That mental picture of my own little girl—it just sat like a rock in my stomach all the time I was processing that house, and it's been with me at every crime scene since then."

The detectives had a moment of hope when they realized that on the back of Jennifer's left thigh was a clear, full handprint—in blood. But their hope faded as soon as Ferguson looked closely at the print. "No good," he said to Wilber. "No fingerprint ridge detail at all. None. It's very probable he had gloves on."

Ferguson went out to his car to bring in his 35mm Nikon and a bag of film. His crime lab supervisor, Sgt. Rick Moore, pulled up just then. With Moore was a brand-new civilian ID tech, Jim Sessa. Sgt. Moore had the lab video camera and told Ferguson that he and Sessa would videotape the entire outside of the house and grounds. Then, the Pasco County medical examiner, Dr. John C. Gallagher, pulled up. With him were not his usual one, but two assistant M.E.s. Dr. Gallagher would make the official pronouncement of death as required by law, but would then hold off any further examination until Ferguson had photographed the entire scene from every conceivable angle.

Bill Ferguson, like many people who live in Florida, was a transplant from up north—a "snowbird," as the native

Floridians call them. He was raised in a little town called State College, Pennsylvania, famous only for being the home of Penn State University. When he was seventeen years old, Ferguson left home and moved to Key West, Florida. He was just a teenager, of course, and he thought he was moving into an easy life of beach blankets, beer, and bikini babes. What he found, though, was economic hard times, and it was a scramble from month to month to eke out a minimum-existence living.

Finally, when he was twenty, Ferguson heard about a job opening: the Jacksonville Beach police department was looking for cadets, young men to act as "gofers" and report-takers—junior police, in effect. Ferguson took the job. A year later, openings came along in Key West for the real police and he took the exam, passed it, and became a Key West police officer. Five years later, in 1976, Ferguson was married, and by then, he was so disgusted with the rampant drug-involved corruption he found in Key West that he transferred up to Florida's Citrus Belt, to the Pasco County sheriff's department. He had to put in his time in the patrol division, like everybody else, but his interest was always in forensics, and in 1982, when an opening in the crime-scene unit came up, Ferguson grabbed it. Pasco County sent him to the Sirchie Lab Crime Scene School in Raleigh, North Carolina, for training, and when he came back, he finally had the job and the life that he wanted.

Now, in the Colhouer house, two hundred photographs later, Ferguson finally packed his camera away and nodded to Dr. Gallagher. The medical examiner crouched down and gently turned Jennifer onto her back. He talked out his initial findings into a miniature tape recorder while his assistants stood by and took notes. Paper bags were fitted over Jennifer's hands in order to preserve any evidence on her fingers or under her nails.

Dr. Gallagher observed that there were several tiny fibers, foreign hairs, on Jennifer's body. Using long steel tweezers, he carefully lifted each fiber and put it into a little plastic bottle, which he snapped closed and then handed to Bill Ferguson. Ferguson marked each piece of evidence with a sequential number and then his initials. The fibers collected by Dr. Gallagher would be labeled nos. 6BF through 10BF.

As Dr. Gallagher worked, Bill Ferguson suddenly leaned forward. He thought he had seen something—or was it a trick of the lighting? He looked closer.

"Dr. Gallagher," he said, "look at this. Is it what I think?"

The medical examiner stepped around to the other side of Jennifer's body and examined the small, silvery translucent spot of liquid on the back of her thigh.

"Yep," he said. "Semen." Both men hid their rage at what the unknown killer had done. Yet at the same time, they had the grim satisfaction of knowing that this tiny bit of liquid might be just the evidence they'd need someday to put the killer away for good. Even before the use of DNA in criminal trials, human semen or saliva had been admissible as evidence, since many men are "secreters"; that is, their blood type can be identified from their semen or saliva secretions. Now, with the new admissibility of DNA profiles, a semen sample was as unique and damning to an individual criminal as his own fingerprints.

Dr. Gallagher opened his bag, and with his gloved hands, took out a little cardboard container and marked the lid with his own evidence codes. Then he dipped a cotton swab into sterile saline solution, and with the moistened swab, collected two samples of the translucent liquid, which he smeared onto glass slides. He placed the slides in the cardboard box, but left it open so that the specimen could dry in air before he sealed the box. Then he picked up his tape recorder and went on with his examination.

When Fay Wilber checked back in with the evidence team, Ferguson told him what they'd found. Wilber was as ecstatic as the forensics experts at the recovery of the usable evidence. "We got him!" he said. "Now, all we have to do is find the son-of-a-bitch."

Sixteen

While the evidence collection was going on upstairs, Fay Wilber was inside, outside, upstairs, and down, coordinating all the other police activities. Across the lane from the Colhouer driveway, a big television van pulled up, and the TV technicians began rigging up their thick, black cables to an enormous portable generator. *Action News* from Tampa was on the scene.

Wilber and his partner, Det. Gary Fairbanks, went next door to interview the Colhouer family. Two other Pasco detectives were already there, assigned to keep watch on everyone until it was determined what part anybody might have played in the tragedy of Jennifer's death. The detectives knew they wouldn't be able to get a whole lot of information, but they did need to establish everybody's comings and goings right away, to begin narrowing down the crime's "window of opportunity."

The Pasco County sheriff's department has two victim advocates on permanent staff. One or the other would always be on call, twenty-four hours a day, to respond with the sheriff's police to serious auto crashes, accidental injuries, or crimes—scenes of tragedy and trauma. Usually, one or the other advocate would respond, but this was no "usual" crime; this was the violent murder of a child. Ellie Calhoun and Jane Stanley were both there now, with the Colhouers, trying to help the family hold onto sanity even while their world was spinning out into horror and madness.

The advocates had to tread a careful pathway in as-yet-unsolved cases like this. No one had yet been ruled out as a suspect, and for all the advocates knew, they might be trying to offer comfort and solace to the very person who had committed the murder. In all cases, their job was to act as liaison between the victim's family and the police; to provide counseling referrals, if they were needed; and to explain to the family—but carefully, carefully—what the police officers were doing at each step of the investigation and why.

"Cheryl Colhouer was frenzied," Ellie Calhoun would say later. "I think I'll hear that poor woman's screams for her little girl for the rest of my life. Tom seemed frozen in shock, like he'd been glazed or something. He'd sit there, staring and staring, and he couldn't seem to understand what anybody said to him or follow what was going on around him."

The medical examiner had taken Jennifer's body to the county lab in Largo. He would do the autopsy the next morning. Wilber told ID tech Curtis Page to go to the morgue, too. Page would collect Jennifer's personal effects, two tiny rings and a watch, and inventory them for return to the family. Then, he would "laser" her entire body for any trace evidence they might have missed at the scene.

Upstairs, ID tech Bill Ferguson was still hard at work. He describes his job as "locating, gathering, photographing, recording, impounding, preserving, transferring, and testing." It is all those things, of course, and a lot more, too.

When Wilber checked in with him, Ferguson was up to evidence inventory no. 61BF. He had taken carpet samples from every room in the house except the living room, where the visible vacuum tracks across the carpet proved that the killer had not walked through that room. He had collected and sealed the kitchen wastebasket with all its contents, as well as the wastebasket in Jennifer's downstairs bedroom, and an empty Coke can that had been lying on her dresser. He collected a bucket and a pair of kitchen gloves from under the kitchen sink, dishrags, dishtowels, bathtowels, rugs, bathmats, and toilet tank covers from both bathrooms. He also unscrewed and inventoried all the sink traps, the elbow-shaped drainpipes under the sinks, and inventoried them.

Ferguson concentrated his special efforts on Jeremy's room and on the killer's "known path of travel," up the stairs, to the left, and into the bedroom. He had to have come back down those same stairs, and Ferguson dusted the entire stair rail, the wall opposite, the wall outside Jeremy's room, and the damaged doorframe. He inspected the tan carpeting in the upstairs hall for bloodstains and finally found a tiny red spot at the top of the stairs. He cut out a one-by-two-foot square of the carpeting surrounding the tiny stain and took that, too.

Most of the evidence being collected, of course, came from Jeremy's room. Jennifer's white shorts, with her blue panties still bunched up inside them, were catalogued. Ferguson took the little yellow racecar next to the knife; the smiling black monkey; all the sheets, pillowcases, blankets, and bedspreads on the bunkbeds; a little boy's red-and-white T-shirt and two pairs of jeans; a baseball cap found on the bedroom floor; and finally, even the bookcase that had held all Jeremy's toy vehicle collection.

The items from Jeremy's room had one thing in common—they were all splattered with blood.

As Bill Ferguson collected each one, he put it into an ordinary brown paper bag. The cheap brown paper everybody knows as grocery bags makes good storage for evidence collection simply because it *is* so cheap, and therefore has little cotton-rag content, like more expensive papers. Plain brown paper allows the evidence inside to "breathe" and dry out naturally; it doesn't intensify or absorb heat from external sources and therefore doesn't "cook" the evidence inside the bag.

Ferguson folded over the edge of each evidence bag with a sharp crease, stapled it, labeled it with his special code, and then sealed it with red crime-scene evidence tape. Evidence tape is different from the yellow "Do Not Cross" tape everyone is familiar with at crime scenes. Evidence tape is red, onionskin thin, nearly translucent, and extremely flimsy. It is impossible to peel off, steam off, remove, reuse, or rearrange in any way because it tears to pieces upon being handled.

Bill Ferguson was on his hands and knees now, using his utility knife to cut out the large square of bloody gold carpet where Jennifer had died. It was now nearly three o'clock in the morning.

"I want the whole thing," said Fay Wilber from the doorway.

"The whole what?" asked Ferguson.

"The whole carpet."

"The whole *room?*"

"The whole room."

So, the whole room it was. The men walked around the edges of the room, lifting the furniture aside. Then they got down with pliers and began ripping out the underlying tacking strips from the wall-to-wall carpet. Finally, it was loosened from all four perimeters. Ferguson went out to the evidence van and returned with a huge roll of butcher paper, also nonfibrous. They carefully rolled up the bloody carpet into a spiral—loose, so as not to crush or break any hairs or other foreign materials. Then, Ferguson wrapped the carpet roll with the butcher paper, around and around. He stapled the length of the wrapping, sealed up both ends, codemarked it, and then put several strips of evidence tape along the length and at either end.

Next, the ID tech and the other technicians who were

helping him began setting up their tripods and gathering together brushes, rollers, and cameras.

"I'm going to laser the entire room for fingerprints," Ferguson told Wilber.

Wilber nodded. "I want the entire house."

"I knew you'd say that. It'll take a while."

"How long?"

"Two full days, maybe, if I have enough help."

"You just ask; you can have whatever and whoever you need," Wilber said. Standing in the doorway, his eyes traveled up the side of the shattered frame and across the top of the jamb. Plaster-encrusted screws protruded between the wall and the ripped-away molding.

"I want this door, too, Bill," he said. "The whole thing, frame and all. Have it cut right out of the wall and take the whole thing to the lab, just as it is."

Ferguson nodded and continued setting up his laser lights.

"Whoever did this, Bill, I want him," Wilber said. "I want him *bad.*"

The ID tech didn't look up, but he nodded. "I know."

Seventeen

"You seen the paper yet this morning?"

It was 7 A.M., and Bill Ferguson was standing in the Colhouer driveway, leaning against his van and sipping at a styrofoam cup of black coffee. Now, he handed the *Tampa Tribune* to Det. Fay Wilber, who had just pulled up.

Wilber took the folded-back newspaper, but before he looked at it, he turned at the approach of a uniformed deputy. When he had finally gone home last night, just a few hours before Thursday morning had dawned, Wilber had ordered an around-the-clock guard on the Colhouer property. The deputy had been sitting in his marked squad car, but he got out now and walked up to the two men in the driveway.

"Anything?" Wilber asked.

"Not a peep." The deputy looked groggy, and now he yawned and ran his hand through his hair.

"Go get yourself some coffee," Wilber said. "We're here now for the day."

The deputy shook his head. "Nah, my relief'll be pulling up in twenty minutes or so. Then I'm heading home and hitting the sack. After maybe a beer or two. You daytime dollies got your schedules all mixed up. I drink coffee at nine at night, when I'm waking up for work. Eight o'clock in the morning is the time for a coupla cold brews."

Wilber and Ferguson walked toward the house. "Remember what that was like, working the midnight shift?" Ferguson asked.

"Yeah, eggs and bacon at night, and meatloaf, mashed potatoes, and beer first thing in the morning. My stomach's turning over just talking about it. How did we do it for so long?"

"We were kids, that's how. Rookies are indestructible."

The two men had known one another for years. They'd both been cops together down in Key West, that colorful, tropical southernmost point in the U.S. that proudly bills itself as "The Last Resort." The history of the island of Key West is replete with pirates and shipwreckers who used to lure the big sailing ships toward shore using false signal lights. The ships, thinking they were approaching nearby Cuba or one of the Bahamas, would tear out their hulls on the coral reef that surrounds the island, and the wreckers would swarm out into the water and claim the salvage. The name itself, "Key West," is an Anglicization of the original Spanish name for the little island. *"Cayo Hueso,"* the Spaniards dubbed the treacherous island—Bone Key. All that ended when the U.S. Navy moved in at the start of World War I, bringing their lighthouse with them.

During the late 1960s and early 1970s, when "flower power" was in all its dubious glory across America, young people everywhere were walking away from what they perceived to be a hypocritical, money-grubbing culture, and walking instead to the beat of a different drummer. Many of these disaffected youngsters headed for California, others left the country altogether, but many headed for the Sunshine State—for Florida, and particularly for the Florida Keys.

One young man who'd followed much the same path, but with vastly different motivations, was a twenty-two-year-old Michigan man named Fay Wilber.

Wilber's father was a pipefitter in their small Central Michigan town, a union man with the steel industry. When his son was born, the boy was named Fay after Wilber's beloved brother, who had died when he was only thirty years old. The first Fay Wilber had been something of an icon in the Wilber family, a sort of ideal young man, and the second Fay, from the time he was a little boy, felt he was expected to live up to that image. In the way of small children, though, little Fay had taken it into his head that if he was, indeed, "just like Uncle Fay," then he, too, was going to die when he was thirty years old. He carried that frightening belief into young adulthood.

Young Fay got a job right out of high school building metal display units. He also married around the same time. Within a couple of years, as the steel industry began to collapse, so did the job, and then the marriage. With not much else to hang onto, young Fay packed up and headed down to Key West to stay for a while with his sister. He worked construction, but it wasn't a steady job. The Key West police department announced they had a few openings. Fay took the exam, was hired, and went to work as a police officer. There, he met another young idealist cop from up north named Bill Ferguson.

Officer Fay Wilber had less than a year on the job when he was approached by his superiors to become a detective. He was appalled; he knew he didn't have nearly enough experience, but they kept pushing, telling him the job brought with it "great benefits." This last was said with sort of a nod and a wink. Wilber did not find the atmosphere in the department to be anything like what he had expected from police work, and within a few years, he was very unhappy and desperate to leave. Another unhappy young cop was Bill Ferguson.

In 1975, Wilber quit the force, along with two other police officers. Within the year, Ferguson would follow suit. Several years after that, in September 1978, the Federal authorities, including Customs, the FBI, and the DEA, moved in and brought drug smuggling charges against four detectives.

Fay Wilber moved up to Florida's Citrus Belt, where he had already applied for a job with the Pasco County sheriff's office. He did his time on the highways as a road deputy, nine years, in fact, and then, in 1984, he became a detective—a *real* detective.

Neither Fay Wilber nor Bill Ferguson had ever regretted pulling up stakes and leaving "The Last Resort" behind. Both men were now steady family guys with wives and kids to go home to, and they were happy to have them.

Now, Fay Wilber looked down at the *Tampa Tribune* in his hand. "PASCO TEEN FOUND SLAIN AT HOME" blared the headline. The reporter had obviously had a short deadline, and the story, though four columns long, was sketchy on details and padded out with paragraph-long quotes from neighbors talking about how shocked they were, and what a lovely young lady Jennifer Colhouer had been.

The article went on to include the first terse quotes by Pasco County sheriff Jim Gillum. All Gillum would say was that Jennifer "was definitely murdered" and that the slaying was "a very, very disturbing crime." He hinted that they had "a few limited leads" and refused to pinpoint the time or manner of death pending autopsy results.

Gillum would remain tight-lipped about details of the case throughout the entire course of the investigation, a stance that is certainly justifiable from a law-enforcement point of view, but which resulted in some rather vociferous backlash of negative publicity from a frightened community.

Wilber stayed by to oversee ID tech Bill Ferguson and the other forensics people getting set up for their lasering of the entire Colhouer house. The lab people had decided to dust the outside of the whole house, too, from ground-level to the height of a tall man's reach. The vinyl siding outside would be damp, and they had to use a special SPR—small particle reagent—which wouldn't smear when applied to a moist surface. The evidence techs also took soil samples and individual blades of grass from the four corners of the Colhouer property. It might seem that dirt is just dirt, but that's far from the case. Urban dwellers add all sorts of things to their lawns—weed killers, turf builders, insecticides. Each different brand name of these products has a slightly different chemical formula, so that over the years, the soil in one person's yard can end up distinctly identifiable, even distinguishable from his next-door neighbor's.

Wilber was out on the lawn, watching the lasering operation, when Det. Robert Hoefs pulled up.

Hoefs parked his unmarked squad car behind Wilber's and stepped onto the lawn, a manila folder in hand. The two detectives stood for a moment watching the evidence techs powder the house. Long sections of matte black striped the horizontal siding panels, as though a color-blind painter had been let loose. The black SPR powder was bringing up myriad light spots on the powder-blue siding.

"I'm always fascinated watching these guys work," Hoefs said. "Think about it—everybody who ever touched that siding left some kind of trace of themselves. The people in the factory who pulled it off the assembly line and put it in a box, the salesmen at the store, the construction guys who put it up. It's all still there."

Wilber nodded. "I spent a year in forensics. There's always that moment when you're snooping along, an inch at a time, and all of a sudden a print pops up, or you find a single hair or a rubber scuffmark or whatever, and you know you got him. It's a kind of rush, like when you're a kid on Christmas morning ripping open that big special present. What's going to be in there? What're you going to find?"

"Well, that's enough nostalgia for the day," Wilber said, turning to Hoefs. "What're you guys turning up?" Teams of detectives were scouring the neighborhood. Others were back at the office in Dade City, pulling out old and pending cases, searching for similarities, searching for patterns, searching . . .

"You're going to like this," Hoefs said, opening the manila folder. "It seems that young Phil Moses . . ."

"The next door neighbor's kid?"

Hoefs nodded. "The fourteen-year-old. Little Phil and his buddies, let's see here . . . Eric Brouard, age fifteen, and Tony Aguilar, age fourteen, are some of our local junior burglars."

Wilber had been staring at the house, but now he whirled and looked at his fellow detective.

"Residential?"

"Yep. Looks like a first time for Eric and Phil, but it seems our little Tony is a regular pro at the breaking-and-entering business. Take a guess how many priors he's got."

"How many could he have?" Wilber asked. "You said he's, what, fourteen?"

"Fourteen years old, and *nine,* count 'em, *nine* arrests for residential burglary. And those are only the ones we know about, of course. How many's he pulled off and got away with? From what everybody says, Tony's a very weird little dude. Most of the other high school kids won't have anything to do with him."

Det. Hoefs explained that a home on nearby Kay Circle had been broken into on January 2, just three weeks earlier. Talk around the area at the time was that some strange rituals had been performed inside the house, ritualistic signs painted on the walls and so forth. Hoefs visited the property himself to get a first-hand look.

"I just came from there," he said now. "There's patches of burned carpet in the living room and one of the bedrooms, like they tried a couple of times to burn the place down. They kicked in a couple of the interior walls, ripped down all the cabinet doors in the kitchen. Just trashed the place."

"What about the ritualistic aspect?" Wilber asked.

Hoefs shook his head. "Hangman! You know that game kids play where you try to guess a word and every time you're wrong, you add a piece to a gallows? That's what they did in there—played hangman with an indelible marker on the guy's living room wall. It's a real mess, but it doesn't look like any of that Satanic cult stuff. Somebody from the neighborhood recognized one of them as they were sneaking out, and that's how they got caught. And get this, Fay," Hoefs said, "their court date was yesterday morning over at HRS in Dade City. We've got somebody on it right now, seeing if they all showed up for court or what."

The two men discussed other aspects of the case, other leads that were shaping up. The night before, while Wilber had been in the Colhouer house with Bill Ferguson and the evidence techs, someone had called 911 to report that the "suspicious" red Ford which had been seen earlier in the afternoon was again circling the neighborhood. In moments, squad cars surrounded the Ford. Out stepped a terrified pizza deliveryman. He readily admitted cruising up and down Wayne Way between 4 and 5, and said he was looking for the address of his delivery. The new subdivision did not yet have clearly marked addresses. He showed the sheriff's deputies his delivery log, which verified his story. Nevertheless, they would check him out further.

Hoefs also said that he and other detectives had driven around Lake Myrtle and talked to the people on the other side whose grounds faced the Colhouer backyard across the lake. This property was a huge thoroughbred horse farm and training center. The owner said that during the afternoon, she'd been out in the barns all day, caring for a couple of sick horses. But she had never looked across the little lake and hadn't seen anything of value.

The sheriff's detectives had been patiently making their

way through a long list of Jennifer Colhouer's teenaged friends. The social dynamics of young teenagers pulses with the high drama and overactive hormone explosions typical of their budding adulthood. Jennifer's circle of friends was no different, and the police already had many tips and clues to follow up, innuendos about who "had it in" for whom, juvenile jealousies, hungry young hearts, and incipient sexual yearnings.

Now Hoefs had added to the pool of possibilities with this follow-up on the Kay Circle burglary ring.

"I need to step back now and take a close, close look at the whole Moses family," Wilber said. "Think about it. The father was out on the lake in his boat when Tom Colhouer got home. How long was he out there? So far, we've only got his word for it. And the oldest kid from the wife's first marriage, Ross—there's another one. Jennifer had a crush on him, even though he's twenty-five years old. Told her friends he was her 'fiancé.' Always blowing him kisses and all that little-girl stuff. He says he was aware of it but never encouraged her. *He* says. And now the fourteen-year-old, Phil, a house burglar."

The two detectives walked back to their cars. "Now that I think of it," Wilber said, "when the Colhouers went to Virginia for a week last month, they said they left their house key next door with Phil, so he could take care of the pets and whatever. They took their key back, but so what? The kid had the run of the place for a week, he knew the layout, he knew what all they had in there. Maybe him and his burglar buddies decided to go in there yesterday and clean it out."

"And maybe Jennifer got in their way," Hoefs added. "I'll check in with you later. Let me know what happens, especially with that Tony Aguilar. From all I hear, that's supposed to be the weirdest kid this side of the Twilight Zone."

Eighteen

"He won't . . . well, clean himself after he goes to the bathroom," his mother said. She was talking about her four-teen-year-old son, Tony, and there were tears of shame in her eyes. And something else: fear.

Mrs. Aguilar said that she had moved from upstate New York a decade before. Her young son, Tony, had stayed in New York with his father and the father's new wife.

"I didn't just abandon my son," she told Det. Wilber now. "It was just that I could never handle him, not from the time he was a little kid. Tony was already strange, even when he was a little boy, and now that he's nearly grown up, he's still strange. But it's scarier now because he's so big."

Mrs. Aguilar said that two years before, Tony's father had called and said he didn't want the fourteen-year-old in his house anymore. He had little kids of his own now and his new family was afraid of Tony.

"What could I do?" Mrs. Aguilar wept. "He's my son, no matter what he is. So we split the cost of the airfare and I brought Tony here to live with me. He has to live *some-where,* doesn't he?"

"When you say Tony was strange as a little kid, Mrs. Aguilar, what do you mean?" Wilber asked. "Strange, how?"

"Well, he was always sort of cold-feeling, I mean, for a little kid, you know? Like all the other little kids would 'ooh' and 'ah' over a new puppy, or something like that. But not Tony. He'd just sort of stand there, looking on. He wasn't ever outright mean to the animals or the other kids, not that I saw, anyways, but it was like he just didn't feel anything."

"What else?" Wilber could see that Mrs. Aguilar was talking around something else, something she was reluctant to say.

"Well, mostly it was the bathroom thing. I couldn't ever potty-train him. He just wouldn't go on the pot, he'd go in his pants. I read all the women's magazines and talked to the other mothers about how they did it with their kids. I tried everything, really, but it didn't matter. Tony wouldn't do it. Sometimes, I'd make him sit on that little pot for a couple of hours, even. But he'd just hold it, and then do it in his pants. Not only number one, but number two. He did number two in his pants all the time until he was, oh, let's see, maybe ten years old. We could be sitting on the couch, watching TV, and all of a sudden, I'd smell it. Tony'd be sitting there, going in his pants. And he'd just walk around like that. Sometimes, he'd be just walking along, and pee would come running down his leg. I'd have to drag him in the bathroom and make him clean it off. He hated taking a bath, too. Still does. It's awful. I mean, the bedsheets, my furniture, everything."

Wilber scribbled a few notes in his blue spiral notebook, but actually, he was giving the embarrassed mother the opportunity to talk without having a cop staring right in her face. Sometimes it's easier that way.

"Did you ever take Tony to a doctor about this?" Wilber asked.

"Of course I did! Not lately, he's too big now and he won't do anything I tell him. But when he was little, of course I took him to doctors. We didn't have any insurance . . . what insurance company is going to pay, anyway, because you tell them he goes to the bathroom in his pants? Would you like a cup of coffee or something?"

Wilber said no, thank you, he was fine. Actually, his stomach wasn't feeling so great all of a sudden, but he didn't say that.

"I took him to a doctor first when he was, I think, about four years old. Four or five, maybe. A pediatrician. He gave him an examination, and they took blood tests and everything, but finally, the doctor said there wasn't anything wrong with Tony, nothing wrong with his body, anyway. He said sometimes little kids develop what he called 'social skills' later than other kids. He said maybe Tony was just a slow developer in this bathroom business, and I should just keep after him about it."

Mrs. Aguilar said that once Tony started school, life became a nightmare for her. "The teachers would call me and tell me to come and get him, all snotty and mad at *me,* like it was my fault, what Tony did. They said the other kids would move their desks away from him and hold their noses. Stuff like that. They said the other kids made fun of him, called him 'Pooper.' "

She said that her marriage was falling apart all during this time. Some of the problem was their constant arguments about what to do with Tony, but there were other problems, too, like her husband's drinking.

"Sometimes a case of beer a day. It's funny if you think about it—Tony wouldn't go to the bathroom, and his father was in there all the time. You can't win."

There were other women, too, she said, and she finally filed for divorce. Her husband said that all the problems they'd had with Tony were her fault; she was too lenient, she was too soft with the boy, she was too this, too that.

"He said he'd take Tony, straighten him out, make a man of him, and all that," Mrs. Aguilar said now. "You know the rest. Most times now, he'll use the bathroom. *Most* times, but you can never tell with him whether he's going to or not. And even when he does, sometimes he just won't clean himself afterward."

Like all parents, Fay Wilber thought about his own kids while he was listening to the woes of other parents: his eleven-year-old boy, and his pretty little seven-year-old daughter—both good kids, smart, loving, obedient. Clean.

"Can you tell me about Tony's movements on Wednesday?" he asked. "What did he do, what time did he come and go all day? Whatever you know." Wilber already had Tony's schedule down pretty tight, from checking and crosschecking with the other teenagers. But he wanted to see if the mother could add anything. She did.

Mrs. Aguilar nodded. "I was late to work on Wednesday, because I had to take Tony over to Dade City for a hearing on that burglary. That's another thing about Tony—all that breaking into people's houses. I keep trying to get him to tell me why he does it, and all he says is he likes the feeling of looking around through other people's stuff. He says it makes him feel good." Tony's mother sighed and shook her head.

"Anyway," she continued, "we were there in court about an hour and a half, then we stopped back here so Tony could get his books and school stuff. I dropped him off at school at, oh, about 11, and then I went to work. I got home about 6:30."

"And when you got home, was Tony here?" Wilber asked.

Mrs. Aguilar nodded. "He was here, and when I came in, you could have knocked me over with a feather!"

"And why is that, Mrs. Aguilar?"

"When I came in, Tony was in the bathroom, taking a shower!"

"I didn't kill that damn girl," Tony said.

Wilber had gotten Mrs. Aguilar's permission, and he sat down now across from Tony, notepad in hand. When he asked about the burglary on Kay Circle, Tony readily admitted his part in it. Wilber asked him why they had done it, and Tony said, "it was something to do." But he denied having anything to do with the murder of Jennifer Colhouer.

"Nobody said you did, Tony," Wilber said. "We're interviewing everybody, you know that. So tell me what you did Wednesday, where you went, who with, and what time."

Tony said his mother woke him up about 7 A.M. They had to be in Dade City at 9. After the hearing, he said, they'd come back to the house for his school stuff and his mother dropped him off at school at 11.

"I had a problem with one of my teachers on Wednesday," Tony said. "You're probably going to find that out anyways, so I figured I might as well tell you."

"What kind of problem?" Wilber asked.

Tony shrugged. "One of the other guys was ragging at me; he always does, and finally I told him to go fuck himself. Everybody else in class thought it was pretty funny, actually, but *she* got all bent out of shape, the teacher. Made this really big deal about it." Tony shrugged again, as though there was no accounting for adults.

Tony said he'd left school at 2:10, as usual, and got home at 2:30. He had a sandwich and then rode his bike down the street to Eric's house, where they'd stayed inside, watching the news, for about fifteen to twenty minutes. Then he went back home, hung around awhile, and took his dog out into the back yard to "do his thing." Tony said he rode his bike back to Eric's about 3:30, and he and the other guys practiced "jumping their bikes" in front of Eric's awhile. Then he went back home.

"What time was it when you left Eric's?" Wilber asked.

"I don't know. How would I know? What do you think, I go around looking at my watch every five minutes? Just in case you guys might be coming around later to check on me?"

"Watch the mouth, Tony," Wilber said. "I'm sitting here, talking to you with respect, aren't I? Do the same."

"Well, I don't know what time I left Eric's. I was just there awhile and then I went home. Later, I saw the ambulance go by," Tony said. "It stopped at Jennifer's house. I took my bike and rode back over to Eric's, and then we both rode over to Jennifer's. We were just hanging around on the sidewalk, minding our own business, but Jennifer's dad started yelling at us. He was standing outside his house, on the grass, and he told us to get out of there, quit hanging around."

Tony looked aggrieved at this.

"You ever been inside the Colhouer house, Tony?" Wilber asked.

Tony said no, he had not.

"How did Jennifer die, Tony? I mean, what do you think happened to her?"

Again, Tony shrugged. "She was raped. But I hear you guys got some fingerprints off her shoulders. What else . . . there was blood all over the walls."

"Anything else?" Wilber asked, noncommittally.

"He probably choked her out first."

Wilber told the boy that he needed hair and blood samples from him. "If you feel you have a problem with that, Tony, then I'll go see a judge first and get a court order. But either way, we're going to test you and the other guys."

"Hey, whatever turns you on, man," Tony shrugged. "Do whatever you want."

After Tony and his mother walked out of the office, Wilber pulled out his notes to double-check. And there it was.

Eric Brouard said that Tony had left his place at 5:15. He remembered the time exactly because he had chores to do before his parents got home at 5:30, and he had had to race around getting them done, looking at his watch every few minutes.

Tony's mother said she had come home at 6:30 and unaccountably, found him taking a shower.

Tony Aguilar, a residential burglar who liked sneaking into other people's houses because it "made him feel good," obviously a seriously disturbed young man, could not be accounted for from 5:15 until 5:45, when Tom Colhouer had pulled into his driveway.

Nineteen

"RESIDENTS ON EDGE," read the *Tampa Tribune* on Friday, and the newspaper did not exaggerate. Fear pervaded the neighborhood. Who had done this terrible thing? And, as the hours and then days passed with no one in custody, "Where is he?" became the question on everyone's lips. The police had searched the neighborhood Wednesday night, of course, and the whole block had been crawling with cops ever since. But still, what if he was there all along, hiding out, and the police had missed him somehow? What if he was in one of their garages, curled up on the back floor of a car, or up in the rafters, even, waiting to attack some other kid? Waiting to sneak into a house, grab some cash and maybe a hostage, and make his escape?

That morning, the principal at Lake Myrtle Elementary School, Monica Joiner, made an announcement to the students and faculty. Ms. Joiner said that for the next few weeks at least, teachers at the 850-pupil school would be escorting home those students who didn't take the bus or get picked up in a car. The students were to gather in groups based on where they live. The group, with its teacher-escort, would walk each child to the front door of his house, and if no one was home, the student would be taken to a neighbor's home.

That plan went into effect immediately, and for the next weeks, the only children to be seen on the streets and sidewalks around Wayne Way were in large groups, with an adult walking next to them.

On Wednesday evening, the evening of Jennifer Colhouer's death, the local community action council had held their monthly meeting. Tom and Cheryl Colhouer had been missed at the meeting, and now, of course, all their neighbors knew why. One of the neighboring women who chaired the meeting said that on Thursday afternoon, she'd called in a locksmith and had new heavy-duty locks put on all her doors and windows. "I have an eighteen-month-old daughter," she said, "and my husband's gone all day at work. I'm terrified to go out of the house, even to the store. Until they catch this maniac, I'm just giving my shopping list to my husband and he can pick up the groceries on his way home."

Another neighbor said she and her husband had called his boss at the local auto parts store and insisted that his hours be changed so that he could be home with them by midafternoon when the kids got out of school. "What would I do here, alone with our little kids, if this lunatic decided to break in? I'll stay alone during the day, I have no choice, but when the kids are here, I want my husband here, too." His boss went along with their request, and said that temporarily, her husband could adjust his hours.

By now, the local locksmiths, alarm companies, and hardware stores couldn't keep up with the demand for security devices. "I live here alone," said one woman. "I bought this Doberman from one of those guard service companies in Tampa. He's attack trained and I have secret command words for him if anybody tries to come after me." She said she also acquired a gun and carried it with her now from room to room. "If I'm going into the kitchen to make a sandwich, I put it right on the counter next to me. When I go to bed at night, it's right there on my nightstand, loaded and ready. It feels kind of stupid to be walking around my own house with a gun like this," she said, "but it feels kind of good, too. If he comes in, he may get me, but I'll get him, too. I'm not going down without a fight."

Professional counselors had been called in at Land O'Lakes High School, where Jennifer had been a freshman. On Thursday, the day after her death, hundreds of high school students were absent from school, their parents calling in to say they were keeping their children home until they knew what was going on. By Friday, the absentee roll had doubled. Of those who did go in, nearly 300 asked to talk to counselors. Wild rumors rippled up and down the halls, and many students asked counselors and teachers for details about how Jennifer had died. But the staff had no more information than anyone else.

On Friday evening, January 22, Sheriff Jim Gillum issued a press bulletin through his department spokesman, Bob Loeffler. "Be on the lookout for a late-model red Chevrolet Corvette," the bulletin advised. By Saturday morning, Loeffler was still answering reporters' questions. He said that the car had been seen by a number of residents around the Colhouer neighborhood between 4 and 6 on Wednesday. "The man is not necessarily a suspect," Loeffler stressed. "It's just that we know that car was seen in the area, and we want to talk to the driver, to ask him some questions about anything he may have seen. We're asking him to come forward."

Loeffler described the Corvette's driver as white, late twenties to early thirties, with dark hair, and described by witnesses as "extremely good-looking."

Reporters were hungry for details, and they quickly picked up on the gender being described.

"You're on the lookout for a male driver," one reporter asked. "Can we assume that the killer was a male?"

"He's a male," Loeffler answered.

"How do you know that for sure?" the reporter persisted.

"I can't elaborate any further," Loeffler answered. "The killer was a man."

What he couldn't say, of course, was that semen had been recovered from Jennifer's body. He also could not disclose that a whole vanful of evidence from the Colhouer house was already on its way to the FBI crime lab in Washington, D.C. for analysis. Or that the hair and blood samples taken from Tom Colhouer, Bill and Phil Moses, Russ Clarke (another neighbor), Tony Aguilar, Eric Brouard, and the pizza man in the red Ford, were on their way to Cellmark Diagnostic Laboratories in Germantown, Maryland, for DNA profiling. Cellmark had been given a portion of the semen found on Jennifer's body and would use that as a comparison against all the others.

Also on Saturday, the Blount Funeral Home began releasing details of the services planned for Jennifer. They would be held the following Wednesday and would be open to the public. In lieu of flowers, Tom and Cheryl Colhouer were requesting that donations be made to MADD, SADD, or the National Honor Society. The donations were to be sent to the Land O'Lakes High School, made out to the Jennifer Colhouer Memorial Fund.

Jennifer's teacher had gone to see her parents. "I think you'll want to have this," she said sadly. "It was her last assignment on Wednesday afternoon."

The teacher had assigned her class to do a paper entitled "After High School."

"After I graduate from high school," Jennifer had written in her round, back-slanted script, "I want to go to college for as long as it takes . . . I want to be a psychiatrist. I love to work with people and to help them in any way I can. I would also enjoy to work on a teen hotline if and when I become stable as far as money is concerned. In elementary school, I remember always wanting to be a guidance counselor. Now I feel I would rather work with adults. I wouldn't mind working in a mental institution and helping them with their illness and problems. I feel I understand things and can look at them from all sides of the situation."

And then Jennifer ended her last assignment with these words: "I just want to help."

Twenty

Red Corvettes seemed to be springing up all over Central Florida like brilliant tropical flowers. Sheriff Jim Gillum had issued a statewide all-points bulletin for the car, stressing again that detectives just wanted to talk to the driver. The calls poured in.

A real estate agent in Land O'Lakes called to say that a good-looking young man driving a red Corvette had been cruising their new nearby subdivision, looking at homes. She and the other agents "freaked out" when he first drove up, and when he asked to be shown around one of the model homes, two agents went inside with him, instead of the usual one. Then, a few minutes later, two other female agents from their office, worried about the first two, followed them into the house. All four women stood together in a group in the doorway as the prospective buyer looked into each room.

"He was looking at us funny," the real estate agent now told the detectives. Then, as he drove away, all four women took down his license plate number.

He was a thirty-four-year-old mechanical engineer from nearby Lutz, and when detectives interviewed him, he admitted "looking funny" at the real estate agents.

"There were four of them, all standing shoulder to shoulder, glaring at me. Every time I'd look into a room and then turn around to come back out, all of them would jump and start backing up. I thought they were nuts. I was afraid they were going to attack me or something."

The detectives asked if he'd ever looked at the vacant houses in the Colhouer neighborhood, and he said he couldn't remember, he'd looked at so many. So the detectives followed him to Wayne Way.

"No," he shook his head. "I've never been over here in my life."

They checked him out anyway. He had been a hundred miles away from the Colhouer house when Jennifer'd been killed.

Hillsborough County detectives called Pasco. A fourteen-year-old girl had been walking home from school in Thonotosassa, in Hillsborough County, when a Corvette with two young men in it had pulled over in front of her. The driver had jumped out with a knife in his hand and demanded that the girl get into the car. He'd grabbed her and started dragging her toward the car, but she'd screamed and fought. He'd let her go then and run back to the 'Vette and peeled away.

"She didn't get the plate; she was too scared and didn't even think of it," police said.

The Thonotosassa girl's mother wouldn't let Pasco detectives interview her daughter. She'd been through enough, said the mother. Hillsborough sent what reports they had on the incident to Pasco. But the car in this attempted abduction was described as "dark red" or "maroon," and it was an older, smaller 'Vette, probably a 1970. Also, it had a luggage rack on the trunk. The Colhouer neighbors were positive that was not the car they'd seen on January 20.

Similar reports were pouring in from all over the state. The problem was that without a more comprehensive description of the driver than "late twenties, early thirties, good-looking," the investigators had no way automatically to rule anyone out. Every 'Vette driver's alibi for the afternoon of January 20 had to be checked out by a detective, which meant making appointments with employers, getting copies of time and attendance records, and looking up friends, families, bartenders, and girlfriends, each of whom would be asked to give a statement. More appointments, more time and paperwork. Within the first week, over a hundred red Corvettes were under police scrutiny, and just that part of the Colhouer file had grown to over 3,000 pieces of paper.

Corvette drivers began putting signs in their car windows: "I have been stopped twelve times! I am not the killer!" It was a clever ploy, thought many police officers, who then made it a point to pull those cars over and check them out again.

A Land O'Lakes man who had the misfortune of living four blocks from the Colhouer house and the further misfortune of owning a red Corvette finally had enough and went to the sheriff's office to see what could be done.

"I know how important this is," he said, "and believe me. I want to cooperate fully. But you guys are virtually rui ing my life. My boss is threatening to fire me because I can't get to work on time. And then my wife's mad because I can't get home, either, sometimes for hours. The question is not *will* I get stopped every time I leave the house, but how *many* times I'll get pulled over before I get to wherever I'm going. I tell every cop that pulls me over that I've been checked up one side and down the other—hell, you guys know more about me now than my own family does! The cops on the street don't believe me, of course, and I understand that, too. But something has to be done here!"

The sheriff's police listened to the man's tale and then, like all good cops, detained him while they name-checked him, just to be sure. Finally, they made out another field interrogation report, made a Xerox copy, and told the man to carry the FIR with him whenever he went out in the car.

"I hope it helps." He sighed resignedly. "I'd sell the damn

car if I could, just to get my life back together again, but thanks to you guys, the resale value of red Corvettes in Florida ain't worth spit just about now."

One of the calls about a Corvette came from Cheryl Colhouer. She said that she and Tom had remembered a man they hadn't seen in some time who owned a late-model red Corvette. He lived in the Land O'Lakes area and was active in the local Sertoma Club, which sponsored a Cub Scout pack. Cheryl said he had been to their house only a couple of times, to drop something off related to the kids' club activities. But now, looking back on it, it seemed suspicious that he'd not only driven the Corvette but had also worked closely with kids through his scouting activities. Pasco detectives went out on it immediately, and he, too, was added to the burgeoning file.

Jennifer Lynn Colhouer was laid to her final rest on Wednesday, a week from the date of her death. Hundreds and hundreds of mourners jammed the Blount Funeral Home for the moving 4 P.M. service. Jennifer's classmates and friends had written notes and poems of remembrance, and many of the kids laid these, along with single flowers, in her casket.

Among the mourners were Fay Wilber, Gary Fairbanks, and many other representatives of the sheriff's department. They were here in a double capacity, actually. Many of the detectives, family men themselves, shared the Colhouers' grief at the loss of their child, and they had, in fact, come to be personally fond of the whole family. In their official capacity, the detectives were there to film the service. Later, they would sit down with Tom and Cheryl Colhouer and view the film to see if anyone or anything looked out of place.

Tom Colhouer had written an elegy to his adopted child, and the Baptist minister now read it aloud: "I was always amazed at your wealth of love and caring for the people in your life," the tribute began. "As a flower blooms, so did your life. I saw you change from a young girl into a woman, as a seed grows . . ."

The elegy recalled Jennifer's earnest desire to help others and then concluded, "Yes, my darling, we will grieve, but we will also smile." It was signed, "Your dad."

Jennifer's remains were cremated, according to her wish.

"For some reason, my sister and I had been talking about funeral arrangements a couple of weeks before. I don't remember the exact details," Cheryl Colhouer says. "Jennifer overheard us and she told me then that she wanted to be cremated. She said if something happened to her, I should scatter her ashes over the lake behind the house, so that she would always be there with us. We all laughed about it at the time, of course. Whoever thinks that your own child will die before you do?"

Jennifer's mother said that despite her daughter's wish, she did not feel it would be appropriate to scatter Jennifer's ashes over Lake Myrtle, not after such a violent, horrible death. "But she's with us, anyway," says Mrs. Colhouer. "I kept a portion of the ashes, and the rest are in a niche at the cemetery. Tom and I bought the niche on either side of it for ourselves, so that when the time comes, Jennifer will rest between us for all time."

By the day of the funeral, Jennifer's parents were anticipating the arrest of their daughter's killer. Det. Wilber told them that the police had zeroed in on a severely disturbed young man in the neighborhood. He was referring, of course, to Tony Aguilar. The department was only waiting for lab test results to come back. This was momentous news, and Cheryl Colhouer was hardly able to concentrate on the details of her daughter's funeral, so intently was she focused on the fact that the killer was soon to be in custody. The detectives had told Tom and Cheryl to keep the information to themselves, so when friends and neighbors at the service kept asking about the investigation, they repeatedly had to answer in vague, roundabout terms, and the effort was exhausting.

The Colhouer family had moved into a relative's vacant house after the murder, and as soon as the police were through with the Land O'Lakes house, they would put it up for sale. It had once been their dream home, but now none of them ever wanted to see it or step into it again.

Cheryl's brother, Gary, who was single, moved in with the family. Tom was adamant that his wife and kids weren't going to be left alone again. They also went to the dog pound and brought home a big Doberman/shepherd dog. "Sarge" became a member of the household.

Neither the dog nor the family's move served to ease little Jeremy's terror. He refused to go into any room in the new house alone, he panicked at being more than a few feet away from his mother, and he would not sleep alone at night.

All of the Colhouers went into counseling at the Life Center in Tampa, a clinic that provides grief therapy to help people deal with the loss of loved ones. Tom and Cheryl sat in on several sessions together, and then each continued with an individual counselor. Jeremy, and to a lesser extent, baby Megan, were seen by child psychologists.

Megan was still too young to understand the concept of death, and besides, she had her own wise, baby way of dealing with Jennifer's loss—she simply wouldn't let her go. "Sissy," as Megan had called her older sister, still "visited" with three-year-old Megan and still "talked" to her, and often Megan carried on "conversations" with Sissy and then translated for the rest of the family. Sissy also visited Megan in her dreams, and the little girl would tell her mother about places that she and Jennifer had visited overnight. Much in the same way that Jennifer had had her imaginary "Cathy" when she was a toddler, so now Megan kept her beloved Sissy alive and with her.

Jeremy, at eight years old, was not so lucky. He had found

his sister's body in his bedroom. He not only knew that Jennifer was dead, he saw how she'd died, and it was a sight that badly injured the little boy's emotional vision of the world.

Jeremy's psychologist, after a few weeks, told Tom and Cheryl that it was time to *make* Jeremy sleep in his own room at night. The theory was that Jeremy couldn't begin to get past his fear until he was made to confront it. His parents tried sticking to this advice for a few nights, but it became a horror—they were locked in their room, and their little boy was out in the hallway, curled up on the floor, screaming and begging to come in.

"We didn't care what the psychologist recommended," Cheryl said. "That was awful, and we went back to letting Jeremy stay in our room at night, for as long as he needed to."

The sheriff's department victims' advocates, Ellie Calhoun and Jane Stanley, had told Tom and Cheryl on the night of Jennifer's death that even if they had a perfect marriage, they were now going to start having some problems. They said that all of the subtle dynamics of the family would have instantly changed with Jennifer's death, and it was going to take time and patience for them to work through it all. The advocates recommended that they begin extended counseling right away.

"They were right," Cheryl says. "For instance, Tom had always chewed tobacco, which never bothered me before, but all of a sudden it made me so angry. And then, even with the funeral arrangements, we found ourselves butting heads. I wanted a closed coffin because to me, Jennifer's face looked like she had died in pain. Tom said the coffin should be open, and maybe that would help squash some of the wild rumors that were going around about how she had died. Some of the teenagers were saying she had been decapitated and all sorts of other things. I wanted a Catholic service, and he wanted a

Baptist service. Everything just seemed so magnified, so out of proportion, all of a sudden."

Tom Colhouer, for his part, suddenly couldn't stand it that Cheryl was an immaculate housekeeper. "Forget the house," he would rage. "Who cares about the house? Let's spend our time together having fun, doing things together, instead of you cleaning all the time."

The grief therapists at the Life Center helped them realize that they were sublimating—directing huge quantities of anger, fear, and feelings of helplessness at one another, feelings that were boiling just below the surface because of the murder of their daughter.

Another tremendous stressor for the family in these dark days was the fact that Tom Colhouer was still a suspect. He was a stepfather, after all, and Jennifer was a budding, attractive girl. He had had alcohol on his breath when the police had arrived at the murder scene, and they'd had only his word that he'd had just the one beer.

Cheryl had gone right back to work the week after Jennifer's death, and Fay Wilber and Gary Fairbanks stopped in to see her several times and to talk to her about Tom. She was certain in her own mind that "Tom Terrific" had had nothing to do with the murder, but "if I'm wrong, and he did this," she told detectives, "I want him to get the death penalty, and the day you arrest him is the day I file for divorce."

The detectives drove Tom's route from his job to his house and back again, checking the times, looking to see if maybe he could have sneaked away before quitting time, killed Jennifer, and then hurried on to the next job. They asked Cheryl about Tom's conduct around her daughter. Was his attitude that of a father, or was there something else?

"I felt like everything I said only buried him deeper," Cheryl would say later. "I told them he was always proper and appropriate around Jennifer, that he didn't even want her walking around in her bathing suit, which she liked to do. But as soon as I said it, I realized even *that* made it sound like him seeing her in her bathing suit affected Tom, and why should it, right? If he's thinking of her only as a daughter . . ."

One night, several days after Jennifer's death, Tom suddenly turned to his wife and said, "What if the DNA tests come back positive?"

Cheryl was thunderstruck. "Tom, they won't! How could they?"

But Tom couldn't seem to get off this track. He would wander around the house, a lost and mourning soul, and say it over and over: *"What if the DNA comes back positive?"*

Finally, even Cheryl's rock-hard faith in her husband began to crumble. Why did he keep saying that? What was he so worried about? The counselors explained that in addition to grief, Tom was experiencing deep, deep guilt. He was the man of the household, the father and protector, and his daughter had been murdered. So somehow, he had failed, he was *guilty*—and his DNA would prove it.

Tom Colhouer's DNA profile came back negative. Also negative were the samples taken from Russ Clarke, Bill and Phil Moses. Tom Colhouer's brothers were all negative for a match, and Cheryl's brothers were negative, as well. Eric Brouard was also negative.

The semen swab taken from Jennifer's thigh was classified as O-secretor with an H blood group.

Tony Aguilar, the investigators' number-one suspect until now, was classified as ABO type B-secretor, BH group.

Back to square one.

Twenty-one

Mrs. Opal Russo was going from one Land O'Lakes day-care center to another, checking them out, comparing prices and facilities. It was March 16, 1988, and she had just moved, with her little girl, from up north—another "snow-bird" sick of brutal winters, come to seek warmth in the Sunshine State.

She was at one of the local preschools now, talking with Helene Harmen about what the school could offer her little girl. Mrs. Russo was due to start her new job the following Monday and she wanted to be certain her child would be in safe, caring hands during the day.

"How is this area for kids?" Mrs. Russo asked. "I mean, is this a safe neighborhood?"

"Safer than most," Helene Harmen said. "In fact, the last time I remember even hearing about anything awful involving a child was back in January. That Colhouer girl over on Wayne Way. Just awful."

"I haven't heard about it," Mrs. Russo said. "We just moved in last week, and I really haven't gotten around much yet. What happened to that . . . what was the name again?"

"Colhouer, Jennifer Colhouer."

Helene Harmen told her about the murder—at least, as much as was known by the public. The sheriff's department was still being extremely tight-lipped about specific details of the child's death. Sheriff Jim Gillum, responding to public pressure, had recently held a community meeting at the

Lake Myrtle Elementary School, where he'd confronted dozens of angry residents.

"Something needs to be said," one woman argued at the meeting. "I would rather hear that you guys don't know anything than to keep thinking there's still someone in my neighborhood. Everybody's still so nervous, you feel like you're living in limbo."

"People want to know bad," added another resident. "Whatever anyone says around here is getting blown all out of proportion. The things I've heard about her death are totally bizarre. I don't think they're true, but I need to know what *is* true."

A local Pasco County commissioner, Curtis Law—whose district included the address of the murder—gave a statement to the newspapers demanding some sort of public announcement of facts from the police.

"There are people out there who are almost on the verge of panic," Law said. "I think there needs to be some kind of statement from law enforcement to calm these people down."

Sheriff Gillum, at the community meeting, listened to everyone's complaints, but he defended his stance on keeping details of the case a closely guarded secret.

"There are always going to be rumors," Gillum said. "But whatever we give away, whatever we release into public knowledge, hurts the case."

People then raised their hands and asked Gillum specific questions. Had Jennifer been disemboweled? Beheaded? Raped? Did the room she'd been found in show evidence of a total bloodbath? Was the murder some kind of occult Satanic ritual?

Gillum would only shake his head, refusing to confirm or deny anything. "The only thing I can tell you," the sheriff concluded, "is that a van full of evidence has been sent to the FBI lab in Washington for analysis. I had my own detectives drive it all the way to D.C. We're still awaiting some results, and as those results come in, we're able to eliminate certain suspects. That's where we're at right now."

"But it's common knowledge," Helene Harmen now told Opal Russo, "that whoever killed Jennifer Colhouer cut her stomach open, and that there was some kind of sex thing, too."

"How terrible," said Mrs. Russo. "That poor, poor child. And her family. My God, what must they be going through?"

Mrs. Russo went on to say that it was odd to hear that the Colhouer child had had her stomach cut open.

"It's odd," she said, "because the little town I just moved from, Griffith, Indiana . . . we had a case like that in Griffith last fall, a sixteen-year-old, Windy Gallagher. Her sister found her in the bedroom of their apartment. It was in the afternoon, too, just like this one. And her stomach had been cut open."

Mrs. Russo explained that her closest friend in Griffith was Becky Grimmer. Becky's husband, Karl, was a detective with the Griffith police department and had worked day and night for months on the Gallagher homicide.

"Becky said it got so she hardly ever saw Karl all last fall," Mrs. Russo said. "Becky said she'd wait up at night as late as she could, after midnight, usually, but he'd still be out on the case. Then she'd get up in the morning with the kids and there'd be Karl, sprawled out on the couch, still in his clothes from the night before. He'd jump right back up in the morning, grab some coffee and a doughnut, and head back out again."

"That's rough on the kids, never seeing their dad like that," Helene Harmen said. "I have a friend who's married to a cop, too, and I tell her I don't know how she does it. I wouldn't be married to a cop for anything in the world, would you? There'd be no such thing as a normal life. Did they catch the guy, finally?"

Mrs. Russo shook her head. "Nope, never did. And the funny thing is, the night the Gallagher girl was killed, another woman was found cut open down in Vincennes, in southern Indiana. They don't know if the same guy did that one, but they're still investigating it."

"You all must have been scared to death," Helene said, "it's like the world has gone crazy. You don't feel really safe *anywhere* anymore."

"Exactly," said Mrs. Russo. "They even circulated a drawing of what the guy looked like. They knew because he attacked some woman in Chicago and she fought him off. He grabbed her purse and ran, and then later, they found her purse with the Gallagher girl's purse and that's how they put two and two together. But even with the picture, they never got the guy. Everybody in town's been a wreck all these months."

"Here, too," said Helene Harmen. "I watch my kids now every second."

The two women went on to discuss the daycare center's programs and rules, and Mrs. Russo left, saying she'd probably be back the next day to sign her daughter up.

That evening at home, Helene Harmen told her husband about the conversation she'd had with Mrs. Russo.

"Maybe I should call the sheriff's office," she said. "You know, that number they keep advertising if you know anything about the Jennifer Colhouer case?"

"You do as you think best," her husband said, "but they're probably flooded with calls like this."

"Maybe you're right," his wife said. "I shouldn't bother them." But a few minutes later, she changed her mind. "I'm going to call it in. What can it hurt? It's only one phone call, and you can never tell what it might lead to, right? I mean, stranger things have happened."

She telephoned the Pasco County sheriff's office.

* * *

Det. Fay Wilber sat at his desk at 3 P.M. that afternoon and placed a long-distance call to Griffith, Indiana. He asked for Det. Karl Grimmer.

"Grimmer here."

Wilber introduced himself and explained why he was calling. "It's probably got nothing to do with you guys' case up there," Wilber said. "This stuff is happening all over the country, right? But, hey, no harm in checking it out."

Grimmer agreed, and the two exchanged highlights of the case: both Windy Patricia Gallagher and Jennifer Lynn Colhouer had been murdered on weekday afternoons, after returning home from school. Both were "perky" young female teenagers with short dark brown hair. Windy's liver had been deeply, raggedly incised and had bled copiously, meaning that she'd been alive at the time. Jennifer's liver had been cleanly severed in two. Each girl had been killed in a bedroom of her own home, and no forcible entry had been found at either location. Jennifer had been sexually assaulted, probably after death. Windy had not.

"But so what?" both men agreed. "Maybe the guy's graduating as he goes along."

Karl Grimmer told Fay Wilber to hold on a second, his boss was going to want to be in on this. Wilber heard him shouting excitedly, "Lieutenant? Hey, somebody find Lieutenant Mowery. Get him in here right away!"

And a moment later, "John Mowery here."

Wilber again introduced himself and the two men began to talk.

As to what the killer had left behind at each scene, Lt. Mowery explained that they had two "beautiful" full-palm handprints from the wall of Windy's bedroom, fingerprint-ridge detail and all. He talked about Joyce Wilson and the finding of both purses in the burning trash barrel on the

South Side of Chicago. He told Wilber they'd had a composite drawing made, based on Joyce Wilson's description of the man who'd attacked her.

"Good-looking guy," Mowery said, "that's what she describes him as—extremely good-looking. Tall, slim, dark blond or light brown hair, parted in the middle. Neat and clean looking. I get the idea of one of those guys who always looks like a rich, movie star kind of guy no matter what he's wearing."

"Our guy is described as good-looking, too," Wilber said. "At least, *one* of the guys we're looking for is described that way."

Wilber told Mowery about the intensive statewide search for the good-looking man in the red Corvette. "You wouldn't believe how many red Corvettes there are in the State of Florida," Wilber said tiredly. "I never want to see another one as long as I live."

"Uh-oh," Mowery said, "our guy was driving a late model silver-blue car, we think a Datsun. And that's a definite ID from Joyce Wilson in Chicago. That's the car he was driving when he attacked her in the alley, and it was just the next day that Windy was killed here in Griffith."

"Well," Wilber said, "we're probably looking at two different guys. But, hey, it was worth a try."

Mowery agreed to FedEx crime-scene photos and a detailed description of the Gallagher case to Wilber in Florida. Wilber said that on March 3, he had put together a package for the FBI VICAP people at Quantico, Virginia. He had included a full set of the Colhouer crime-scene and autopsy photos, videotapes, and case reports. He was awaiting a reply.

Mowery said that one of the FBI-trained serial killer profilers was a Chicago police captain, Thomas Cronin. He'd called Cronin in on the Gallagher case, and Cronin had come up with a psychological profile.

Mowery said, "It says here in the profile that—and I'm

quoting here—'the killer probably inflicts some of the neck wounds initially and with slow, deliberate torture. He watches the terror in the victim's eyes. This terror is part of his fantasy, he has the ultimate power, the power of life and death.' The profile also says we're going to find a guy who likes to brag about himself, and who'll probably put a lot of mileage on whatever car he's driving."

Mowery had also submitted the prints taken from the Gallagher scene to the FBI via AFIS, the new computer-driven Automated Fingerprint Identification System just then being put into use in police departments around the country. That was looking to be a slow process, though. New arrestees' prints were now routinely being done via AFIS, but the many millions of hand-inked fingerprint cards already on file—decades' worth from every police agency in the country—would have to be hand-fed into the new computer system before any one could hope for a possible match to a new arrest. The backlog was mind-boggling; there were enough 6¢ x 6¢ fingerprint cards to fill an enormous warehouse to the rafters. It would take years to enter them all into AFIS.

"We had a real good suspect," Mowery said, "a Chicago guy—convicted sex offender. Chicago actually had him in custody and charged with the Joyce Wilson attack, but then she backed off on the ID, which she had never been too happy with in the first place. She says this guy, Joseph Rinazzi, *isn't* the man, but he looks enough like him to be almost a twin. I'll send you his mug shot, and our composite drawing, just on the off-chance yours is somehow connected."

Mowery promised Wilber that the copy of the Gallagher case file would be at the FedEx office and on its way to Florida before the end of the day. The two men thanked each other and said they'd be in touch.

* * *

In Indiana, Lt. John Mowery hung up with Wilber and immediately picked up another phone call waiting for him, from an Indiana state trooper in Gary.

"One of our informants is telling us a story about some guys he was in the Lake County Jail with a couple of weeks ago," the trooper told Mowery. "It seems his cellmate was bragging about how he and his pal 'offed' a couple of young girls. My informant thinks one of the girls this mope was beating his chest about was that little Gallagher girl you guys had."

Mowery listened a few moments longer and then made arrangements to drive to Gary the next morning to meet up with the trooper and his informant.

In Florida, Det. Wilber hung up with Lt. Mowery and then grabbed his jacket and headed out for yet another interrogation. A young man from the nearby town of Lutz had come forward to talk about his former roommate.

"I got a little place, not a farm, really, just an acre or so with a mobile home on it," the young man told Wilber. "In December, I wanted to go back up north, to see my family for Christmas, you know? But I have about a hundred chickens and a few turkeys, and I didn't have anybody to take care of the animals. I knew this guy, Choochie Morales, on account of he's always hanging around the Phillips 66 station where I work."

"Go on," Wilber said, taking notes.

"Well, it didn't seem like Choochie really had any place to live, he was always just hanging around somewhere or another. So I made a deal with him—he could come and stay at my place for free, and in return, he was to take care of my chickens while I was gone. He thought that'd be great, and he brought his stuff over, what little stuff he had, about the middle of December."

He gave Choochie instructions about how to care for the

chickens and turkeys, and showed him where the fusebox was and whatever else he'd need to know. Then, he left to head north on December 21.

"I got back the second week of January, somewhere around the eleventh or twelfth, and all my chickens and turkeys were dead. I mean, they weren't just dead, Choochie had *killed* them all."

"What did he say about that?" Wilber asked.

"He said he needed food, he got hungry. But over a hundred chickens and a dozen turkeys? And he's full of shit anyway, because it looked like he killed them all at the same time. I mean, there were chicken heads and feathers and beaks and feet scattered all over the place, like a giant chainsaw went through my place. He knew I was pissed, and he didn't come around then for a few days. I was sick of him by then, anyway. I mean, the guy never washed his clothes and he wouldn't, you know, take a bath or anything."

"Not another one!"

"Pardon?"

"Never mind," Wilber said. "Go on."

"Well, on the night that little girl was killed, about 9:30, I was at my job, at the little store in the Phillips 66 station, and Choochie came in, all full of blood. It was all over his hands and his shirt and jacket. I remember especially the jacket, because it was this cool Spuds McKenzie jacket I always liked, and now it was full of blood."

Choochie Morales told his roommate that he'd gotten into a bar fight, and then he'd wandered back out again.

"He's always just *wandering*," the roommate said. "That's all he does. After that night, all of a sudden, the Spuds McKenzie jacket was gone. He said he traded it to a guy in some bar for some drinks, but I don't know."

"What about the shirt?" Wilber asked.

"I think that's still at the house, and I know he didn't wash it. He never does, I don't care what's on his clothes."

Wilber put the young man into his squad car and they drove to Lutz, out to the little mobile home.

"Here it is," the young man said, holding up a rumpled dark green T-shirt. Wilber laid the shirt flat on the kitchen table and studied it. There were dark stains around the collar and one sleeve. He put a few drops of MacPhail's reagent 7812, a "blood finder," on the spots, and they all tested positive.

Wilber took the shirt into evidence, but first he cut out small, bloodied sections from the collar and the sleeve and packaged them separately. He was going to have two detectives personally take the shirt to the FBI lab in Washington. Another detective would deliver the cut-out sections to Cellmark Diagnostics, for DNA analysis comparison against the semen found on Jennifer's body.

"So where's Choochie at now?" he asked.

The roommate shrugged. "I only wish I knew. I'd tell him to get his filthy stuff out of here—the place'd smell a hell of a lot better. But I haven't seen him, and neither has anybody else. It's like he all of a sudden just *poof!*—disappeared."

Twenty-two

The next afternoon, St. Patrick's Day, Wilber was sitting in his office, buried in Colhouer paperwork. He had issued a "Stop and Hold for Questioning" order for Choochie Morales, but Morales had not been seen around town since the night of Jennifer's murder, and Wilber was afraid the Mexican national had fled the country.

"Hey, Wilber, you got a call!" one of the other detectives sang out from across the room.

"Wilber here."

"This is Lt. John Mowery. From Griffith, Indiana? We talked yesterday."

"Sure, sure, your case file got here this morning, and thank you. We're going over the whole thing, checking off all the variables. You're calling to make sure it arrived?"

"That, too," Mowery said, "but we've got something else going—something I think you guys are going to want to sit up and take a good, hard look at."

Mowery told Wilber about his meeting with the Gary state trooper and the confidential informant.

"I'm just walking back into the office now," Mowery said, "still got my jacket on, but I wanted to get on the phone to you guys right away. Took forever to get back here, there's St. Paddy's parades going on all over the place."

Mowery said that the informant had spent two weeks in a cell on the fifth floor of the Lake County Jail on a charge of possession of stolen property. In the cell next to him was a guy named Billy Rae Brown, who was there on a minor drug charge, and who insisted on being called "Duke."

The days and nights are long inside a twelve-foot cage, and Duke and his neighbor were soon exchanging stories of the street. Duke said that the second they opened the cell door, he was going to be out of town but fast, and he wasn't coming back. He had to split, he said, because he'd been involved in a murder a few months back in some dumpy little burg about an hour from Gary, a little town called Griffith, Indiana.

Duke said that he and his "runnin' partner," who went by the name "Lefty," were the perfect examples of American entrepreneurs—they were self-employed hitmen.

"We thought about offering our services to the Mafia," Duke said, "but I thought—shit, man, what kind of a deal is that? You do all the dirty work—take all the chances—and they get all the cash and the credit. No way! That's like a hooker out there selling her ass and then turning all the money over to her pimp. You gotta be a goof, right?"

So, Duke said, he and Lefty had gone into business for themselves. Their first big "contract" was from a woman in Dyer, Indiana. Her fourteen-year-old daughter had been raped, she said, but the man had beaten the rap and was still out on the street. She wanted them to track him down and "beat the dog spit" out of him, break his legs, knock out his teeth, that sort of thing.

"Well, we found his sorry ass, okay?" said Duke. "Couldn't miss him, hanging around in all his same places, the goof. We waited for him out back, and then Lefty jumped him and we dragged him into the alley to do him."

But, Duke said, they had "gotten carried away" once they'd started "stomping" him, and he'd died right there in the alley.

"No great loss, right?" Duke said. "Raping a little girl like that."

After the fatal "stomping," Duke and Lefty were sitting in a bar one night, looking at pictures. Lefty had broken into a coroner's van in Lake County and stolen a briefcase, which had turned out to be full of crime-scene and autopsy pictures. Many of the photos were of several crime scenes involving young women, and it was these that held Duke's and Lefty's attention.

"It got to be, looking at those pictures, Lefty said it was like, you know, almost a turn-on."

They decided to find a young girl to rape. Duke said they drove around in Lefty's white AMC Matador, and that's when they saw the little girl walking in Griffith.

"Lefty followed her for weeks," according to Duke. "He said she had a sweet ass. We scoped out the apartment building where she lived, and then I got in downstairs and used the internal phone to call her. I said I was a maintenance man and needed to get inside her apartment."

Duke said they only intended to rape her, but once again, Lefty "got carried away" and killed her. Duke said he and Lefty had killed someone before, though he didn't say who, and that they had buried that body at his mother's farm in Kankakee, Illinois. But the little girl in Griffith, they'd just left her body where it was. Duke said the bayonet Lefty had used to kill her was buried in a swampy area not far from her apartment complex.

"Lefty headed right down for his dad's place in Florida," Duke said. "I had some unfinished business to take care of up in Minneapolis, so I went up there. Then I flew to Tampa and stayed awhile with Lefty on his dad's farm. But I needed to make one more stop up here—my connection, you know, then I'm out of town for good."

That was just about everything that the informant could remember of his conversations with Duke, Mowery told Wilber.

"Oh, great," said Wilber. "Self-employed hitmen. Did the

informant say where in Florida this Lefty's father lived? Presumably near Tampa, right? That's where they flew in?"

"He said New Port Richey sounded familiar," said Mowery. "And he said they dumped the AMC Matador at the long-term parking at Chicago's Midway Airport. I'm going to get on the phone with them right now and see what I can do to follow the rest of this up. But I thought you guys would want to be in on this right away, given the Florida connection."

"And I appreciate it," Wilber said. "Please keep me up on whatever rocks you're able to turn over, looking for these guys. I appreciate your help. As soon as you know the father's name down here, and where his farm's supposed to be at— call, okay? We'll put together a few carloads of deputies and go over the place like Grant taking Richmond."

Calls like those from Mowery in Indiana were coming in sporadically from other jurisdictions, other states. That's always the case when word of a particularly heinous murder, such as the murder of a child, begins to spread along the police grapevines. One cop knows a cop in another town, and he knows somebody in another state, and somebody remembers somebody he knows who had a similar case.

The Pasco County sheriff's office got a call in late March from a detective in Stowe, Ohio, who said they had a twenty-four-year-old guy in custody for a particularly brutal home invasion, rape, and attempted murder. His name was Chuck Schroeder and he had broken into a young woman's apartment in the middle of the night, raped her at knifepoint, and then slashed her, repeatedly and savagely, leaving her for dead. She'd lived, and Schroeder was soon in the hands of the police.

The Ohio detectives told Wilber that he might want to come up to Ohio. Schroeder was a real bad-ass hardcase and he "didn't have nothing to say about nothing," but his fifteen-year-old girlfriend, Cindy, was a different matter. She was so relieved that she was finally safe from him, according to the Ohio detectives, she was talking her head off. And she was talking about Florida.

Fay Wilber and Gary Fairbanks flew to Ohio. They tried talking with Schroeder, but as predicted, he had nothing to say. They all met with fifteen-year-old Cindy.

Cindy said she was from Tennessee; she'd met Chuck there. He was a lot older than her, she said, but he seemed lonely, and anyway, he was "cute." She started keeping time with him, and finally moved in with him. Then things started changing.

"He always talked about his ex-girlfriend during sex," Cindy told Wilber and Fairbanks. "She was from Knoxville, and I guess she must have really hurt him bad, or something, because he'd be getting it on with me, all the time screaming her name and yelling 'bitch' and 'whore' and other dirty words I won't say. Then he'd start slapping me around while we were in bed, and sometimes he'd tie me up and hit me. That seemed to get him real excited. Movies, too. He liked to watch those dirty movies all the time and he'd make me do all the stuff they were doing in the movie whether I wanted to or not."

Cindy said that she was afraid of him and didn't think he was cute anymore, but she was afraid to leave. He told her he'd hunt her down like a dog and kill her if she ever tried to run. In August 1987, a girlfriend of Cindy's called her from Clearwater, Florida, and invited her to come and stay as long as she liked. Chuck thought that would be a good idea; both of them would leave Tennessee, where they had nothing going anyway. Besides, cops in several counties were looking for him for some burglaries, and it seemed a good time to skip town. Chuck was into burglary, according to Cindy.

The weather was nicer in Florida, but their relationship continued to worsen. Cindy said that Chuck kept getting scarier and scarier about sex, which he wanted all the time, "like an animal." He forced her into anal sex, which she hated, and he hit her all the time. They stayed in Clearwater until February, when Chuck got fired from his job at a gas station because $180 came up missing. The owner said he was going to charge Chuck with the theft, and Schroeder decided it was time to hit the road again. They decided to go to Ohio, where they could live off Chuck's aunt for a while.

Cindy told the detectives that while they were in Florida, in fact, no matter where they were living, Schroeder would come and go as he pleased, sometimes for days on end. She didn't dare ask where he'd been or what he had been up to, or she'd face yet another beating. In truth, she told Wilber and Fairbanks, she was glad when he'd disappear and always hope he'd just never come back. When they asked Cindy if her boyfriend had any access to a red Corvette, she said that there was a nice black woman who worked at the McDonald's near the gas station, and she let Chuck drive the car sometimes while she was at work.

With the help of the Ohio detectives, Wilber and Fairbanks appeared before Summit County judge Frank J. Bayer and were granted a court order allowing them to "extract blood, hair, and saliva exemplars from the person of Chuck Schroeder." Those, like all the dozens of others, would be sent to the FBI lab in Washington, D.C., and to Cellmark in Germantown, Maryland, for DNA comparison to the semen on Jennifer Colhouer's body.

Wilber and Fairbanks went out for dinner with their Ohio hosts before flying back to Florida to continue working on the Colhouer case. While they ate, the detectives talked about a cop's life in their respective jurisdictions. Police officers all over the world do this, because, stripped of geographical influences, the nature of police work is much the same anywhere. Over and over, year after year, the cop steps into the middle of human crisis, tries to set to right all that he or she can, and then steps back out and into the next situation. But benefits are different, working conditions are different, and the willingness, the courage, of your community and your department's bosses to back you up when you need it—those things are vastly different from city to city and county to county. A cop talks about those issues with other cops whenever he travels outside his jurisdiction.

While they were at dinner, Wilber and Fairbanks told their Ohio counterparts about another "snowbird" who had migrated to Florida, this time from Louisville, Kentucky. Wilber had several friends with the Saint Petersburg Police Department, and one of them had contacted him after Jennifer Colhouer was murdered.

"We've got a guy living here now," said the Saint Petersburg detective, "who has no more business being released into an unsuspecting public than a mad dog. It isn't a question *if* this guy is going to start tearing women apart here; the only question is *when*. And there isn't a damn thing we can do about it—we can't even warn people who they got living next to them."

Ross Prettyman Webster was 5⁊¢ and 220 pounds, had thinning brown hair, and was born in 1942. In 1979, Webster had been found guilty of sixteen counts of first-degree sodomy, seven counts of first-degree rape, six counts of residential burglary, and attached counts of robbery and assault in Pinellas County, Kentucky. In all, twenty-six different women testified against him. In nearly every case, he stalked his victims, sometimes around-the-clock for weeks at a time before he struck. His crimes were so brutal, so perverted, that he was sentenced to eighty years at the Kansas State Penitentiary in Frankfurt. He served less than eight.

On December 3, 1987, Webster was released from prison into the custody of his elderly mother in Clearwater, Florida. He now had a college degree, with a particular interest in police procedure and interrogation techniques. Law enforcement officers in Kentucky, who knew Webster well, were appalled. "They released him to his *mother?*" one cop asked. "You don't have to be a shrink to know that this particular kind of wacko is probably all messed up in his head about his mother anyway. And now he's forty-five years old, he's been stalking and attacking women all his adult life, getting more sophisticated and more brutal every time. He admits he was a voyeur and a world-class masturbator even as a kid. So now he's sentenced to eighty years, he's released after eight, and they send him home to *Mom?*"

The Kentucky investigators produced a case file for their Florida counterparts on "the Prettyman." In it, they conclude: "It is the opinion of investigators who are familiar with Mr. Webster that he will probably continue to engage in rapes/sodomies . . . gaining greater sophistication and awareness of police techniques and tactics . . . he will probably select areas which have little or no police service and [he] will be careful regarding evidence. If identified and questioned, he will undoubtedly attempt to taint any interrogation in anticipation of a trial."

Now, as their Ohio hosts drove them to the airport for their return trip to Florida, Wilber couldn't help getting in one last jibe.

"You know, we'd surely appreciate it if you northerners could see to keeping your maniacs up here in your own frozen wasteland. We like to take life easy down in Florida—sit around in the sunshine, sipping a cold beer and dangling our feet in the pool."

The Ohio guys laughed and groaned at the same time. It was a raw, blustery day. Frozen rain pelted the car, and beyond the *clack, clack* of the wiper blades, all the world looked cold and dismal.

"Hey," one of the Ohio detectives said, "maniacs like sunshine, too, you know. I mean, they aren't necessarily stupid—they're just . . . maniacs!"

Twenty-three

"We just have to start over, that's all," said Maj. Bogart. "Right from the very beginning—pull out every old file, every old piece of paper, see if you missed anything. Reinterview everybody you've already talked to . . ."

"Even the old lady who keeps her toilet lid closed so the alligators don't come out of the sewers and get her, like they did Jennifer?"

The last of the lab reports had come back. Neither Choochie Morales, nor Chuck Schroeder nor Prettyman Webster was a genetic match for the semen stain found at the Colhouer crime scene.

A tired chuckle went around the detective squad room. It *was* a sound decision, they knew, but the paperwork! There were boxes and boxes of case reports, formal interrogations, informal interviews, notes and telephone message slips, and torn scraps of paper with phone numbers jotted on them.

"Just the Corvette sightings took up two full boxes of paper," says Fay Wilber. "Lord, how I hate that car!"

The detectives got down to work. They cleared off a desk in the squad room and heaved all the cardboard boxes up onto it. Then they started dividing up the work by sector and by subject. Fay Wilber and Gary Fairbanks started back on the trail of the elusive red Corvette. Each reinterview would now have to have a new cover sheet on its file and would be reclassified to ensure that they didn't end up re-reinterviewing the same people.

Wilber started with the sightings in the immediate area around the Colhouer home. Again, Adam Santiago told of seeing the 'Vette zooming down the street one way, and then back up the street the other way. Other people reiterated their description of where and when they'd seen the Corvette; or rather, *a* Corvette. Wilber was beginning to feel like he and his fellow detectives were the only males in Land O'Lakes who *didn't* drive red Corvettes.

In the "Corvette box" of files was a notation of yet another sighting. This one had a business card stapled to the back of it, and the narrative part of the report stated that the driver of the 'Vette had stopped for a moment and spoken to the interviewee. Wilber went back out on that one.

"Oh, sure," said Joey's buddy. "I remember that guy now. He pulled up just for a minute or two and said something about buying Joey's car."

Joey's memory of the incident was much clearer, as it would be, since the Corvette driver had mentioned the sum of $5,000 for his Cougar. He gave another statement about the conversation, remembering a few more details now.

"The guy said he was from Missouri—Saint Louis, I think," Joey said. "And I remember now that the 'Vette had a third taillight, you know? The kind in the back window that lights up when you hit the brake? I saw it when he was leaving. And I think he had a Missouri plate on the car, too. I remember when he said he was from Saint Louis, I glanced down and sure enough, the license plate was from out of state."

These were just scraps of information, of course, but they were *new* scraps, and Wilber absorbed them hungrily. He tracked down the owner of the mysterious business card, which wasn't easy, since the address was a now defunct post office box, the corporate name on the card was no longer listed with the state, and the telephone number was out of service . . . all the things that make a policeman's life interesting.

"It's my wife's card," said the Zephyrhills real estate developer. "She had this little business going for a time and got cards made up for it. Then her business folded and we just continued using the card for notes and so forth."

The developer remembered the red Corvette, but he couldn't really describe the driver, other than being "young, I think, polite, and nice looking." The driver had pulled up and asked about renting one of his apartments; thus, the column of figures on the back of the card.

"I think he said he was from out of state somewhere. Isn't everybody? I don't remember if he said he'd get back to me about the apartment or what, but I never saw him again."

This was all exciting, new input into the mystery of the red Corvette. The detectives had no way of knowing whether the driver had even had anything at all to do with the Colhouer murder; or if he hadn't, whether or not he'd even seen anything worthwhile to the case. But at this point, the 'Vette was the only lead they had going, and Wilber and the others kept after it.

One of the residents on Wayne Way, half a block down from the Colhouer house, was a young woman named Jeannie. She had initially given her statement to the police. It fit right in with what everybody else in the neighborhood had said. Jeannie had been working in her front yard a little after 4 P.M. when she'd noticed a red Corvette driving by. Then, she thought it was about forty-five minutes later, she heard the squeal of tires and there came the 'Vette again, back the other way—from the direction of the Colhouer home.

Jeannie thought now that she could give a pretty good description of the driver. She'd only glimpsed him for a moment as the car had driven past, but she remembered him because he was so good-looking. Another woman who lived on nearby Collier Parkway also agreed to try and provide a description of the driver.

Wilber had the women come in and sit down with Det. Longworth, their department artist.

When he looked at the finished composite sketch, Wilber's first thought was that the guy looked familiar. Then he realized that the man was a dead ringer for the photo and composite he'd gotten from Mowery in the Indiana murder case. The new composite showed a young man with handsome features and an attractive, open expression. The man's most distinguishing characteristic, though, was his hair—brown, streaked with natural blondish tints, parted in the middle, and feathered off to the sides, exactly like the Indiana composite and exactly like the mug shot of the guy Chicago had initially picked up for the Joyce Wilson attack.

Wilber had the department artist run off hundreds of copies of the new composite. Several road deputies clustered around the Xerox machine, grabbing copies as they came off the tray.

"I know this guy!" said one deputy. He mentioned one of their local ne'er-do-wells, and two other deputies agreed with him.

"So, what are you waiting for?" Wilber said. "Go find him. Check him out six ways from Sunday." But Wilber was afraid to be too hopeful. He remembered Mowery telling him that once Indiana had issued its composite, they'd been suddenly inundated with suspicious young men who parted their hair in the middle and feathered it off to the sides. Indiana had dozens of photos of such men, each of whom had to be checked out "six ways from Sunday," and each of whom looked like he was competing in a "Look Like the Composite" contest.

While all this activity was going on, another detective turned up two more little scraps that electrified the entire sheriff's department.

Two people who had been reinterviewed now said they remembered seeing the red Corvette parked in the driveway of the vacant house next door to the Colhouers'! No one was in the car, they said, and neither one had any idea what kind of license plate the car had. Their remembrance of the time they'd seen it differed by an hour or so, which meant that either one of them was off on the time, or that the car had been parked there for at least an hour. And, logically following that thread, while the 'Vette had sat unattended for an hour, the car's driver could well have been inside the Colhouer home—murdering Jennifer.

All this new input provided a stunning shot of adrenaline to the investigation. On Wednesday, May 4, Sheriff Jim Gillum held a press conference.

"We have not identified or targeted this individual as a suspect," said the sheriff, holding up a composite.

Flashbulbs popped all over the room, and the sheriff turned from side to side, holding the photo up before him. Gillum explained that their decision to seek the man in the photo was the result of several different groups of sightings in the Colhouer neighborhood. According to Gillum, several witnesses had reported seeing the car in the neighborhood, and recalled a Missouri license plate; another group, he said, had seen a red Corvette in the driveway next door, but hadn't seen a license plate. The sheriff said they were going on the assumption that all the sightings were of the same car, and that, therefore, they were looking for a 'Vette with a Missouri tag.

The sheriff described the driver as a white male between 25 and 35 years old, between 5'10" and 6'. "He is described as extremely handsome," said Gillum. " 'Extremely good-looking' were the words used."

Wilber had had his graphic arts people put together a color photo of the type of Corvette they were looking for, with an example of a Missouri license plate superimposed on it. Missouri tags are deep burgundy, almost purple in color, with white lettering. The photo that Gillum passed out to reporters along with the composite sketch of the driver had, in place of actual license plate numbers, the white letters "S-A-M-P-L-E" drawn on the deep burgundy background.

The press conference was carried on the news that night by every television station in the State of Florida, and by the next day, the information and the composite drawing appeared in newspapers across the state. The sheriff's office was once again flooded with calls—with alleged sightings. By Friday, sheriff's spokesman Bob Loeffler had to issue another press release correcting, or rather explaining, the first.

"Many people have called in sightings of the car we're looking for," said Loeffler dryly, "but according to several people, they've seen a red Corvette driving around Tampa with Missouri tags that read 'SAMPLE.' "

Loeffler patiently explained that "SAMPLE" isn't a real license plate listing—it's just a . . . *sample.* Still, calls kept coming in, about one in twenty callers reporting that they'd just seen a red Corvette with dark burgundy license plates that read "SAMPLE."

Fay Wilber and Gary Fairbanks in Florida, and John Mowery and Karl Grimmer in Indiana, felt fairly confident by now that they were looking for the same man—the "extremely handsome" young man with the feathered, center-parted hair. None of them could figure out the car angle. Mowery was looking for a late model silver-blue Datsun, and Florida, of course, wanted the red Corvette. But they had put together a comparison chart of the "variables," the different aspects of each case, and it came up looking as if the two murder scenes, Windy Gallagher in Griffith, Indiana, and Jennifer Colhouer in Land O'Lakes, Florida, had been stamped out of the same cookie-cutter. They were "signature crimes" in every respect.

But *whose* signature? Indiana had fingerprints, Florida had semen stains, but thus far, neither had a definite suspect, let alone an arrest.

Where was he, this "extremely handsome" young killer with the flashy cars, the nice clothes, and the heart of a troll? Where was he, and *who* was he?

The answer came, finally, on June 6, 1988, with a telephone call to Fay Wilber from a police officer friend of his in Saint Petersburg.

"Hey, have you seen the latest ROCIC bulletin?" his friend asked.

"Get real," Wilber answered. "I haven't had time to read the morning paper in months, let alone some police journal."

"Well, you're going to want to read this one. There's a profile in here about a guy who shot a police officer to death back in March, in someplace called Beaumont, Texas."

"And . . . ?"

"And, take a guess what the cop killer was driving."

Wilber held the phone away from his ear and looked at it for a moment. Then he put it back to his ear. "Please tell me this is not a joke."

"No joke, my friend. He was driving a 1986 stolen red Corvette!"

"Missouri plates?"

"Nope, even better. Florida plates. *Stolen* Florida plates. But if you really want Missouri plates, you can have them, too. The Texas guys found them in the trunk of the 'Vette."

Wilber sighed and closed his eyes, pressing two fingers against the bridge of his nose.

"Can it be that somebody up there loves me, after all?

Can we finally be getting near the end of this thing? What's this guy's name? And where in Texas did you say they got him?"

"He's in Beaumont, Texas. And his name's Lockhart. Michael Lee Lockhart."

Part III

TEXAS

* * *

PAUL DOUGLAS HULSEY, JR.
BORN: APRIL 13, 1958
MURDERED: MARCH 22, 1988

Twenty-four

Beaumont police officer Paul Hulsey was working alone on a Tuesday afternoon shift. His beat was in the north central section of the city, in a neighborhood which was commonly known to Beaumont residents and cops alike as "Dope Town." Dope Town was a ten-square-block area that consisted mainly of ramshackle three-room wooden shanties with tin or tarpaper roofs. Each little house was raised up off the ground on brick footings, to keep the untreated wood floors off the damp ground, and to keep out the rats and the snakes.

Weekdays, during the morning hours, Dope Town looked like a deserted wasteland; but as the afternoon lengthened and the humid, subtropical South Texas heat began to bear down in earnest, people, mostly black, began to come out of their houses. They stood in little gatherings around the storefront doorways, or they sat in mismatched kitchen chairs, dragged outside for that purpose. The women mostly sat, talking out the latest neighborhood gossip and maybe sipping cold beer as they kept an eye on their kids. The little ones, usually wearing only diapers or shorts, and usually barefoot, ran around in the road or played in the dusty, garbage-strewn patches of ground that passed for lawns.

As nightfall closed in, activity in the neighborhood picked up. Dealers began to deal, users used, drinkers became boisterous, and the young black would-be gangsters strutted about in pairs or threes, flashing hand signals back and forth, ready to explode into violence.

Officer Hulsey was at ease in this neighborhood. It was his regular beat, and he knew and understood its people—the dealers, the users, the gangbangers and burn-outs and penny-ante hustlers. And the good people, too, who lived here only because they were too hardscrabble, rock-bottom poor to live anywhere else.

The nightlife people in this kind of neighborhood don't generally refer to each other by their given names. Everybody has a "street name," and they can know one another for many years and never once hear whatever name came with the birth certificate. A "street name" is different than a nickname, and it is a phenomenon unique to the poverty-blasted sections of American cities. A street name takes on an identity of its own, one which the bearer may then spend much of his time and energy trying to live up to, or grow into. An urbanologist once likened the granting of "street names" to the naming rituals of Native Americans—in that a man is called by a name that befits what he does, or the way he looks.

Just as Officer Hulsey knew the people of his beat, they knew him, too. He was a part of their world, a daily presence in their streets and businesses and homes. They did not hate Hulsey, or even fear him overmuch; living with "the man looking over your shoulder" was the only way they knew how to live. And, as cops went, Hulsey was one of the better ones. If he caught you dirty, then sure as God made little green apples, he was going to take you down. But that was an accepted part of life, too, and Officer Hulsey always treated men or women with respect, no matter what charges he was bringing against them.

Hulsey was so much a presence in Dope Town that he, too, had a street name. They called him "Blade," because of his tall, whip-thin physique.

Now, Hulsey was cruising the side streets of his beat,

making sure everything was quiet on this Tuesday afternoon, and looking around to see if any new faces had turned up lately. Beaumont patrol officers are occasionally detailed to specialized detective's units, to broaden the scope of their police experience and to provide the department the opportunity of seeing where an officer's hidden talents might lie. Officer Hulsey had just completed a ninety-day detail with the detective burglary team; he'd returned to his beat only yesterday. Today was his second day back in a patrol car.

Hulsey had enjoyed working with Det. Sgts. Chuck Little and Jim Evans on the burglary team. Investigatory techniques fascinated him, but his first choice in police work was not with the burglary squad—it was in narcotics investigations. In fact, he had made application to the DEA, the Drug Enforcement Agency, had passed all their preliminary requirements, and was due to report to Quantico in September, to begin training as a DEA agent.

Paul Douglas Hulsey, Jr., was as much a born-and-bred cop as he was a born-and-bred Texan. His father, Paul, Sr., from Beeville, Texas, had been wounded in the Korean War, and, suffering gangrene, had been shipped to a military hospital in Tokyo for three months. He came home with a Bronze Star and a Purple Heart, and immediately became a police officer in Plainview, Texas. Paul, Sr., married his childhood sweetheart, Mary Jo Alsobrook, of Rio Hondo, and Paul, Jr., was the first of their four children. Paul Hulsey, Sr., earned a reputation for incorruptibility and fair-mindedness in law enforcement, and by 1968, he was chief of police in Kingsville. Over the years, he served as chief of police in Amarillo, then Orange, and then, in 1982, he became chief of the Galveston Police Department. Galveston is one of the jewels of the state's Gulf Coast resort towns, whose usual population of 80,000 swells to nearly a million during the summer tourism.

During Paul's early years, his father would take him riding on his police motorcycle out on the famous King Ranch, the legendary 1,300-square-mile private empire that gave Kingsville its name. The King Ranch, established by two steamboat captain brothers in 1853, is bigger than the state of Rhode Island. Mr. Hulsey's great-grandmother had herself been a King. Every year, the King family descendants would hold an enormous outdoor barbecue for all their employees and all the law enforcement personnel in the surrounding towns and county, and the Hulsey family were honored attendees.

"They were wonderful to people who they felt were loyal," says Chief Hulsey, "and absolutely brutal if you messed with them."

Paul Hulsey, Jr., had grown up in a home full of love, religious devotion, pride in his Texas heritage, and respect for law enforcement work. From the time he was a little boy, he mimicked his father's police expressions, and he listened avidly to anything he could pick up about what it was like to be a policeman. A cop was what he wanted to be. When he graduated from Little Cypress High School, Paul joined the Army. At Fort Polk, Louisiana, he became an M.P. and was assigned to do undercover narcotics investigations, which he found interesting and worthwhile. He carried that interest with him when his tour of military duty was over and he joined the Beaumont Police Department.

In 1979, Paul married Barbara Jean Hanley, a tall, willowy gentle woman, in a double-ring ceremony at the Community Church. Their daughter, Ashley was born in 1982, and little Amanda followed four years later.

Cruising his beat now, Officer Hulsey glanced at his watch. Soon, the dispatcher would take him out of service for his dinner break. He would call Barbara to let her know he was on the way, and then head home for dinner with his family. He was looking forward to that precious hour at home. Working the afternoon shift meant that he was rarely home during the evening, except when he could get away for dinner. Tonight his little girls would be all excited and

Windy Patricia Gallagher, murdered in her bedroom by Lockhart. *(Courtesy of April Gallagher)*

Windy (left) was captain of the Calumet High School dance team, shown here practicing with her sister Chrissy (right). *(Courtesy of April Gallagher)*

Windy Gallagher at age 16.   (Courtesy of April Gallagher)

Victim Jennifer Lynn
Colhouer at age 4.
(*Courtesy of
Cheryl Colhouer*)

Jennifer (right) with her little sister Megan.
(*Courtesy of Cheryl Colhouer*)

Officer Paul Douglas Hulsey, Jr. with wife Barbara and younger daughter Amanda. He was shot to death by Lockhart in a Beaumont, Texas motel room. *(Courtesy of Hulsey family)*

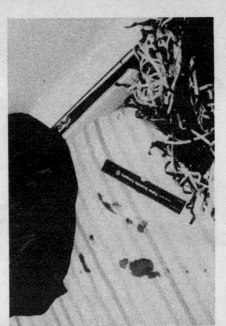

The bloody outline of a Buck knife on the bedsheet can be seen below the police ruler. One of Windy Gallagher's red and white pom-poms is in the upper right corner. *(Courtesy of Griffith Police Department)*

The 12" knife Lockhart took from the Colhouer's kitchen and used to kill Jennifer was found on the floor near one of her brother's trucks. *(Courtesy of Pasco County Sheriff's Department)*

After gunning down Officer Hulsey, Lockhart led police in a
high speed chase that ended when a deputy smashed into
Lockhart's red Corvette.
(*Courtesy of Beaumont Police Department*)

Commander Robert Hobbs stands next to the Toyota Celica
Lockhart stole. Its carpet fibers matched those found on
Windy Gallagher's body.
(*Courtesy of Beaumont Police Department*)

Composite drawing of man who attacked and robbed Joyce Wilson. The contents of Windy Gallagher's purse were inside Wilson's purse when it was later found. *(Courtesy of Griffith Police Department)*

Michael Lee Lockhart. *(Courtesy of Beaumont Police Department)*

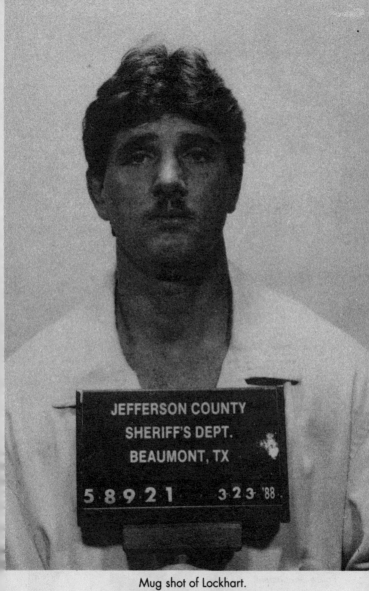

Mug shot of Lockhart.
(Courtesy of Beaumont Police Department)

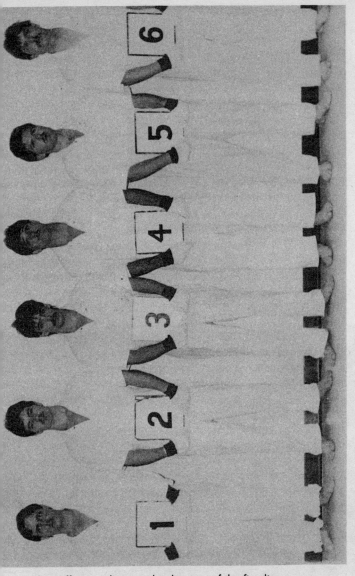

Police officers volunteered to be part of the first line-up following Officer Hulsey's murder. Dressed in identical prison jumpsuits, they wore white gloves to prevent the bite mark on Lockhart's (#4) hand from showing.
(Courtesy of Beaumont Police Department)

During the trial in San Antonio, Lockhart suddenly jumped from his chair and dove head first out the window (upper right). By the time he landed, a dozen guns were pointed at him. (*Courtesy of Bexar County Sheriff's Department*)

Karl Grimmer was a rookie detective with the Griffith, Indiana Police Department at the time of Windy Gallagher's murder. He has since become a Chief of Police. (*Courtesy of Karl Grimmer*)

Lt. John Mowery spearheaded the Gallagher investigation and spent three years coordinating the Indiana portion of the multistate case against Lockhart.
(Courtesy of John Mowery)

Texas Prosecutor Paul McWilliams put together the airtight San Antonio legal case that resulted in the death penalty for Lockhart. *(Courtesy of Paul McWilliams)*

District Attorney's Investigator, now Commander, Robert L. Hobbs. On the wall is a plaque showing the fingerprints and DNA evidence against Lockhart. (*Courtesy of Robert Hobbs*)

Jefferson County Texas Judge and Law Professor Larry Gist presided over Lockhart's trial for the murder of Officer Hulsey. (*Courtesy of Larry Gist*) full of stories about having spent their afternoon at a little neighbor friend's birthday party.

Hulsey rolled past the intersection of Gladys and Magnolia and then looked, and looked again. Now, what was this?

It was a red Corvette, with Florida plates and a young white guy behind the wheel, and it was as out of place as a palomino in a herd of sorrels.

And, somebody in the passenger seat? Familiar, somehow . . . one of the regulars . . . ah, yes. George McBride, a small-change neighborhood drug dealer.

Hulsey drove to the corner and waited for traffic to clear so he could make a U-turn. He spoke into the radio mike clipped to his shoulder, giving the dispatcher his location and a description of the 'Vette. There could be only one logical explanation for *that* guy in *that* car in *that* neighborhood—a drug deal was going down.

Hulsey U-turned and drove back down the block, then stopped. The 'Vette was gone. Damn! He sped up to the next corner and slowed to look down the street. Nothing.

Hulsey crisscrossed his beat in a quick grid pattern, but it was no use—the 'Vette had gotten away. He pulled up to a group of the regulars hanging out in the parking lot of Salem's Liquors. Had they seen the 'Vette? Did it come by this way? Nobody knew anything.

Then Hulsey looked in his rearview mirror and saw McBride. He was hanging near the rear of the squad car, trying to hear what was going on, and trying not to be seen at the same time.

"McBride," Officer Hulsey called out the window.

He came up to the driver's side of the car.

"Where's your buddy?" Hulsey asked.

"What buddy? I don't got no buddy."

"The guy in the red Corvette. Where is he? Where'd he go?"

"Oh, him! He ain't my buddy. I just hitched a ride with him, that's all."

Hulsey shook his head; this was going nowhere. He pulled away and continued the search, but the 'Vette was nowhere to be found.

His dinner hour was scheduled for 7 P.M. At 6:45, he stopped by the Sabine Tabernacle Church at Hazel and Forrest to see a friend, Det. Larry Thomas, who was working there off duty. He told Thomas about the incident with the red Corvette, and the detective told him to put the squeeze on the drug dealer, pressure him a little, and he'd give up the guy in the 'Vette.

"I will," Hulsey said. "McBride and I are going to have a little talk." He glanced at his watch. "I'm going to check out the motels. The guy had out-of-state plates and he's got to be staying somewhere."

Beaumont, Texas, a Jefferson County city of just over 100,000, lies ninety miles east of Houston. It nudges hard against the Gulf of Mexico to the south and Louisiana to the east. On the Louisiana side of the border stretch a hundred miles of beautiful, treacherous bayou swampland. Known as the Sabine National Wildlife Refuge, the wetlands are a steaming, cypress-enveloped jungle of mystic otherworldliness, breathtaking beauty, and toxic death. Cottonmouth snakes up to six feet long, their fangs concealing enough neurotoxin to paralyze a bull, glide in silence through the shadowy, bacteria-rich green muck. Alligators wait in perfect silence, only their eyes exposed above the slime, to explode upon an unwary great blue heron or careless marsh duck. Splendid butterflies hover like stemless flower petals over pink and purple waterlilies as big as dinner plates; and the female black widow spider, tiny as a baby's fingernail, possesses the power to inflict such wrenching muscle spasms upon her victim that a bitten man's heart and lungs will convulse him to death.

Along with Port Arthur and Orange, its sister towns to

the south and east, Beaumont sits on what is known locally as the Golden Triangle. The Southeast Texas area came by its name during the years following World War II, when returning servicemen, hungry for work, flooded into these towns by the thousands. Anybody who wanted to work could find a job here, and the population doubled in less than two decades. Port Arthur is a major deepwater port of entry on the Sabine-Neches and Gulf Intracoastal Waterway, and the landscape throughout the Triangle is dotted with sprawling petrochemical plants, shipyards, and oil refineries. During the early 1980s, the bottom fell out of the U.S. oil industry and countless thousands of blue-collar workers suddenly found themselves destitute. The Golden Triangle had turned to brass, but the euphemism stuck.

Next door as they are to Louisiana bayou country, Texans in the Golden Triangle "talk Texas" but "eat Cajun." Filé gumbo, dirty rice, blackened catfish, shrimp étoufée, and pecan pie are staples, and bottles of Tabasco sauce are to be found on every table in the restaurants.

Beaumont is bisected cleanly by Interstate 10, a highway that has molded the shape of law enforcement in the Triangle. I-10 runs 2,553 miles across the lower border of the United States, all the way from Jacksonville on the East Coast to Los Angeles on the west. It is the number-one drug-transportation highway in the country, and its path through the center of Beaumont has a profound effect on crime conditions in the area.

The rule of thumb in Beaumont about drug traffic on I-10 is that if they're going west, they're carrying money. If they're heading east, they're carrying narcotics.

Houston, to the west of Beaumont, is a major regional receptacle and processing center for illegal narcotics coming up through Mexico. The drugs are cut, repackaged, and sent out all across the country via cars, trucks, vans, planes, and boats like lethal tentacles branching out to deliver killer cargo to every city in the United States.

For narcotics shipments leaving Houston, the one high-speed, nonstop direct route is I-10—right through the Triangle. Every level of law enforcement, from local to federal, has come together in the Triangle to spread a net across the drug highway. And some spectacular catches land in that net. The Jefferson County narcotics task force puts out interdiction cars on I-10, high-power road warriors bristling with computerized tracking capabilities and the ability to outrun anything else on the highway. They've developed their own profiles of who and what they're looking for eastbound on I-10, and then again westbound on I-10, and these aggressive young cops know everything there is to know about how drug traffickers can take a car apart, pack it with narcotics, and put it back together again.

Paul Hulsey was looking forward to becoming a part of this antidrug effort, and he had only six months to go before he would head for the DEA school to become a federal agent. The white guy in the red Corvette with Florida plates had only one reason for being in town, and Hulsey knew it. He left Det. Thomas at the Sabine Tabernacle Church and headed for the cluster of motels that hug the Beaumont exit off I-10.

It was 7 P.M., coming on to dark now, as Hulsey in his white marked squad car wove in and out through the various motel parking lots on Eleventh Street, along either side of the I-10 overpass.

The dispatcher signaled him: "312, you're clear for lunch."

Hulsey acknowledged the call and decided to head home for dinner with Barbara and the girls.

And then—there it was. The red Corvette, Florida license plate BQH83X, parked in the lot at the Best Western Motel.

Twenty-five

Hulsey looked around, but there was no one near the 'Vette. He raised the dispatcher again and told her to hold off on lunch, that he had found the Corvette he'd been investigating earlier.

"312, do you need a back-up?"

"Not right now," Hulsey answered. He ran the Florida plate: "Boy-Queen-Henry-8-3-X-ray," and within seconds, the dispatcher radioed back. The plate was stolen. The dispatcher now asked on the air for another unit to provide back-up for unit 312, Officer Hulsey, at the Best Western.

Officer Keith Goudeau responded—he was close, he'd head on over.

Hulsey drove around to the front of the Best Western and went into the lobby. He called home to tell Barbara it looked like he was going to be late for dinner, but there was no answer. She was probably across the street with the kids at the party.

Hulsey asked the desk clerk about the Corvette. She pulled out the registration log and told him that a "Rick Treadwell" had checked in the day before, and that he'd asked for a room toward the rear of the motel. She'd given him room 157. She said that "Mr. Treadwell" (Lockhart) had just left the office. He'd come in and said he'd forgotten his key in his room. She gave him a duplicate, which he used, and had just then returned.

Officer Goudeau pulled into the Market Basket parking

lot next door, facing the motel parking lot. Hulsey came out of the motel office and, seeing Goudeau, told him on the radio to switch from channel 4, which carried all the ongoing police radio traffic, to channel 5. Channel 5 was an auxiliary channel, and they'd be able to carry on a conversation without disturbing regular radio traffic.

On channel 5, Hulsey directed Goudeau's attention toward the rear of the Best Western lot, and Goudeau said he saw the 'Vette.

Then, Goudeau said he saw someone who looked like the suspect Hulsey had described. The man was heading down the walkway alongside the motel, toward the rear.

"He just went down the corridor and I don't see him anymore. He's headed south along the sidewalk," Goudeau radioed.

"Okay," Hulsey said, "okay, I think that's our guy. I'm not sure. It sure looks like him."

Right then, the dispatcher broke in to assign a pedestrian hit-and-run accident on Eleventh Street, just a half block down. An old woman had stepped out into the street and been hit. She was seriously, perhaps fatally, injured and lying in the street. The driver had sped off.

Officer Goudeau could see people shouting and running into the street toward the accident scene. "I'm on 5," he radioed, "I'll be checking that location." He backed up and rushed to the accident scene, where the woman was now dead in the street.

EMS was responding to the accident, too, and now sirens could be heard all over the place.

At 7:12:01, Officer Hulsey got on the radio and requested a back-up to "sit up on" the Corvette; that is, to make sure nobody drove off in it while he was continuing to check around the motel for information on the driver.

At 7:12:33, the dispatcher requested a back-up for 312 at the Best Western Motel. Several cars responded that they were en route.

At 7:13:41, police officers all over Beaumont were stunned to hear garbled screaming on the radio: "I need assistance! I need assistance!"

Chuck Little and his partner, Joe Ball, were just pulling off I-10 onto Eleventh Street. "That's Hulsey's voice!" Little shouted. He slammed on the siren button and plowed into traffic, driving the wrong way down Eleventh Street and up over the curb into the Best Western parking lot.

People were running out of their motel rooms into the parking lot at the rear of the motel. As Little and Ball screeched to a stop and leaped out of their squad car, a man ran past them, pointing back and yelling: "They're shooting in there!"

The piercing shriek of a fire alarm radiated from one of the rear rooms. The two burglary detectives were drawing their guns even as they raced past the frightened man.

"312," the dispatcher kept calling. "312, please respond! 312?"

Radio traffic approached chaos as squad cars from all over the city flipped on their lights and sirens and keyed in with their unit numbers that they were on their way to the Best Western.

"312?" called the dispatcher again and again. "Officer Hulsey, respond, please."

At 7:17.22, Sgt. Little's voice took over radio traffic. "Officer down!"

"Officer down!"

Twenty-six

Sgt. Ray Beck and his wife, Susan, strolled around the grounds of the Beaumont Fire Training Center with a visitor from England. The woman was in town as the guest of Judge Larry Gist, one of Jefferson County's two criminal court judges. The judge was going to be busy on this Tuesday evening, and he had asked Ray and Susan to show his guest around Beaumont. They were glad to oblige.

Beck had his police radio with him, as he did no matter where he went. When the radio traffic around the Best Western started, he was listening with half an ear even as he kept up a conversation with his wife and guest. He heard Goudeau head toward the motel as Hulsey's back-up, and then he heard Goudeau get called off for the fatal hit-and-run. Hulsey then asked for another back-up, and without even having to think about it, Beck was mentally clicking off who was responding and where they were coming from. That tinny, squawky radio voice is so much a part of a cop's life that many police officers, even fast sleep in their own beds, come instantly awake if the radio on the nightstand sounds out their own call number. Since the police officer knows the habits of his colleagues and knows the area, the traffic patterns, and the previous police history of where they're responding to, his mind is painting a picture of the developing scene even before he gets there.

Ray and Susan and their guest were walking across the grounds, heading toward their car, when Hulsey's agonizing call for help came over: "I need assistance!" It is the second worst call a police officer can hear. If a cop needs more help to handle a large crowd, a fight, or whatever, he says he needs a back-up. If he says "I need assistance," that means that he personally is being attacked.

Without thinking, Beck broke into a trot and started running for his car. Then he remembered and turned toward his wife.

"Go!" Susan Beck said. "We'll grab a ride with somebody!"

By the time Beck was peeling out of the training center parking lot, the dispatcher was begging Hulsey to respond. "312? 312? Officer Hulsey?"

"Come on, Paul!" Beck yelled, slamming his fist into the dashboard as he raced toward Eleventh Street. "Answer the damned radio!" He had chided Hulsey before about getting so involved in what he was doing that he didn't pay attention to his radio calls. Beck kept trying to tell himself as he drove, that that was the case now.

More voices, and more voices—cars responding from all over the city.

Beck was still ten minutes from the motel when Chuck Little's voice broke in with: "Officer down! Officer down! Officer down!"

The worst call a police officer can hear.

Squad cars were parked at awkward angles all over the motel parking lot, many of them with their front doors still wide open, their Mars lights still turning. Beck saw a cluster of uniforms around an open motel room door at the very rear of the building, and he rushed to join them.

"Where's Paul? Is he okay? What the hell happened?"

Keith Goudeau was there, as were Chuck Little, Joe Ball, and many other police officers. All looked stunned and white-faced with rage. Some were crying.

"Hulsey's dead," said one.

"You don't know that!" yelled another. "The paramedics were still working on him when they left—maybe there's still a chance."

"Forget it. Paul's dead."

Their radios were mad with traffic. The red Corvette had screamed out of the motel parking lot and up onto I-10 eastbound, toward the Louisiana border. Witnesses were saying the car was already approaching 70 miles an hour as it flew up the ramp. Beaumont officers were in hot pursuit and were being joined on the highway by state troopers and county constables.

Now, police officers at the motel shook off their tears, their frozen shock, and ran for their cars. Lights and sirens screamed their grief, their rage, as they headed east on I-10.

The Corvette thundered eastward through the dark like a sleek red bullet, for more than twenty miles, the highway behind it lighting up with blazing red lights here, blue lights there, as more and more squad cars raced up entrance ramps and onto the highway.

Then the 'Vette suddenly veered to the right, crossed three lanes, dived down the exit ramp at Sixteenth Street, and hurtled, at 110 miles an hour, into residential Orange, Texas.

Squad cars from Orange and the surrounding towns were grouping around all the exit ramps as the chase sped by on I-10. When the 'Vette left the highway at Sixteenth Street and flew toward Orange, it was plowing through a moving gauntlet of police cars. Pedestrians and civilian traffic scattered as the 'Vette cannoned along, heading straight for the downtown center of Orange.

As the 'Vette sped east, Orange County constable Jack Thompson was speeding toward it westbound. The distance between the two cars closed, and at the last moment, the

'Vette swerved to the right, trying to get around Thompson's squad car.

As the Corvette thundered past him, Thompson cut his wheel hard to the left and smashed into the driver's side of the speeding red bullet.

The impact drove the nose of his car downward and then flung the car backward, pieces of the squad car's radiator grill and headlights clattering into the air.

The shock of the squad car ramming into its left rear quarter-panel nearly lifted the speeding Corvette off the ground. Shards of red fiberglass exploded, and the left rear tire was instantly crushed out of shape into the car's steel undercarriage. Considerably slowed, but still speeding like a projectile, the Corvette plunged toward the traffic circle and spun out into a full 360-degree turn, and then half around again.

As the 'Vette leaped the curb surrounding the grassed-in center of the traffic circle, the driver flung open his door, leaped from the car in an expertly executed tuck-and-roll, and jumped to his feet, already running.

The empty, speeding Corvette, its driver's door hanging open, its left side dragging sharp-edged rags of metal, plowed across the grass, its left rear tire now shredding itself to pieces. The car bumped over the curb on the opposite side of the circle, crossed the street inches in front of a passing motorist, and plowed into the brick wall of an abandoned pizza parlor.

Dozens of squad cars converged. Police officers squealed to a stop and leaped out of their still-running cars, guns in hand. The Corvette driver, the cop-killer—a slim, long-legged, fair-skinned man in a red jersey and pale blue ice-washed jeans—ran across the street, leaped over a deep ditch, and disappeared between buildings in the Sussex Manor apartment complex. Behind the Sussex Manor buildings stretched a dense line of trees and thick shrubbery. Police officers poured into the buildings, up into hallways

and stairwells, and down into storage rooms and laundries.
Others made their way out back into the trees, their flashlight beams crisscrossing the dark undergrowth.

Back at the Best Western Motel in Beaumont, Ray Beck
had called his partner, William Ruby Gates, at home. Gates
rushed to the motel and the two men, along with all the
other cops, took a moment to try to pull their shattered
emotions together. Det. Larry Thomas had just talked to
Hulsey at the Tabernacle Church, and he knew as soon as
he heard the frantic radio call that the voice was his, and
that something had happened involving the red Corvette.
Paul Hulsey wasn't just a nameless uniform; he was their
friend, their partner, a wonderfully funny and gentle young
man only twenty-nine years old.

"Okay, guys," Beck said, "let's try to handle this like the
professionals we are."

He motioned to several patrolmen to rope off the crime
scene with yellow tape and got permission from the motel
to use room 135 as a command center. Telephone calls
could be made from there, and activities coordinated.
Crime-scene technicians were on the way, and everyone
wanted to be certain that nothing in room 157 would be
contaminated by all the police activity. Patrol Lt. Basil arrived and assigned several officers to begin a canvass from
room to room. "Find out what everybody heard, what they
saw, and the exact times everything went down," the lieutenant ordered.

With the scene under control, Sgts. Beck and Gates
jumped in Beck's squad car and headed east on I-10. They
were halfway there when the radio traffic announced the
'Vette had crashed in the traffic circle in Orange and the
murder suspect was now on foot, being hunted by what
seemed to be half the police in Southeast Texas. Other po-

lice units were still pouring into the area, and the Orange town center looked like a Christmas parade gone berserk.

Beck and Gates went up to the Corvette, which was being guarded by a female officer from the Orange Police Department. She said that the crime lab was on the way. Gates looked into the car and saw a stainless-steel .357 magnum lying on the passenger seat, its barrel pointed toward the front of the car. The gun was splattered with blood, and blood smeared the outside of the driver's door handle. Amazingly, a group of high school kids had been driving past, on their way to a basketball game, when the Corvette had smashed into the building. They'd jumped out of their car and run to the 'Vette, peering in to see if anyone was hurt. A sixteen-year-old girl, seeing the bloody gun on the front seat, and seeing all the squad cars screeching into the traffic circle, told her friends: "Don't touch anything!" She reached in and turned off the 'Vette's ignition, pulled the keys, and locked the car door. Then she turned the keys over to a police officer.

A group of people was standing at the windows of Whip's Creamery ice cream shop to one side of the traffic circle, watching all the police activity, wondering what was going on. The store manager had been out on an errand, and now, when he came back in, everybody started questioning him. He said a cop had been shot to death in Beaumont and the killer had bailed out of his car here in Orange. The cops were all over town looking for him. He was supposed to be a tall young guy wearing jeans and a red jersey with white trim, said the manager.

"Wait a minute!" said a young woman. "A guy like that came in here just a little while ago! His hand was bleeding, and he said the engine of his car had gone out and he'd cut his hand trying to fix it. He said he *had* to get to Beaumont right away, he was late for an appointment, or something, and he offered $50 to anybody who would drive him. I told my boyfriend to do it, and I gave him my car keys. They just left!"

The manager got on the phone, and within seconds, police officers, including Sgt. Beck, were at the ice cream shop.

The girl said her car was a gray Ford Futura, but she didn't know her license plate number. Beck stepped outside and tried to reach the police dispatcher in Beaumont, but they were more than 25 miles away, and the static was too heavy. Then, he remembered that Sheriff Huel Fontenot had a mobile telephone in his Bronco. Beck ran to the Orange County sheriff's car and phoned the Beaumont radio room, telling them to have squad cars set up along I-10, watching for the gray Ford. This new information flew from cop to cop, and many of them now peeled away from the traffic circle in Orange and headed back up onto I-10 westward— toward Beaumont. Other squad cars were still coming eastbound on the highway, and now they sped past one another in the night.

In Orange, sightings of the suspect kept pouring in. Somebody told one of the searching police officers that there was a man on the roof of the nursing home on the next block. He radioed for back-up, and cops swarmed into the home and shinnied up onto the roof. Someone else said that a man fitting the description had come racing into Kmart, knocking shoppers aside and fleeing out the back door. Cops surrounded Kmart. Still, the sightings kept coming in.

A short time later, Beck and Gates were outside the ice cream shop when the gray Ford Futura pulled up. The young driver stepped out of the car and was shocked to find himself instantly surrounded by police officers.

"I had no idea," the young man said, in answer to their questions. "He walked into the shop so calm and all. He just said he had car trouble and had to get to Beaumont, and could somebody help him out. I figured it was a fast $50, and so what? On the way, we chatted a little about his car trouble. His finger was bleeding pretty bad, and he said he'd cut it trying to fix the car. Then I dropped him off and came back here, and that's all!"

"Where?" demanded several cops at once. *"Where* did you drop him off? Come on, come on, where *is* he?"

"He told me to drop him at Bennigan's Restaurant. It's at . . ."

But the cops were already running for their squad cars.

"I had no idea," the shaken young man said, to no one in particular. "He was a perfect gentleman."

Twenty-seven

A half dozen squad cars pulled up at Bennigan's, several of them circling around to cover the rear exit.

"He's gone," said the hostess. She said that the man they were describing had walked in and asked them to call a taxi for him. They'd put in a call to Flanagan's Taxi Service.

"He had a bad cut on his hand," the young lady now told police. "It was bleeding pretty awful, and he said his car was broke down and he'd cut his finger trying to fix it. We called the taxi for him, and then he went into the men's room. When he came out, he asked us if he could have a couple of aspirins."

She said that she and a couple of the waitresses looked in their purses, but no one had any aspirin on them. Then he astonished everyone.

He pulled out a wad of money from his pocket and peeled off a bill.

"I've got $100 here for anybody who can give me a couple of aspirins."

To be sure, the Bennigan's employees searched again, but no one had any aspirin. Then Flanagan's taxi pulled up. Two of the young women from Bennigan's walked outside with him, concerned that he was in such pain with the wound on his hand.

"Where did he go?" the police now asked. "He wanted a taxi to where?"

"I don't know," the hostess said. "He never said where he was going."

This latest development went immediately over the police radio, and the search was on all over Beaumont for Flanagan's taxi.

The Flanagan Taxi Service belonged to two brothers, middle-aged black men who ran the business out of their home. Their "dispatcher" was their home telephone number. If anybody was home to answer the telephone, they got a taxi; otherwise, they didn't.

Larry Thomas spotted it, driving through downtown, and it was occupied. He radioed in his location, pulled the taxi over, and approached it with his gun drawn.

"Out of the car! Everybody out! Hands up on the roof, and *nobody* make a wrong move!"

The driver, and several terrified passengers in the back seat, spilled out of the taxi and did as they were told. Other squad cars were pulling up now.

"Y'all want my brother's taxi," said Jimmie Flanagan. "Marvin Murl tole me on the radio that he picked up a fare at Bennigan's. He said he's takin' him to Houston."

Houston! The police officers were stunned. If the killer got to Houston, ninety miles west, he could disappear into the enormous city and they might never find him.

"But jest 'cause he *said* he's goin' to Houston don't mean he's *goin'* to Houston, necessarily," said Flanagan in his soft East Texas drawl. "We got us this secret code we use sometimes, like if we say we're goin' one way, it might be that we're really headin' out jest the other way, do you see?"

No, the cops did not see.

"Well, Marvin Murl, he's got a coupla friends—over to Louisiana? And sometimes it might be he don't want nobody knowin' he might be headin' over there like, so he might say he's headin' west, to Houston or suchlike, when he's really headin' out east, Lake Charles, or even New Orleans, maybe."

"Well, which is it this time?" asked Det. Thomas. "Was he really heading for Houston, or what?"

"He might be," said Flanagan. "Yes, sir, he just might be heading straight for Houston, at that. But then again, he might not be. Y'all jest cain't rightly tell with ole Marvin Murl."

Now what? Thomas put out the information, with the strong possibility that Marvin Murl Flanagan's taxi, with Officer Hulsey's killer in it, *was* heading for Houston. The killer would not likely ask to be taken back eastward, toward Orange and the Louisiana border. That whole area was still crawling with police officers, and the killer had paid the kid at the ice cream shop $50 to get him out of town. Would he head right back that way? Maybe, but not likely.

Everybody ran to their squad cars again and headed back up onto I-10. Most of them went west. Toward Houston.

Many miles to the west, Texas Highway Patrol (THP) troopers Scott Garrison and J. L. Najera had a traffic violator stopped along the shoulder of I-10. A name-check on the man came back with several minor traffic warrants, and Garrison was processing the necessary tickets.

Then, the THP dispatcher relayed the information from the Beaumont Police Department that they were seeking a taxi whose passenger was wanted for the murder of a Beaumont police officer. The passenger was described as a white male wearing a red-and-white shirt and blue jeans. Several descriptions of the vehicle were given; one was that it was an older yellow taxicab with the words "Flanagan's Taxi" on the doors. The taxi was thought to be heading west on I-10, destination Houston.

The troopers handed the traffic violator's license back to him and told him to take care of the warrants on his own. Then they set up along the shoulder of the highway, noted their location as milepost 813, Chambers County, and watched westbound traffic.

Within minutes, a tan four-door Chevy went past. Garrison saw some kind of small, square plate on the door, and he pulled into traffic to check the car closer. Following the Chevy now, the troopers ran the license plate, but the dispatcher said that the MVD computer was temporarily down.

Garrison pulled into the lane left of the car and the troopers looked over at it as both vehicles continued westward. They could see that the driver was an older black man and that no one else appeared to be in the car. But there was no taxi company name on the driver's door—only two small stick-on numbers that read "71." Trooper Najera relayed this to his dispatcher and added that he could see a red glow reflecting from the car's dashboard, which might indicate a radio or other electronic device.

The Highway Patrol dispatcher patched in to the Beaumont frequency. Then she came back on and told Garrison and Najera that the wanted vehicle was now described as an older Chevrolet that was supposed to have "Flanagan's Taxi" on the door and the number "71" on the trunk.

Close enough.

The state police car fell back behind the tan Chevy, and the troopers called in their location to the dispatcher. Reception with Beaumont was extremely poor this far away, so Garrison requested other THP units to set up ahead of them, and to be ready as the taxi approached. Several squad cars responded almost immediately that they were in place at milepost 802, just west of the Old and Lost Rivers Bridge. With the assisting squads in place up ahead, Garrison activated his lights and siren.

The old Chevy pulled immediately to the right shoulder and was instantly surrounded by state troopers with guns in hand. They were less than twenty-five miles from metropolitan Houston.

"Step out of the car," the troopers ordered. "Keep both

your hands in sight. Just step out, turn around, and place your hands flat against the roof of the car. *Do it!"*

An older black man, wide-eyed with fear, shakily stepped out and put his palms flat on the roof. He gazed around in wonder at all the flashing red lights, the incomprehensible babble of the police radios, and the bright flashlights shining in his face.

"Well, I'll be dogged," said Marvin Murl Flanagan. "Have the UFOs landed?"

Then, the back door opened and the troopers stepped back a pace, guns trained. No one had been visible in the back seat.

He was a tall young white guy wearing a red-and-white Adidas jersey and blue jeans. He stepped out with his hands up, turned, and put his palms to the roof.

"I'm the one you want," he said loudly. "I'm the one you're looking for. He doesn't have anything to do with this."

"Identify yourself," said Garrison. "What's your name?"

"My name's Rick."

The troopers patted down both men. Then, waiting for Beaumont to arrive, they put the taxi driver in one squad car and walked the passenger over to another. Trooper Najera read him the required Miranda warnings from a card.

As he got into the back seat of the car, the passenger turned to the troopers.

"I'm sorry I killed your guy," he said.

And then, "I killed him because he fucked up."

Twenty-eight

On Tuesday evening, March 22, Robert L. Hobbs was playing basketball in the Port Neches High School gym.

Hobbs was a district attorney's investigator for the Jefferson County D.A.'s office, and on this night, he and the others from the D.A.'s office were playing against the Port Neches Police Department. These basketball games were regular monthly events, with the D.A.'s office taking on different teams of cops from police departments around Jefferson County.

The game was hot and heavy. Both teams were made up of competitive, strong-willed men who, by the very nature of their professions, don't like to lose. Good-natured insults went back and forth across the floor, as always. Then, just before half-time, Assistant District Attorney Paul McWilliams dived for a loose ball, slipped on the glassy gym floor, and fell hard on his right arm, breaking it.

The game stopped while everyone crowded around McWilliams. Embarrassed at all the fuss, McWilliams, a slim, boyish-faced thirty-six-year-old, brushed away all the attention. But it was clear that his arm needed attention. Several of the men offered to drive him to the hospital, but McWilliams, in his low-key drawl, insisted he was perfectly able to drive himself, that they should just continue on with the game.

Paul McWilliams had been born in the little Texas Panhandle town of Silverton. He'd attended SMU and then transferred to and graduated from Texas Tech in Lubbock. He and his fellow prosecutor, Jim Middleton, had for months now been preparing to go to trial with a capital murder case that was due to start in less than two weeks. A Vietnamese man in Port Arthur had walked into the Tam Game Room in December 1986 and started shooting. When he was through, three people were wounded and two lay dead. The state was seeking the death penalty, and both McWilliams and Middleton had been spending long hours buried in pretrial paperwork. They had been enjoying this evening out on the basketball court until McWilliams had fallen.

Now, with McWilliams safely on his way to the hospital, the basketball game went into the second half. With McWilliams gone, the D.A.'s team was down to a dozen men, including Hobbs, Middleton, and first assistant D.A. Wes Rivers.

Middleton was Jefferson County's senior coprosecutor, along with Paul McWilliams. A tall, attractive dark-haired man, he held degrees in both forensic chemistry and law, and though brilliant in both fields, he was a self-effacing man and shunned the spotlight.

The basketball game was just gearing up again when the men stopped as one and looked toward the sound of an approaching police radio.

It was a Port Neches patrolman, coming through the door of the gym.

"There's been a shooting," he said. "A Beaumont police officer. I don't know which one, but I know it's bad. He may be dead. He's over at St. Elizabeth's, and they said they want the D.A.'s office over there right away."

Wes Rivers had his own car with him. Robert Hobbs rode along with Jim Middleton. The men had toweled themselves off and pulled on their jeans before hurrying out of the gym, but they were still hot and sweaty, still breathing hard and coming down off the adrenaline rush of vigorous physical activity.

Hobbs's stomach was knotted with fear as they drove the twelve miles back to Beaumont. His twin brother, Ron, was a Beaumont cop—and Ron was on duty right now.

Robert Lavelle Hobbs, a tall, wide-shouldered thirty-one-year-old Beaumont native, had been an investigator for the Jefferson County district attorney for six years, and a Jefferson County sheriff's deputy for three years before that. His reserved, inborn watchfulness and his ability to paint devastatingly accurate pictures with words made him a natural for the D.A.'s office. His job as investigator was to work with police officers, victims, witnesses, and outside experts after a crime to put together a clean, comprehensive case that prosecuting attorneys could feel confident taking into court. Hobbs had a fascination with the myriad subtleties and nuances of human behavior under stress, and he didn't miss much that went on beneath the surface of any group he was in. He loved his job with the D.A., and he was good at it.

Hobbs and Middleton were halfway to the hospital when Wes Rivers called on the radio and told them that the Beaumont police officer was Paul Hulsey, and that he was DOA at St. Elizabeth's. Middleton said they were minutes away.

Both men rode along in haunted silence for several minutes. They both knew, and were immensely fond of, the slim young cop known as "Blade." That any police officer had been murdered was a tragedy; but that it had been Paul Hulsey was nearly unthinkable. Neither man had ever heard a harsh word spoken, by anybody on either side of the law, about Hulsey; nor had they ever heard an unkind word *from* him.

"I just saw Paul last night," Hobbs said.

Hobbs had been on his way home from work when he'd heard a "burglary-in-progress" call just a few blocks from his Beaumont home. He'd driven by the address, and Paul

Hulsey had been there. Hulsey'd said the call was unfounded, and the two men had stood awhile and talked. Hulsey talked about the DEA Academy appointment that was coming up for him in six months. Hobbs himself was scheduled for the FBI National Academy in July. Both men were eager for the opportunity, but it was going to mean a dramatic career change; it was a big decision to make. Hulsey said that while he'd pretty much made up his mind that he was going to take it, he was still mulling over his other options. Those options were either to stay with the Beaumont Police Department and work his way up through the ranks, or to go to work with his father. Chief Hulsey had retired and moved to DeSoto, a suburb of Dallas. He was a private investigator now and would be pleased and proud to have his son join him. Hobbs and Hulsey spoke for a few more minutes, and then each went his own way.

And now Paul Hulsey was dead.

At St. Elizabeth's Hospital, Wes Rivers briefed them on what was known so far. The suspect was still at large, and Hobbs could hear, on the radios of the cops coming in and out of the emergency room, the beginnings of the rapid-fire, frantic search for Hulsey's killer.

Barbara Hulsey was there, in the emergency room. Next to her, holding her hand, was Officer Clare Rivers. Rivers would stay right next to the distraught young widow through this most terrible night.

"I want to see my husband," Barbara Hulsey sobbed. So far, she had been told only that Paul had been badly injured. There was no putting it off any longer.

Dr. Herman Gerhardt, the emergency room physician, took Barbara Hulsey's arm and led her into a little side room.

Gerhardt, a ruddy-faced man with strawberry-blond hair, had rushed to treat Paul Hulsey as soon as the paramedics had wheeled him in. When he'd seen that any life-force was already gone, Gerhardt had taken drastic, last-ditch action.

The fatal bullet had entered the left side of Hulsey's chest, five inches beneath his armpit and just behind the protection of the Kevlar vest. Not even stopping to pull on gloves, Dr. Gerhardt had scalpeled Hulsey's left side wide open, hoping to reach in and try manual heart massage. But the internal damage was catastrophic: the large-bore bullet had torn through ribs, muscle, and lung, shattering Hulsey's heart.

Dr. Gerhardt told Barbara Hulsey that the damage to her husband's body had simply been too great. He did not go into details about the drastic procedures he had taken.

"I want to see him!" Barbara sobbed. "I want to be with my husband!"

Dr. Gerhardt asked her to wait a moment, with Officer Rivers. He had the emergency room staff take away all the blood-drenched sheets, knives, and instruments. They put a thick padding across Officer Hulsey's ruined chest and covered him with a clean white sheet, leaving only his quiet, sleeping face exposed. Then Dr. Gerhardt and Officer Rivers led Barbara Hulsey into the room.

"Stay on top of this case tonight, Robert," Wes Rivers told Hobbs. "Emotions are running high, and we can't afford to have anything go wrong on this one."

Hobbs hitched a ride to the Best Western Motel with a police officer. Sgt. Bill Tatum, the Beaumont ID tech, was already at work in room 157. Hobbs was glad to see him; they had worked together on murder investigations before and were comfortable together with what would be needed by the D.A. from each scene. When Hobbs asked Tatum if he needed any help, the ID tech said that he had everything under control. Tatum said that all the Beaumont ID techs, on or off duty, were being called in to assist him.

Satisfied that the murder room was secure, Hobbs walked over and talked with Det. Lt. Steve Basil. Many squad cars were pulling in and out of the parking lot, and crowds of people were beginning to gather along the sidewalks. The area around room 157 was taped off, but now the men decided to cordon off the whole parking lot and front of the motel. By this time, everyone still on the scene was listening intently as the pursuit of the red Corvette headed into Orange.

Lt. Basil said that he had assigned a couple of police officers to take witnesses, particularly the people who had seen the fleeing suspect, or who had been staying in rooms adjoining 157, back to the Beaumont police station for witness statements. Hobbs offered to assist, knowing that getting a comprehensive, factual chronology from someone who's just witnessed a murder can be a tricky process.

Again he hitched a ride with a cop. As they drove to the D.A.'s office, where Hobbs wanted to pick up his laptop, the police radio crackled with activity. The pursuit had ended in Orange with the crash of the red Corvette. Many officers were combing the center of town, while others were now heading back toward Beaumont after learning the killer had hitched a ride from the ice cream shop.

Before he got to the police station to help with witness statements, Hobbs heard the news that the suspect had been captured at the Old and Lost Rivers Bridge and was being taken to the justice of the peace in Mount Bellvieu.

Whoops of relief went back and forth from town to town over the police airwaves, along with some comments and suggestions about what should be done with the cop killer—comments that the FCC would certainly not have approved for transmission over the air—suggestions that the ACLU would certainly not have approved of under any circumstances.

Hobbs drove up the ramp onto I-10 westbound and headed for Mount Bellvieu—to meet Paul Hulsey's killer.

Twenty-nine

Retired chief Paul Douglas Hulsey, Sr., was sitting in the living room of his gracious home, watching an old World War II movie that featured dangerous take-offs and landings of little fighter planes on an enormous aircraft carrier.

It was early evening, and while he watched the movie, the chief smiled, thinking about his son, Doug. The family called Paul, Jr., by his middle name, Douglas, to distinguish between the two of them.

Dougie had always loved airplanes. As a little kid, toy airplane in hand, he would run through the house, flying the plane up and down, up and down. *Z-o-o-m-m-m* . . . across the kitchen table, and up his mother's arm. Out of the kitchen, then, *z-o-o-m-m-m* . . . crash landing on the coffee table and miraculously recovering to dive-bomb the jungle enemies in the carpet, another miraculous recovery, and slam-bang—out through the screen door, around the house, and back again into the kitchen.

Chief Hulsey watched the old movie and thought back to those days. Dougie wasn't that little boy any longer, of course; he was a grown man now—a husband, a father, a police officer to be proud of. But he was still their little boy, his and Mary Jo's, and he still loved airplanes. Dougie often talked about getting a pilot's license. He wanted to be up there, *z-o-o-m-m-m* . . . through the clouds, flying fast and free, with the whole sky in front of him.

The telephone rang at 7:30.

"I'll get it, Dad," said Tamara, the family's only daughter.

"That's all right, I'm right here," the chief said. Taking his eyes away from the action on TV, he picked up the phone.

"Hello?"

It was Chief George Schuldt, calling from Beaumont.

"Mr. Hulsey, I am sorry to have to tell you this, sir, but I'm afraid something's happened. It's your son. I'm afraid Paul's been shot."

Chief Hulsey's knees collapsed.

"Daddy? What?" said Tamara. "What's wrong?" She and her brothers Steve and Danny crowded around the phone.

"How bad is it?" Chief Hulsey asked.

"Bad, I'm afraid. Paul's at St. Elizabeth's Hospital, here in Beaumont. Should we send someone up there to bring you down here?"

"No, thank you," the chief said. "That would just take twice as long. We'll be right there. Does Barbara know yet?"

"We've sent a police officer to pick up Mrs. Hulsey and bring her to the hospital," said Chief Schuldt. "And again, I'm so sorry."

As the family held one another, trying to absorb the shock, the chief groaned. "What am I going to tell your mother?"

Hulsey asked Steve and Danny to stay at the house. Calls would be coming in. Then he and Tamara drove to the furniture store where Mary Jo Hulsey was working.

Paul, Sr., and Mary Jo Hulsey were about halfway through the five-hour drive southeast to Beaumont. They were on I-45, which cuts a diagonal slash down the state from Dallas to Houston. They would pick up I-10 from Houston to Beaumont. As they drove, the Hulseys, deeply Christian people, prayed with all their hearts, asking that their merciful Lord spare the life of their firstborn son. They were just passing Huntsville, where the chief had received his degree in criminology from Sam Houston University. Coincidentally, Texas's maximum-security penitentiary, housing the state's death row, is also at Huntsville. The Hulseys had their car radio on and were listening to the developments from Beaumont.

"Officer Paul D. Hulsey was declared deceased at St. Elizabeth's Hospital at 8:30 P.M. At this time, the suspect wanted for his killing remains at large."

Thirty

Captain Gary Breaux came up to Det. Sgts. Ray Beck and Bill Gates. They were still in Orange, and the news had just come over the police radio that the murder suspect had been captured by the state troopers at the Old and Lost Rivers Bridge and was being taken to the justice of the peace in Mount Bellviu.

"You two handle the arrest and processing from here on," said the captain. The troopers would be turning the man they had captured into the custody of Beaumont. Beck and Gates, as the case officers, would have the responsibility of walking the prisoner through the formal arrest and processing procedures, guarding his personal safety, and then beginning on the volume of paperwork the case was going to require.

On the two-hour drive west to Mount Bellvieu, both men tried to put a cap on the flood of emotions pouring through them. Grief kept welling up, but there wasn't time for grief right now. Or rage—a man's rage at the senseless murder of another man who is his friend. But all of that had to be swallowed now, put to one side, to be dealt with later. They both knew it would never be more important to handle every procedural detail perfectly than it would be this night. Every moment would end up in the glare of a courtroom some day. All Beck and Gates could do now for Paul Hulsey was to make sure—make *damn* sure—that his murderer didn't get away with murder.

Ray Elliott Beck was a third-generation Beaumont man whose older brother was a doctor up in Maine. His younger brother and sister-in-law had made the care of foster children their life's calling, and the Becks were involved in child-welfare activities. Beck, at thirty-six, had prematurely silver hair that formed an attractive frame for his tanned skin and blue eyes. He was an avid hunter and fisherman, and among his great pleasures were his ongoing bass-fishing tournaments.

Beck's partner, William Ruby Gates, preferred to work in his comfortable jeans, checked flannel shirts, and well-worn cowboy boots. He looked like every dusty rangehand cowpoke in the movies, and he knew it. Bill took a lot of teasing from his fellow cops, both about his appearance and about his unusual middle name.

"Ruby? Son, you're so all-fired yella-dog ugly, how'd you ever come by such a *bee*-utiful name as *Ruby?"*

"Well, when I was born," Bill would drawl, settling happily into the story, "my mama looked at me and said 'I'm goin' to name this here boy *Ruby,* 'cause ah know a *jewel* when ah see one'!" A lot of the guys called him by his middle name, *"R-u-u-b-b-y,"* to tweak him and try to get a reaction, but Gates would just nod and smile. "That's all right, y'all go right on ahead. Even you peckerwoods and goobers got to recognize a *jewel* when y'all see one."

"At first he said he was a juvenile, and he told us his name was Rick," the state troopers said now to Beck and Gates. "He's no more a juvenile than I am, and he gave that up right quick. But all the way over here, he kept talking. First, he'd say, 'I'm sorry I killed that guy,' and then,

right after that, 'I killed him because he fucked up.' Don't
that just beat all? Like he's trying to convince us that him
killing a cop was the cop's *fault,* somehow. Judge Cryer
just officially administered the warnings, and set no bond.
We put him in a room down the hall, waiting for you guys.
We've got an officer from Port Arthur guarding him."

Beck and Gates had come into the Cedar Bayou Community Building, where justice of the peace Larry Cryer
had his offices, and they were now standing in the lobby.
It was 11:30 P.M. The building had glass doors, and they
could see more squad cars pulling up in front. Reporters
were beginning to arrive, too, and a police officer was
standing at the door to keep them out.

Beck and Gates greeted Beaumont ID tech Boyd Lamb,
who had just arrived with his video camera. Beaumont tries
to tape as much of the proceedings as possible during every
major arrest to forestall later defense charges of improper
conduct.

As the men walked down the short hallway, the trooper
said that the suspect had changed his name several times.

"At first, he said 'Rick.' When we wanted to know 'Rick'
what, he said his name was really Mike Locke. Now, he
says he's Michael Lee Lockhart."

They walked into the small, stark interview room.

He was cuffed behind his back and talking when they
walked in. Beck, Lamb, and Gates looked at him for a long
moment. He was tall, slim, and long-legged, with attractive
features, hazel eyes, and dark blond hair parted in the middle and feathered off to the sides. His red Adidas jersey
and pale blue jeans were stained with splotches of blood.

Beck told ID tech Lamb to turn on the camera. Then he
walked up to the man, who had finally stopped talking, and
told him they were going to videotape all contact with him.

"I got no problem with that," he said calmly. He looked

at the police officers with wide, clear, long-lashed eyes that revealed no fear, no evidence at all of inner turmoil, as though they were all standing around small-talking about the weather.

Beck said that they wanted him to undress so they could videotape his physical condition, and again he agreed. Gates took off the cuffs, and the police officers took each piece of bloody clothing as he removed it. Beck recorded his observations for the camera's microphone, and each time he made a comment, Lockhart would jump in and start talking, even though no one was asking him anything. He just couldn't seem to stop talking about himself They would later learn that Michael Lee Lockhart loved to talk, sometimes for hours on end, about his favorite topic in the world—Michael Lee Lockhart.

As Lockhart undressed, the police officers could see that he was in excellent shape: he had a hard, flat stomach, strong, well developed chest and shoulders, and muscular arms, like someone who works out or lifts weights. Beck noted for the record that the suspect had scratches on his arms. Lockhart said he'd gotten them crawling through the brush after he'd bailed out of the Corvette.

For the video, Beck noted that the suspect's right index finger had a bad cut just behind the first knuckle. Lockhart volunteered that the police officer had bitten him during their struggle. Then he began to complain of pain in his right shoulder. He said that he had fallen and dislocated it years before, and started telling them about how he'd gotten the injury.

Beck asked Lockhart, for the camera, if he had been advised of his rights. Lockhart said he had, several times, and that he understood them perfectly. The cops let him get dressed again, and then they stepped out into the hall to discuss their next move.

Robert Hobbs was there, and then prosecutor Paul McWilliams arrived, his right arm in a cast. Outside, the parking lot in front of the building was filling up with television trucks. Klieg lights flipped on outside every time the group inside the lobby moved.

The men stood in the lobby and conferred. The police officers said that Lockhart, if that was really the suspect's name, seemed to be pretty upbeat and talkative, and maybe they should try to get a statement now about the killing of Officer Hulsey.

Hobbs went into the room and introduced himself to Lockhart, asking if he was willing to give a statement about what had happened at the motel. But the words "district attorney" must have had an effect, because Lockhart said he preferred to wait until he could talk to an attorney.

"Let's get him over to a hospital," Beck said. "Let them treat that finger, and look him over so we've got it on paper what his condition is."

They decided that Beck, Gates, and Port Arthur detective Cartwright would take Lockhart first to St. Elizabeth's and then to the Beaumont police station. Robert Hobbs said he would take the cab driver with him to the station, where he would take down the driver's statement.

As they brought Lockhart out into the lobby, television lights went on outside and reporters pressed close to the glass doors. Lockhart, again cuffed behind his back, saw the cameras outside.

"Can you guys cover my head when you take me out?"

They looked at one another and shrugged. Why not? It is always a mystery to police officers why criminals insist on covering their faces for the television cameras. The affectation was first seen on national television during the McCarthy hearings in the late 1950s, when movie stars would dramatically cover their faces as they rushed past the same cameras they spent their lives in front of. During hearings into organized crime in the late 1960s and early 1970s, mobsters took up the habit, taking off their fedoras and holding the hats against the sides of their faces closest to the cameras. From then on, the criminal class seems to have taken its cue from these early celebrities about how to run the gauntlet of cameras in appropriately dramatic style.

Bill Gates pulled Lockhart's red jersey up in back, and Lockhart tucked his face down into the collar in front. Leaning forward, with only the top of his head showing, he was escorted by Beck and Gates out through the lobby doors.

As they walked the short way to the squad car, reporters rushed in. Bill Gates held up his free hand. "Please!" he said.

One of the reporters thrust a microphone in Lockhart's direction.

"Got anything to say?"the reporter called out, skipping backward in front of them.

"Yeah," Lockhart called back, "I'm going to die in the electric chair. That's what I'm going to do."

"Why?" yelled the reporter.

"Why?" Lockhart repeated. "Because I killed somebody and I'm guilty."

"Who did you kill?"

"That's pretty irrelevant, isn't it, sir?" Lockhart said, his head still tucked into his shirt.

"No," said the reporter. "Why did you kill him?"

"It was an accident."

By this time, they were at the squad car. Beck opened the back door and put Lockhart in. Cartwright went around and got into the back. Beck and Gates got into the front seat and prepared to pull away. From the back seat, Lockhart looked out his window, and seeing the cameras still trained on him, he squirmed his shoulders back and forth to straighten out his shirt.

"Now, why did I say that?" Lockhart said, as the squad pulled out.

None of the three police officers answered. They were being extremely careful not to initiate any conversation until this killer got the lawyer he had asked for. But even beyond that, they were keeping a tight hold on their hatred, rage, contempt, and grief. They would not give this cop killer the respect of pretending to hold an ordinary conversation with him. They all three stared straight ahead, rigid and cold as stone.

None of which fazed Michael Lee Lockhart.

"Well, it don't matter, anyway," he said, as he relaxed back against the seat.

Then, he turned to Cartwright, next to him.

"Did that cop have a family?"

"He had a wife and two little girls," Cartwright said, still staring straight ahead.

"I have a wife and daughter, too," Lockhart said, still chatting. "Well, an *ex*-wife and a daughter. Was Paul a friend of you guys?"

Paul! Lockhart had obviously heard the group talking about their friend, and now he felt entitled to use the first name of the police officer he had just assassinated.

"We all worked together in Narcotics," said Cartwright tightly. "We knew him very well."

"Well," said Lockhart, "your friend really fucked up tonight! I mean, why did he come to my room without a back-up?"

No one answered. Beck's knuckles were white as he gripped the steering wheel. Did this man really think they were all going to join together in a philosophical discussion about proper police procedures?

"I knew he didn't have a back-up, because I saw him out there by my car in the parking lot, and I knew he was looking for me. So why didn't he have a back-up?"

No one answered.

"I mean," Lockhart continued, "that was really stupid!"

None of the police officers had to look at one another or exchange one word among themselves to know what they were all telling each other—don't lose it; don't lose control, don't give in to the rage. Lockhart's cool, brazen arrogance was unbelievable. But they were not just men, men who could just let go and take swift vengeance for the murder of a friend. They were police officers, and they didn't have that choice.

Michael Lee Lockhart was perfectly oblivious to the unspoken dynamics going on around him in the squad car.

"So, if you guys are his friend," he said now, "how come you're not crying or anything? I mean, I know about cops, the brotherhood and all that." When no one spoke, he continued talking about how Paul Hulsey had "fucked up." He said this so many times that Bill Gates said later he thought he would go crazy hearing it.

"It was as though he was *bragging,*" Gates said. "Like he was feeling high that he'd gotten over on the police officer and killed him, and he wanted to keep talking about it over and over, the way you do when you want to relive some great moment in your life."

Lockhart went on to say that the cop had come to the door of room 157 and asked him for identification.

"I told him to wait, that my wallet was in the room. He stood in the doorway, and I went over to the dresser, like I was looking for it, but I knew I didn't have any identification. Then, he stepped into the room, and I saw him look at my gun on the dresser. He pulled his gun and told me to put my hands up on the wall."

Lockhart said he put his hands on the wall and the police officer stepped behind him, pulling out his handcuffs.

"And that's where he *really* fucked up!" Lockhart said. "I had my hands up on the wall, but looking to the right, there's a mirror on the wall there, and I could see him behind me. He put his gun back in his holster, and that's when I turned and hit him."

Lockhart said he grabbed his own gun, the officer pulled his, and the two men fought and struggled back against the bed.

"I told him over and over to drop his gun." Lockhart

shrugged now. "But he wouldn't do it. So that's when I shot him."

Hulsey had been wearing a bulletproof vest, and though injured, he was still conscious.

"He laid there on the floor and begged me not to shoot him again," Lockhart said. Tears blurred Ray Beck's vision as he listened, and all three officers were now taking deep, slow breaths. *Hold it in, hold it in, hold it in.*

"I'll never forget the look in his eyes, begging me like that not to shoot him," Lockhart continued. "I stood there, but then I said 'Hey, you started this. I'm going to finish it.' And I shot him again. He was dead when I left the room."

The silence was thick in the car. Lockhart seemed to be casting about for something else to say that would keep his one-sided conversation going.

"How'd you guys know I was in that taxi, anyway?" he said now.

No one spoke.

"Ah, it must have been Bennigan's. They called the police, right?"

No one spoke.

Finally, Lockhart seemed to be getting the message. He shrugged and rested his head back against the seat, closing his eyes.

At St. Elizabeth's emergency room, Lockhart told the nurse that the injury to his finger was from a human bite. He and the three police officers were directed to a curtained-off treatment section. The detectives told Lockhart to remove his clothing, that it would be taken into evidence. ID tech Bill Tatum had finished his work at room 157 of the Best Western Motel and was here now at St. Elizabeth's, waiting for the suspect's clothing. Then Ray Beck asked if he would sign a waiver allowing the hospital to take blood samples. Again, Lockhart said, "No problem."

When he brought in the waiver, Beck handed it to Lockhart with a pen and asked if he could read and write. At this, Lockhart instantly bristled.

"I am *very* educated," he snapped, grabbing the waiver and reading the entire text out loud, proving his point, before he signed it.

Dr. Herman Gerhardt was still on emergency room duty. Barbara Hulsey had been taken home by Officer Clara Rivers, who was helping with telephone calls and arrangements to gather the family together. There was still the task of trying to explain to the two little Hulsey girls why their daddy wouldn't be coming home anymore.

As Dr. Gerhardt strapped on the blood pressure cuff, he listened to Lockhart complain about the pain in his shoulder. "Well, his blood pressure's 138 over 88—perfectly normal," said the doctor.

A dramatic rise in blood pressure is the body's physiological response to stress, fear, pain, threat, or excitement. The body automatically pours more adrenaline and other "fight-or-flight" chemicals into the system so that the muscles and brain can function at maximum efficiency to meet the perceived emergency. All of these physiological responses are unconscious. Only one factor is necessary before these internal emergency systems kick in—a person must feel stressed, fearful, in pain, threatened, or excited. Michael Lee Lockhart had just murdered a police officer in cold blood, led his pursuers on a 110-mile-an-hour chase all over Southeast Texas, been captured at gunpoint, and then recounted the entire "adventure" to a carful of cops— and his blood pressure was perfectly normal.

Dr. Gerhardt could find nothing at all wrong with the shoulder, but the deep bite to the right index finger needed treatment.

Michael Lee Lockhart was sitting up on one of the high

portable gurneys in the emergency room, surrounded by police officers, as Dr. Gerhardt treated the injured finger. Lockhart watched in silence as the doctor finally began bandaging his finger.

"Well," a chipper Lockhart said to Dr. Gerhardt, as he jumped down from the gurney, "this should liven things up a bit around Beaumont. It's a little dead around here, isn't it?"

Thirty-one

"Please sit down, Mr. Flanagan," said district attorney's investigator Robert L. Hobbs.

They were in one of the small interview rooms at the Beaumont police station, and Hobbs was preparing to take the taxi driver's formal statement. Marvin Murl Flanagan was somber and downhearted, now that the terror of being pulled over and surrounded by armed, angry police officers was over. He had been born in 1936, and in all his life, no police officer in this town had ever before been shot and killed in the line of duty. It was simply unthinkable, and Flanagan, like all of Beaumont, was stunned at the murder.

The last time a Beaumont police officer had been murdered on duty was back in 1920, before the Depression, before World War II, more than a half-century earlier. That he had been so close to the killer, and in fact, had unknowingly helped him nearly to escape capture, saddened the cab driver. Robert Hobbs reassured him that of course, no one blamed him for any part of it. Hobbs asked Mr. Flanagan to please recall every detail of the time he'd spent with Michael Lee Lockhart, and the statement began.

Flanagan said that about 8 P.M., he was called to pick up a fare at Bennigan's Restaurant on I-10. He told the caller to have the passenger wait near the front door of the restaurant and said he would be there in about ten minutes.

The cab driver now told Hobbs that when he'd pulled up, a young white man had come out of the restaurant. Two young ladies in uniforms had walked with him to the doorway. Flanagan said the man came to the passenger window of the taxi and asked if he could sit in front, which the cab driver said would be okay.

"He told me he wanted to go to the airport," said Mr. Flanagan. "And I asked him which one. He said which ones are there, so I told him there's the Jefferson County Airport and the Municipal Airport, and he said I should take him to whichever airport was bigger."

As they headed for the airport, the man next to him told the driver that before he went to the airport, he wanted to stop at a shopping mall, but first he wanted to know how much the fare was to the airport. Flanagan said that airport was sixteen miles away, and $18 dollars should cover it. How much more to go to a shopping mall first, the man wanted to know. Flanagan said the Central Mall was right near the airport, and the fare wouldn't be much more if they stopped there.

"If I have you take me to the mall, wait for me while I buy some clothes, and then take me on to the airport, will $30 cover the whole thing?" asked the passenger.

Flanagan said that was more than enough, but then he looked at his watch. It was 8:54, and he told the man that the mall closed at 9 P.M. The man seemed upset at this and asked what he could do about getting some new clothes. He said he had blown the engine on his car, and while he was looking around for somebody to fix it, someone had gotten into the car and stolen all his clothes. He also repeated, several times, that he had slammed his finger in his car door and cut it.

"Are there any hotels near the airport?" the man asked. "I guess if I can't get any clothes tonight, I'm stuck. I might as well find a hotel for the night."

Flanagan said there was a hotel right near the airport. Then, as they continued driving, the passenger spoke up again.

"Houston is where I really have to go," he said. "But it's, what, about a three-hour drive?"

Flanagan said that Houston was ninety miles away, and that it would take about an hour and a half to get there. He would have to ask $90 for the trip, and for that sum, he would take his passenger anywhere in Houston he wanted to go.

"You got a deal," the man said. "Look, I've got the money right here. I'm not trying to pull anything over on you." He pulled out a wad of money and peeled off a $100 bill.

Flanagan pulled into a gas station at Cardinal and Highland and filled the tank. While he was doing this, the man got out of the front seat and climbed in the back, saying he was tired and wanted to try and catch a nap. He stretched out on the back seat, and Marvin Murl Flanagan drove up onto I-10 and headed west through the night, toward Houston.

After a few moments, Flanagan now told Hobbs, the man started talking. He complained to Flanagan about what a bad day he had had, going over and over the details about his car breaking down, his clothes being stolen, and then cutting his finger so badly.

"But I'm not mad about what happened today," the man said. "It could have been a whole lot worse."

Flanagan said it was good not to get too angry about things. After a bit, the man fell silent and the driver assumed he had fallen asleep.

Suddenly, there were lights and sirens all over the place. Flanagan told Hobbs that his passenger sat up then. "I know I'm going to jail," he said.

Marvin Murl Flanagan finished his statement, and Robert Hobbs told him he was going to have to confiscate the $100 bill Flanagan had been given for the trip to Houston. Then, he asked Flanagan how the passenger was behaving during this time. Was he upset? Did he seem to be frightened or acting strangely?

"No, not at all," said Mr. Flanagan. "He was very calm the whole time."

After he had the taxi driver sign his statement, Hobbs issued a receipt for the $100 bill and walked Flanagan out of the police station. Then he went into the detective squad room, which was abuzz with activity. Ray Beck and Bill Gates had brought Michael Lee Lockhart back from the hospital, now dressed in a white paper hospital jumpsuit.

Judge Harold Engstrom, the Jefferson County justice of the peace, had just arrived to reissue the Miranda warnings to the prisoner and to set bond. These procedures had already been done by justice of the peace Larry Cryer, of course, but that had been in Chambers County, the site of the capture. Since that time, the prisoner had been moved out of Chambers County and taken into custody by Jefferson County, so the whole process started over.

In Texas, justice of the peace, an elected office, provides a sort of first-line judge on an around-the-clock basis. A justice of the peace can place charges, set bond, issue warrants, and marry people, often stepping in to provide these judicial services during odd hours on holidays and weekends when courthouse judges are not available. One police officer described the office of justice of the peace as a sort of "7-Eleven of judges," the place you went when you needed something and all the regular stores were closed.

Judge Engstrom Mirandized the paper-suited Lockhart, who was standing in the midst of his guardian police officers. Robert Hobbs, wearing down now like the rest of them after the exhausting night, stood leaning on the doorjamb, watching the proceedings.

After Judge Engstrom issued the constitutional warnings, he officially charged the suspect.

"Michael Lee Lockhart, you are charged with the capital murder of a police officer. I am setting your bond at one million dollars. Do you understand the charges against you?"

"Yes," said Lockhart, "I understand."

"Do you have any questions about these proceedings?"

"Well," said Lockhart, "I'd like to say that I'm guilty, and I'm sorry for the trouble I've caused here."

As soon as Lockhart said the words "I'm guilty," all the police officers in the room took out notepads and began writing.

"Also," Lockhart said, "I would like to represent myself, to act as my own defense attorney. But I realize that the technicalities of the law here in Texas probably won't allow that, will they?"

The police officers were writing furiously.

"Mr. Lockhart," said Judge Engstrom dryly, "I am advising you that this is not the time or the place to be making statements about your guilt or innocence. You will have that opportunity at a later time."

Lockhart was put into a guarded office while Beck and Gates did the necessary booking-in paperwork. Then they took him to the lock-up, where Gates instructed the lock-up personnel to keep a very close eye on their prisoner. He was to be put into a cell by himself and kept in full view of the jailkeepers at all times. Even though he was wearing only a paper suit, nobody was going to take a chance on his trying to hang himself or otherwise harm himself. He was going to go to trial for the murder of Paul Hulsey, and he was going to do it as fully healthy as he'd been when he'd pulled the trigger on the fallen policeman.

The men all left the Beaumont station together. It was 5 A.M. the morning after the most emotionally brutal night of their lives.

Dawn was just breaking, and the morning was chilly and

damp. Everyone was yawning and shaking his head, trying to stay awake for the drive home.

"Dang," said Gates, as they stood outside the front door of the police station. "My mouth tastes like a stable."

"Ruby, ole jewel," said his partner, Ray Beck, "y'all got about an hour to get home, brush your teeth, and get back here. We got us a mess of paperwork coming up."

As the men walked to their cars and pulled out into the still deserted streets of Beaumont, they were feeling an exhausted sense of resolution: they thought they would do the necessary paperwork to bring Michael Lee Lockhart to trial for the murder of Paul Hulsey, then they would be able to step back a bit as police officers and step forward again simply as ordinary men who had a friend to bury and to mourn.

They were wrong.

Thirty-two

"The gun he killed Paul with was stolen from a police officer," Robert Hobbs said.

It was 6:30 on the morning after Paul Hulsey's murder, and Hobbs was sitting in on the morning roll call at the Beaumont police station. He, Ray Beck, Bill Gates, and the others who had worked all night had taken an hour or so after booking Lockhart into a cell to go home, take a shower, say hello and goodbye to their wives and kids, and come back to the station. Other officers were just coming on duty for the day shift. Their uniforms were fresh, but their faces were haggard; many of them had come in during the night, off-duty, to help. One young policeman especially hard hit was Jimmy Ellison; Officer Paul Hulsey had been his FTO, his field training officer.

Ellison had stood guard over Lockhart for a short time during the night in one of the interview rooms, while the processing was going on.

"I wasn't in that room for more than a few minutes," Ellison said, "before I felt like the hairs on my arms were standing on end. He just keeps this sort of blankly pleasant expression on his face, but when you look into his eyes—I mean, really *look*—that's when your instincts start setting off alarm bells and you say 'there's something *missing* inside this guy's head.' A soul, maybe. After what he'd just done, his eyes reflected no more feeling than a shark, or a doll. Not like he was crazy, or drugged, or anything like that. Just empty."

The ancient Hebrews recognized the same frightening phenomenon that Officer Ellison described. Their legends spoke of a "clay man," a *golem,* who looked and acted like everyone else from the front, but who, when he turned sideways, couldn't be seen. The *golem* walked among his peers during the day and couldn't be distinguished from an ordinary man; but at night, he would roam the lonely roads, and if he caught you alone and unprotected, he would tear you apart. This three-thousand-year-old legend suggests that even back then, the man with the empty eyes and no soul was recognized by his own tribe. He looked like other men, he talked and acted like other men, but behind the clay mask lay the primitive instincts of a predatory reptile. The ancient Hebrews called him *golem;* today, the term is "sociopath."

Now, at morning roll call, the news about Paul Hulsey's having been killed with a policeman's stolen gun hardened their rage even more; "one of theirs" had been killed, and now they were hearing that Lockhart had violated another "one of theirs" to get the weapon to do it. Everyone took the news in silence for a few moments. They sat drinking strong coffee, cup after cup, some of them smoking cigarettes, others putting a pinch of tobacco in their mouths. No one mentioned their gritty eyelids and sleep-queasy stomachs; the caffeine and nicotine would keep them going through what was going to be a very long day after a very long night.

"Smith and Wesson .357, model 66, serial number 47J7299, chrome service revolver, Officer Richard Armstrong of Elyria, Ohio," Hobbs read from the NCIC response he had just torn off the teletype machine. "Stolen in a residential burglary of the officer's home on, let's see . . . August 4, 1987, along with the officer's coat badge, a Buck knife, and other personal items."

"So, he's had the gun six months or more," said one of the Beaumont cops.

"Yeah, let's see, August to March—more than eight months all told. And the Corvette comes from Ohio, too— stolen in an armed robbery in Toledo last November. Then we've got the Florida plates, also stolen; and Missouri plates hidden in the rear compartment of the car. We're checking on them right now, but it certainly looks like this guy's a traveler. I haven't even started yet on the credit cards, receipts, and all the other evidence we recovered from his room at the Best Western, and from the Corvette. Just from the quick look I had, though, the credit cards are in all different names. The wallet he was carrying has all the personal IDs of a 'Philip Tanner,' of Jacksonville, Florida. We ran a name-check on the name he's given us—Michael Lee Lockhart—and got an immediate hit. Michael Lee Lockhart has done time for armed robbery in Wyoming, and he's got open warrants from Ohio for rape and auto theft. So at least on this one point, his real name, I think he's telling us the truth. Whoever and whatever else he is, we now believe that he *is* Michael Lee Lockhart."

"We've inventoried the money he had on him when the troopers made the capture," said Ray Beck. "$1,489, nine hundred of that in hundred-dollar bills. He also paid the taxi driver with a one-hundred-dollar bill, which we've got. Once everything starts opening up for business this morning, we'll start checking around further into where all that money came from."

"There's also the $50 he gave that kid in Orange," said Bill Gates. "The kid put it in an envelope and dropped it into the night slot of the Wienerschnitzel Restaurant where he works. I'll be waiting there when the restaurant opens to take it into evidence. Kinda looks like everybody who

got paid for taking Lockhart someplace last night is going
to come up short on the deal."

They talked for a few more minutes and then had to let
the day shift people get out into their squad cars. Reluctantly, the day crew would have to do their best to handle
all the normal calls that came into the department in the
days to come, and that was perhaps even more difficult than
being assigned, like Ray Beck and Bill Gates were, to work
exclusively on the Hulsey murder investigation.

"We should put together the line-up as soon as we can,"
Bill Gates said now, as the investigators sat dividing up
their responsibilities for the day. "Some of our witnesses
at the Best Western are from out of state, and they'll want
to be heading out as soon as they can."

"We've got a couple of young policemen who could easily pass for Lockhart's brother," added Beck. "I'll call them
in and then start calling witnesses. Bill, you and I can take
care of transporting everybody over here. And I'll call over
to the lock-up, see if they've got anybody who looks close
enough to stand in."

"And I'll get ahold of Judge Gist," Hobbs put in. "We
need him to appoint a legal representative for Lockhart. It's,
what, 7:30 now; let's schedule it for about 10:30. That
should give us time to get everybody together."

Hobbs put in a call to district judge Larry Gist, who said
he would appoint a local attorney, G. Patrick Black. When
he contacted the man, Hobbs asked that he be at the Beaumont station by 10:15 so that he could spend a few minutes
with his new client and then review the procedures for the
line-up.

When Mr. Black arrived and had spoken with his client,
Hobbs let him view the six possible candidates they had
lined up to stand with Lockhart, which included several
police officers. He let the attorney make the choice which
five men he wanted. He also let the defense attorney choose
which position Lockhart would take in the line-up.

Michael Lee Lockhart and each of the five other stand-ins were dressed in identical white jail jumpsuits. Because Lockhart had a bandaged right index finger, all the men were provided with white cotton gloves; they all had dark blond or light brown hair, parted in the middle for the occasion, neatly trimmed mustaches, and slim builds, and were within an inch either way of Lockhart's height.

There were eleven witnesses police wanted to bring in, including people from the motel, from Bennigan's, and from Whip's Creamery in Orange. Each witness had to view the line-up separately, through one-way glass, so the morning went by slowly as each person was brought in, allowed as much time as he needed for the viewing, and then taken out to have his findings recorded. Several of the witnesses were not going to be available this morning, so the detectives arranged for a second line-up to be held later in the afternoon.

No one had actually seen Michael Lee Lockhart shoot Officer Hulsey. The two men had been in the room alone, so it was doubly important to be able to piece together, from what witnesses *did* see, an airtight identification that would logically carry the entire scenario from one point to the next.

One of the most important witnesses was the man who had been staying next door, in room 156 at the Best Western Motel. Mr. 156 was a New Mexican who had been on vacation in Florida and was returning home. He had pulled off I-10 for the night at Beaumont, where a string of motels cluster around the highway. He had checked into his room around 6:30 and then decided to go jogging; it was a good way to see some of the city, and it would loosen up his legs after the long hours on the road. He got back to his room at 7:02, he told police, and saw a squad car parked in the motel parking lot. An avid workout buff, he knew the exact time because he always clocked himself when he ran.

Once in his room, Mr. 156 immediately got down on the floor and started doing a series of sit-ups. He was on his thirty-seventh sit-up when he heard a series of loud thumps from next door, like someone or something banging into the adjoining wall. Seconds later, he heard several loud "pops," and the smoke alarm next door went off. He rushed out of his room, and just then, the door to 157 was flung open and a young man rushed out. Mr. 156 said that the man was shoving money into his pocket as he ran. Coins were falling all over the sidewalk, but he never slowed down. He raced to a red "sportscar" in the parking lot and peeled out into the street toward I-10.

Mr. 156 looked now at the six men facing him from the other side of the glass. "That's him," he said. He had pointed to Michael Lee Lockhart.

The parade of witnesses continued until lunchtime. Lockhart seemed subdued this morning, turning right and left as he was told, standing still and blank-faced, and not saying anything to anyone. Apparently, he had talked himself out the night before.

After lunch, with the rest of the witnesses now ready to view the line-up, Robert Hobbs and Sgt. Beck called in their stand-ins and called over to the jail for Lockhart to be brought back.

All the detectives stopped talking at once when Michael Lee Lockhart, between two deputies, walked into the line-up room. A crafty little smirk played around his mouth, and he darted sly sideways glances at Hobbs and the detectives, like a cute little boy who'd gotten away with something—as indeed he had. His mustache was gone.

"It was the first indication we had of just how impulsive, almost childishly impulsive, Michael Lockhart could be," Robert Hobbs would say. "We simply had everybody stand by while we lined up five more similar-looking guys *without* mustaches, and we held the line-up anyway. For this second line-up, Robert Hobbs called a neighbor of his,

Darin Cassidy. Cassidy, a former pipefitter whose job had evaporated with the oil market crash, had gone to work as a corrections officer for the city. Hobbs had immediately noticed the physical resemblance between Cassidy and Lockhart—except for the mustache—and now, the corrections officer said that of course he would be happy to help out

In all, nine of the eleven potential witnesses positively identified Lockhart, so he'd shaved his mustache off for nothing. Hobbs continued, "The more I came to know him, to understand something of the way his thought processes worked, the more I realized just how pervasive this impulsiveness was in him. He would get a thought or idea into his head and act on it instantly, without thinking it through or weighing the outcome or consequences. The kids today have a phrase that fits that kind of thinking: 'If it feels good—do it.' That seemed to be Lockhart's credo, as well."

While the Beaumont detectives worked to pull together all the strings of the police case against Michael Lee Lockhart, Robert Hobbs's responsibility was to investigate everything there was to know about Lockhart himself so that by the time prosecutors Jim Middleton and Paul McWilliams were ready for trial, they would have a complete portfolio on him. He also oversaw the collection of physical evidence that might be needed, and would have to provide the D.A.'s office with an accurate chronology of the maelstrom of activity following the murder. It was going to be an enormous task.

Jefferson County district attorney Thomas Maness called Hobbs into his office to talk about the investigation to come.

"This is going to be your case, Robert, your investigation from beginning to end, and I just want to be clear with you right from the start that whatever you need from this office in the way of resources or help, you've got it. If you have to make trips to gather evidence, or get on the phone all day long-distance—whatever it takes to bring us an unbreakable case against him—that's what I want from you. You don't have to clear expenses with me at every step of the way or wait to get my permission before you approve an expenditure. Our trust in your judgment is absolute. We intend to seek the death penalty against this man; your responsibility is to bring us enough to do it.

"I want everybody here in my office tomorrow morning at 9 A.M.," Maness went on. "The police officials, Middleton and McWilliams, the crime lab, the FBI, everybody. We'll coordinate our efforts so we don't end up stepping all over each other, but at the same time, we'll make certain we're not missing anything, either."

As he left the D.A.'s office and headed back to the police station, Hobbs mentally reviewed his "things to do immediately" list.

Over a hundred police officers from six different counties had had some part in the drama that had ended at the Old and Lost Rivers Bridge outside Houston. All those movements would have to be traced. The Best Western Motel, the Orange traffic circle, the ice cream shop, Bennigan's Restaurant, Flanagan's taxi, St. Elizabeth's Hospital, and the bridge where Lockhart was captured were all sections in the crime-scene trail. Anybody who saw anything, heard anything, or did anything would have to be interviewed; all their movements would have to be put into context with everyone else's. Then there would be backtracking to do— the stolen Corvette, the stolen license plates, the stolen gun, the stolen credit cards.

On the car radio, Hobbs listened as the City of Beaumont reacted to the news of their policeman's death. The whole city seemed to be in shock. Before last night, the only other Beaumont police officer murdered in the line of duty in the history of the city had been Alex Ruffis Sterling, who was gunned down in a shootout on Crockett Street on August 7, 1920. Most residents of Beaumont had not even been alive then, and they were shocked and enraged as they poured out their grief.

Within hours of Paul Hulsey's death, the Beaumont law firm of Reaud, Morgan and Quinn established a memorial trust fund for little Ashley and Amanda Husley, which they opened with a $5,000 contribution of their own. By afternoon, the contributions had grown to well over $11,000, with the radio reporting that one little boy emptied his piggy bank and gave his entire savings, $1.17, "to help the policeman's little girls." Within two weeks, the trust fund would grow to well over $60,000.

Back at the police station, Robert Hobbs looked through the growing list of evidence being catalogued from room 157.

"Michael Lockhart seemed to have the world's largest collection of stone-washed denim" Hobbs said. "He had a huge suitcase and a really big garment bag. Pairs and pairs of stone-washed denim jeans, shirts, vests, jackets—you name it, he had it. I wondered how he fit all that stuff into the Corvette."

But who was this man, this cop killer, this *golem?*

Among Lockhart's possessions was an address book. It intrigued Robert Hobbs for two reasons: one, because the people in this book would know Lockhart, his movements, his personality, his history; and two, because in it were many names and many telephone numbers from many different states.

And they were all women.

Thirty-three

"Is Rick in trouble?"

Robert Hobbs sat at his desk with a notepad and started calling the telephone numbers in Michael Lee Lockhart's address book. The first number he tried was in Miami, Florida. Detectives had checked the motel telephone log at the Best Western and found that Lockhart had placed two calls after he'd checked in; one to a Beaumont pizza parlor, and the other to a Miami number. Hobbs was on the phone now with a young woman at that number. She'd identified herself as Cathy.

Hobbs told her that the man she knew as "Rick Tread-well" was in custody in Texas for the murder of a police officer. He asked how well she knew "Rick," and when was the last time she'd seen him.

"I met Rick in November, when I was working at Kmart," Cathy said. "He came into the housewares department and we started talking. He seemed real nice; and of course, he's so good-looking and all. He said he was here from out of state, and did I know anywhere he could stay for a while that didn't cost too much."

She told Hobbs that she and her husband had been in the process of a divorce, and she'd been having trouble paying the mortgage on her condo, where she lived with her twelve-year-old son. She had an extra bedroom and had been thinking of renting it out, and now she and "Rick" talked about it.

"He was there for quite a while. We talked and I asked him all about himself. He said that he was from Ohio, his parents were dead, and he had inherited some money from them. He said he was a college man, and that he would be starting at Harvard Law School next fall. Meanwhile, he was just traveling around, to see something of the country before he had to buckle down and start law school. I said he could rent the extra bedroom at my place for $250 a month."

She said that Rick moved in that same day, with just some clothes and toiletries that he brought in from his red Corvette. Her home was in a nice neighborhood, just across from the Miami Zoo, and at first, everything seemed like it was going to work out just fine. The week after her new tenant moved, Cathy, her son, and Rick spent Thanksgiving Day cooking a huge traditional dinner, and they all sat around the table and ate together.

Over the next month, Rick spent his days exploring Miami, while Cathy worked at Kmart. They spent most evenings together at home, talking for hours at a time. It wasn't until nearly Christmas that she began to think her gentleman tenant wasn't all that much of a gentleman, after all.

Both Cathy and Rick enjoyed drinking. Often, during the evenings, they would have a few drinks—and sometimes, more than a few. Twice during one of these evenings when they were both pretty well buzzed, Rick "came on" to her, and they began kissing and fooling around on the couch. But then, she told Hobbs, Rick wouldn't stop, and he'd ended up forcing rough sex on her. She described "rough sex" as Rick holding her down while he tore at her clothes, and then slamming her back down every time she tried to get up. She also said he put his hands around her throat and told her to lie still.

Cathy said that she hadn't reported these incidents as rape since she had been drinking heavily, too, and felt she was partly to blame. Besides, in each case Rick had apologized the next morning, saying he was so drunk he hardly remembered what he'd done. Then, he would go back to being the perfect gentleman again. He was extremely clean, always showering and washing his hands and taking care of his clothes; and he kept his room in the condo spotless. Cathy decided to overlook the two frightening drunken episodes.

Then, the week before Christmas, her ex-husband had come over. They'd gotten into a loud argument, and her ex had begun slapping her around. He chased her into the kitchen and pushed her against the wall, where he'd begun choking her, yelling that he was going to kill her. She had screamed for Rick to help her, but he'd come to his bedroom door, watched what was happening, and then turned around and gone back into the bedroom, shutting the door. She had eventually broken free from her husband and run to the neighbor's across the hall, where she'd called the police. When she'd stood in her doorway, telling her ex-husband that the police were on the way, Rick had suddenly come rushing out of his bedroom. He'd run out of the apartment and driven quickly away. When he'd returned home that evening, Rick had told Cathy that the reason he hadn't defended her against her ex-husband was that his new girlfriend had told him he should mind his own business and not interfere in the affairs of his landlady and her former husband. He'd never mentioned why he had rushed away so quickly when he'd heard the police were coming.

Cathy told Hobbs now about Rick's suspicious behavior right around Christmas.

"I bought my son a camera for Christmas," she said. "We all sat around opening presents on Christmas morning, and my son was so excited about the camera, he ran all around the house, taking pictures of everything. He took a picture of Rick, and then all of a sudden, Rick got very upset about that. He said he just didn't like having his picture taken. A few minutes later, my son was trying to figure out something about the camera and Rick said to give it to him—that he would help. Well, he took the camera and popped it right open, exposing the film and ruining it. He said he was sorry, that he'd buy more film, but I felt he did it on purpose."

Cathy said that she also took a photo of Rick while he was opening the Christmas present she got him. He looked very angry at that, but she said she always took pictures at Christmas, and he should stop making such a big deal of it. Later, feeling that Rick would try to destroy her film, too, she put her camera in the trunk of her car. She thought no more of the incident until a few days later, when she came home from work early and found Rick in her bedroom, looking through her closet and dresser drawers. He made some paltry excuse for being in her room, and then he left and didn't come back until the next day. She was sure he was looking for her camera, and that he left to avoid being questioned about it.

By this time, Rick was staying away overnight occasionally, and sometimes for two days at a time. Cathy didn't care; he was only a tenant and could come and go as he pleased. But then, on the day before New Year's, he left and didn't come back. She told Hobbs that she didn't hear from him again until the end of January, when he suddenly called one evening and asked if he could come home. She said he could, but that he would have to come up with the rent. Cathy said that sometimes Rick seemed to have no money at all, while at other times, he flashed big bills all over the place. He never got any mail, and he didn't seem to have a checking account; he paid for everything in cash.

Cathy said that when Rick came home now, toward the end of January, he seemed very subdued—moody and brooding, and always wanting to be by himself. But he had a lot of money. She said that when she asked for the rent, he pulled out a stack of cash at least three inches high. He seemed extremely volatile now, and once, in the kitchen, when her son made some smart-aleck remark, Rick reached into a drawer and pulled out a big knife, threatening to go after the boy if he didn't shut up. She threw a fit; they argued, and Rick promised not to threaten the boy again. But the relationship had soured, and his living there was becoming increasingly strained.

By mid-February, Rick told Cathy that he was moving out for good. He packed his few belongings and left, and she now told Robert Hobbs that that was the last time she'd seen "Rick," which would have been about four weeks before this telephone call.

Robert Hobbs thanked her for her candor, and asked would she be willing to testify in court as to what she had just told him if the occasion arose. Cathy said she would; she was appalled that Rick had killed a police officer. Then, she added some thoughts of her own to the interview.

"He was so charming, and I used to love to just sit and talk with him. But as time went on, I started to realize that he was a compulsive liar. He'd start telling me something, and it would be different than what he'd said before about the same thing. A couple of times, I'd say something about it, point out that this wasn't what he'd said before. But he would get very upset when I did that—very upset. He'd go into his room and shut the door and just stay in there for hours, and then be real quiet and cold when he came out. So I just stopped saying anything about his lies; it didn't matter, and it just wasn't worth all the trouble. He seemed more pleased with me after that, like he could say anything he wanted about anything now, without fear that I would contradict him."

Robert Hobbs told Cathy now that he would be in touch soon and would make arrangements to have her formal statement taken. Then, she had one last question:

"Does Rick have AIDS?"

Hobbs said he had no way of knowing that, but would see if he could find out. He thanked her and hung up.

* * *

Monica, from Lawrenceville, Georgia, was next. When Hobbs introduced himself over the telephone and explained why he was calling, Monica's first question was, "Does Rick have AIDS?"

Monica said she met "Rick Treadwell" at the Atlanta Airport in early January; they talked and became close, and she invited him to stay at her home for a few days, which he did. Like Cathy, Monica thought Rick was a college man about to enter Harvard. He told her he came from a very large family in Missouri and that his parents were dead. She told Hobbs that Rick was always a perfect gentleman— kind, considerate, and a wonderful lover. She knew from the first that he was in town for only a short time, but when he left in mid-January, he promised to keep in touch. She said that Rick had called her only once since then.

"Does Rick have AIDS?" asked Denise, when Hobbs telephoned her in Leisure City, Florida. Again, the investigator had to say he didn't know but would try to find out.

Denise said she had met "Rick Treadwell" at the Tropical Bar and Grill in Miami. Denise, a bank teller, was out for the evening with her friends. Rick told her that his full name was Frederick Treadwell, but that he preferred Rick. He always had a lot of money, and she had no reason to doubt that he was just what he said he was—a college student from a wealthy family in Missouri, where his parents were now dead. She dated him while he was living with Cathy in Miami, and sometimes he spent the weekend with her and her mother.

It was obvious to Robert Hobbs from the first moments he talked to Denise that this young lady was in love with the man she knew as "Rick Treadwell." It came through in everything she said, and even though she talked honestly about Rick, Hobbs sensed her reluctance to add anything that might be harmful to the man she loved.

She said sadly that she knew Rick was dating another woman in Miami even while she was seeing him and he was living part of the time at her house. She didn't like that at all, but he was adamant that he wanted to be free. She finally admitted to Hobbs that she caught Rick in more and more lies, and that as she got to know him better, he seemed to be "kind of a fraud"; but that didn't lessen her feelings for him.

Hobbs thanked Denise for her information and said that he would be back in touch with her later for her statement. But it was to be the last time he ever talked with her. Every time he tried to call after that, he would leave a message, but she never called back. Finally, he contacted her mother. Her mother told Hobbs in no uncertain terms not to bother her or her daughter again.

"Rick is a wonderful young man," said Denise's mother. "He loves my daughter and he's been very good to her, and to me. They'll probably be married at some time in the future; and meanwhile, Rick will be welcome in this house anytime at all."

At first, Robert Hobbs thought he hadn't made himself clear. He explained again that "Rick" was really Michael Lee Lockhart, a thief and now a murderer.

"I heard you!" said Denise's mother. "And I don't care what you say. I know Rick, and I know how you police are. I have no use for the police, and I don't believe anything you say. When Rick is able to clear himself from whatever trouble you police are causing for him, he's going to come back here and marry my daughter. Now, don't call here again!"

Jill said she met Rick at Whistler's, a nightclub in Miami. "He doesn't have AIDS, does he?" she now asked Hobbs.

Jill said that she saw a lot of Rick Treadwell for a couple of weeks, but that she hadn't seen him in the last month or so.

"He said he was from New Hampshire, where his dad was a wealthy attorney. He told me he was going to Florida International University, and that when he graduated, he'd go to Harvard Law School, just like his father had done."

Rick always had a lot of money when he was out with her, usually in stacks of hundred-dollar bills. And, of course, he had that red Corvette.

"I always thought it was odd, though," she said, "he always backed that car into a parking space, as though he was always ready to make a quick getaway, like you see in the movies."

Jill said that she would testify against Rick if she had to, but Hobbs noted the reluctance in her voice and told her he didn't think her testimony would be necessary.

Lisa, from Homestead, Florida, seemed to have gotten a little closer to the real man than most of the other young women. She told Hobbs that Rick hinted to her that that wasn't his real name, and that he was in some kind of trouble. She was a single parent, and she said that Rick had been just wonderful with her little girl; the child had come to love him almost as much as she did.

Lisa said that she met Rick at a nightclub. He was with a young woman named Denise, but he told Lisa that Denise meant nothing to him. They were soon dating, and then spending most of their time together. Lisa had fallen very hard, very fast, and finally, in early March, Rick told her that he was leaving her. It was for her own good, he said, he didn't want to hurt her by staying any longer. She hadn't heard from him since then.

"Is Rick in some kind of trouble?" asked Lori, when Hobbs reached her in Duluth, Georgia. And then: "Oh, my God, please tell me he doesn't have AIDS!"

According to the version Lori knew, Rick Treadwell was a political science major at the University of Miami who had been accepted at Harvard Law School. His father was a wealthy Michigan businessman, a claim she had no reason to doubt. Rick always had lots of money, and he spent it freely. She had a great time during the weeks she dated Rick, and now she had nothing bad to say about him.

Angelique of Jefferson, Louisiana, was only seventeen years old. She was a high school student who met Rick at a yogurt store, and unbeknownst to her parents, she spent most of the weekend of March 4 with her new boyfriend, driving around in his flashy red Corvette. Her friends were suitably impressed, especially when Rick told them he was a private investigator from Miami. It all sounded like something out of that television show *Magnum, P. I.* Rick seemed to be just as successful a private investigator as Magnum, too, because he always had stacks of money. He kept the money in a dark green zippered pouch, because it was too thick a stack to fit into his pocket. She hoped her parents wouldn't have to know she had spent the weekend with the rich, mysterious private investigator, who'd then left town on Monday morning.

"Rick proposed to me on our third date," said Mandy, of Coral Gables, Florida. "He was a great guy, but he seemed kind of messed up, and he came on way too strong right from the start."

She was a student teacher at the University of Miami. She met Rick while she was working out in the university weight room. Rick told her that he'd just been turned down for admission to the school because of psychological problems, but that he was going to reapply and hoped to be accepted the second time. That way, they could see each other all the time.

Mandy took Rick home for Christmas dinner with her parents and family. The whole family was charmed with her classy, gracious new friend, and he seemed genuinely to enjoy the family atmosphere, offering to help serve dinner and clean up afterward. Rick talked about himself during dinner, telling Mandy's family he was from Ann Arbor, Michigan, and how much he was looking forward to settling down to his new student life at the University of Miami.

Later, when they were alone, Rick admitted to Mandy that he was having some emotional problems and was seeing a psychiatrist.

"He cried very easily," she told Hobbs, "and seemed emotionally needy and fragile. And he just kept going too far, too fast, with our relationship. He had that beautiful Corvette, of course. I didn't have a car; I just took the bus everywhere. But right away, he insisted he was going to buy me a car. He said he would pay cash for it; all I had to do was pick it out. I didn't want anything to do with that. I didn't want to be beholden, and I'll buy my own car when the time comes for it."

Rick always had stacks of money, according to Mandy, and he showed her a good time, taking her out to nightclubs and shows. The only really dark moment during their relationship came on what turned out to be their last night together, while they were at a nightclub. They were having a nice time, talking and dancing, when all of a sudden, a hostile young woman came up to their table. This woman told her to be careful—that the guy she was with was a pick-up artist. She said that he had been in there just the night before with one woman, while he was trying at the same time to pick up some other woman.

Mandy said that Rick became very angry at this, hotly denying it. He said he'd never even been there before, and he ordered the "stupid bitch" to go back to her own table and leave them alone.

By the next morning, Rick was gone. Mandy never heard from him again.

"He was always real mysterious," she concluded. "And he drank. A lot."

Robert Hobbs closed his notebook and sat back to take in all he had heard. A picture was beginning to come together of the man who was able to murder a police officer in cold blood and then talk about it so blithely afterward. But what picture? Lockhart had women, many of them college educated and intelligent, many of them very fond of him, and some actually in love with him. Each one, with the exception of Denise, thought she was his only lady; and each one had found him charming, personable, and generous. But he had not only been telling lies of convenience to his women; he had been living a lie with all of them—his life was like a masquerade ball that never ended. He was a private investigator, he was a college student; his parents were dead, his father lived in New Hampshire, or Missouri, or Ohio; he was about to enroll at Harvard, or he was about to enroll at Florida International University.

What, if any of it, was true? Why all the lies, all the make-believe, all the *women?* And if Lockhart's props were stripped away—the flashy Corvette, the stacks of hundred-dollar bills, the clean blue-jean image, the aura of Harvard Law School on the horizon—who would they find under all that? Robert Hobbs intended to find out.

Several of the other phone numbers in Michael Lee Lockhart's book were out of service or just didn't answer, and Hobbs made a note to himself to try them again later.

The final telephone number in Florida was answered by an elderly woman, Lisa's aunt, who offered her opinion of "Rick" in a concise, snappish recap.

"I met him *once!* I didn't *like* him! He's a *fraud! Good-bye!*"

One listing didn't show a telephone number, only a name: Betty Markham, at a North Sheridan Road, Chicago, address. Hobbs called Information, but no one by that name was listed at that address. Assuming that Betty, whoever she was, didn't have a telephone, Hobbs typed out a brief letter to her on the D.A.'s office stationery, asking that she get in touch with them as soon as possible. He dropped the letter into the out basket and was just getting ready to leave for the Beaumont police station to check in with Ray Beck and Bill Gates when his phone rang.

It was Cathy, from Miami.

"After you called," she said now, "I went into the bedroom that Rick had been staying in while he was here. He was always so neat and clean, and he left the room clean when he moved, so I just never had any reason to look around in there until you called this morning."

Cathy said that she went through the whole bedroom, but there was nothing at all of Rick's in the dresser drawers or the closet.

"Then, I looked in the wastebasket," she told Hobbs, "and there was this crumpled-up piece of paper, with the name 'Frederick Treadwell,' in writing, over and over and over, like he was practicing it or something."

Thirty-four

Monday, November 9, 1987, was looking to be a really good day for Toledo, Ohio, car salesman Frederick "Rick" Treadwell.

The thirty-four-year-old had come out of the University of Toledo with a degree in finance. He tried one job, and then another, and finally, a good friend of his asked him to come and work with him at his auto dealership. Rick talked over the offer with his wife, who was an attorney with the Lucas County prosecutor's officer, and they decided he should take it. The position offered good benefits, a great salary, and a chance for him to use his skills. In addition to his college degree in finance, a definite plus for the complicated financial management of an auto dealership, Rick had a creative flair for marketing. His employment contract with his friend provided that if he was able to come up with an innovative marketing idea for the dealership, he would share in a percentage of the profits.

With all these details worked out to everyone's satisfaction, Rick went to work for the huge Lincoln-Mercury dealership.

Rick Treadwell spent several months getting settled into his new job as finance director, but he had a clever marketing plan in mind, too, and now he talked it over with his friend. The auto dealer loved it.

Rick had come up with the idea that the dealership should make a big splash advertising the leasing of top-of-the-line *used* cars. New car leases were nothing new, of course, but nobody in the business was promoting the leasing of used cars. Rick thought it was an untapped market, and now, the Lincoln-Mercury dealership was going to give it a try.

Treadwell picked three very special cars to kick off the campaign, each of them a status symbol in its own way—a black, fully loaded BMW, a quietly elegant silver Mercedes-Benz, and a flashy 1986 red Corvette.

The dealership took out an eight-inch ad in the *Toledo Blade* over the weekend, and calls were already starting to come in. Rick had an appointment set up for 11 A.M. with a man who'd called that morning about the ad, wanting to see the Corvette.

His customer walked in right on time, and Rick automatically sized him up, deciding immediately he would be perfect for the Corvette. He was tall, slim, sandy-blond, immaculately groomed, and obviously aware of his own striking good looks. "Mike Locke," as the customer introduced himself, seemed to be one of those lucky people who can wear the most casual clothes and yet still look freshly showered and designer tailored. Even in his carefully faded jeans, tweedy gray sweater, and white athletic shoes, Mike Locke seemed to radiate a feline, movie-star quality. He was a perfect match for one of the world's flashiest high-performance sportscars.

The two men talked for a few minutes, discussing the car and the leasing arrangements. Mike Locke said that he was a salesman and his wife worked for the First National Bank of Toledo, so Rick didn't think money was going to be a problem. The 'Vette had only 14,000 miles on it and was in cherry condition; its street value was about $25,000. Leasing the car on a monthly basis was going to cost somewhere between $400 and $500, depending on the down payment.

All this seemed agreeable to Mike Locke, so Rick put a

temporary dealer plate on the back of the car and went out with his customer for a test drive.

As they headed toward I-475, Mike Locke asked a lot of questions about the car—good questions, Rick thought, about engine size and performance ratios and what sort of warranty the dealership was offering on its leased vehicles. Once on the expressway, Locke handled the Corvette like he was born to it, weaving through traffic easily, not abusing the tremendous power of the car, but not afraid of it, either.

"I really like it," Locke said, as he pulled over onto the shoulder of the expressway. "I'm going to take it."

With his right hand still on the wheel, Locke reached down with his left hand and came up with a big silver gun. He laid it in his lap, barrel toward Rick.

"Give me your money," he said, his eyes steady, his voice as calm as though they were discussing the weather report.

Rick Treadwell, blank with shock, put his hands up as soon as he saw the gun. Now, he reached carefully into his suit jacket pocket and brought out his money clip. Locke took it and opened it into his lap. He used one hand to go through the money clip while keeping the gun pointed at Treadwell's side. There were a couple of credit cards and $15 on the clip.

"You must have more than this," Locke said matter-of-factly. He reached over and patted the salesman down, pulling his checkbook out of the inside pocket of his sports jacket and rifling through it. Then he handed the checkbook back.

"Get out," he said, his voice chilled and businesslike. "And don't be stupid. I'm a pro, and there's somebody behind us watching every move you make."

As Rick turned to get out of the car, he could feel the hairs on the back of his neck prickle, and his back seemed to arch involuntarily, waiting for the crash of a bullet into his spine. He stumbled out onto the shoulder of the expressway.

The Corvette sped away.

Thirty-five

Robert Hobbs was back at his desk at 7:30 in the morning when Det. Sgt. Ray Beck called from the Beaumont police station.

"Major Sibert just called me from the jail," Beck said. "Seems our star boarder is putting up some all-fired ruckus over there, demanding to see us right away."

"Us? You and I? What could he want to see *us* about?"

"I have no idea," Beck said. "Sibert tells me that Lockhart has been spending all his time reading about himself. They get all the newspapers over there, and every time the jailers check on him, he's sitting there surrounded by newspapers, going over and over everything they're writing about Paul's murder. Then, all of a sudden, he starts putting up this big fuss, demanding that he has to see Beck and Hobbs."

"Let me see if I can get ahold of Pat Black again," Hobbs said. "If Lockhart wants to start talking about the case, I truly hesitate to go into the jail and have any statements being made without an attorney present for him. Who knows what spin they might later put on it? Let me call Black's office. I'll call you right back."

The attorney's office said that Mr. Black was out of town. Then, Sibert called Robert Hobbs, asking if they would please come over to the jail. Lockhart's antics—banging on the bars, yelling, and making demands—were upsetting all the other prisoners, and the jailers were having a rough time of it.

Hobbs met up with Ray Beck, and together they went into the jail. Hobbs asked that Sibert sit in on the interview. Then, two jailers brought Lockhart into the interview room.

"You assholes!" Lockhart screamed, as soon as he saw Beck and Hobbs. The jailers stood on either side of him, holding his arms.

"I'm tired of reading all this *bullshit* about me being some kind of dope dealer! You assholes are just trying to cover your own asses, and I know why! Because your guy *fucked up,* that's why, and now you're trying to blame me!"

"Get him out of here!" Ray Beck shouted back.

"You can go fuck yourselves!" Lockhart screamed, as the jailers hauled him out of the room. "You had my complete cooperation! I was going to help you guys out all I could! But now you can just go fuck yourselves, you fucking *assholes!"*

Hobbs and Beck could hear Lockhart's tirade all the way down the hall. Then the steel doors slammed and quiet returned to the room.

"Well, sir," said Ray Beck, "I guess we just saw something of the real Mr. Lockhart."

The newspapers all over Southeast Texas were carrying the murder of Officer Paul Hulsey as front-page news. The *Beaumont Enterprise,* the *Orange Leader,* and the *Port Arthur News* covered virtually nothing else in the days following the murder. "POLICE OFFICER SHOT AND KILLED," read the Beaumont headline. "FORMER POLICE CHIEF'S SON MURDERED," blazoned the *Orange Leader.* Chief Hulsey, young Paul's father, had been chief of police in Orange for four-and-a-half years, until his retirement in 1980. In Houston, the *Chronicle* headlined: "OHIO FUGITIVE HELD IN MURDER OF BEAUMONT POLICEMAN." The murder also made news 400 miles away, down in the Rio Grande Valley, where the Hulsey family had originally lived. "VALLEY NATIVE SHOT," reported the *Harlingen Morning Star.* And up north in Dallas, the *Morning News* announced, "SUSPECT IN OFFICER'S SLAYING CAUGHT IN TAXI."

But it was in Beaumont, of course, that Officer Hulsey's murder was most extensively reviewed. The *Enterprise* interviewed neighbors and friends of the slain cop, who all talked about what a gentle, upstanding young family man Paul D. Hulsey, Jr., had been. His fellow police officers, too, praised him as a good man, a good partner, and a good cop.

On the morning following the murder, Beaumont city manager Al Haines and police chief George Schuldt held a news conference at City Hall. Flags on all city buildings were ordered flown at half-mast. Many business owners around Beaumont dropped their flags, too, in a show of respect, as did hundreds of private citizens.

"Officer Hulsey was an exceptionally qualified officer who exhibited leadership ability, dedication, and a desire for excellence in providing police services to citizens," said Mr. Haines. "I join with all city employees in extending my heartfelt condolences to Officer Hulsey's wife, Barbara, their two children, parents, and family."

Chief Schuldt praised the professionalism of Hulsey's fellow Beaumont officers, and he thanked officers from other departments who had rushed forward to aid in the investigation that resulted in the quick capture of the murder suspect. Chief Schuldt had worked alongside the young cop's father in Galveston, and later, in Orange.

"This is the most difficult thing to do as chief of police," said Schuldt. "Our deepest sympathies go to his family. We've lost a professional officer. I want to thank the tremendous cooperation exhibited by all law enforcement officers whose assistance made this investigation successful."

Then attorney Wayne Reaud stepped forward to talk about the Hulsey Memorial Trust Fund he had established. He said that according to the contract between the Beaumont Police Officers' Association and the city, police officers are entitled to a life insurance policy of just $22,500. He hoped that the whole city would come together now to contribute to the benefit he had established for the stricken family.

"Barbara Hulsey has just lost her husband," Mr. Reaud said. "Their little children just lost their daddy. They've got two car notes and a house note. I don't see any way for her to keep her house. We owe this man enough to see that his children never have to go begging for bread."

Chief Hulsey and his wife, Mary Jo, held hands as they gave a brief statement of their own.

"Even though, at this point in time, our hearts are saddened, our son is a very special guy," Chief Hulsey said, his voice cracking. Next to him, Paul, Jr.'s mother wept softly, her head bowed.

"What he was doing was in the cause of good and of helping people," Chief Hulsey continued. "Our hearts go out to all the police officers all over because that's their task—to be a benefit to mankind. Doug was doing that and he gave his life. Doug's wife, Barbara, has asked us to extend her heartfelt feelings and gratitude for the showing of love and compassion that you've all had for our loved one."

Following the initial news reports of details of the crime and the upcoming funeral services, articles and letters to the editor began to appear in the papers, written by police officers concerned and unhappy about certain conditions of their job. "POLICEMEN QUESTION SAFETY OF ONE-MAN PATROL VEHICLES," headlined the *Beaumont Enterprise*. And then, "ONE-MAN PATROLS ENDANGER OFFICERS," and "POLICE WANT MORE OFFICERS ON THE STREET."

The issue of one-man versus two-man patrols was an ongoing discussion in Beaumont, with the city saying they simply couldn't afford to staff two-man cars, and the officers saying that their lives were needlessly endangered every day that they drove out to begin their shifts alone. The one-man, one-car policy had been instituted in 1984 by chief of police John K. Swan, who said that the policy would create more visibility on the streets.

The Beaumont Police Officers' Association received at least sixty calls from police officers concerned about their safety in the two days following Paul Hulsey's death. A city council meeting was scheduled for April 5, and many of the officers said they planned to attend.

Another issue the police officers were angry about was the matter of bulletproof vests. If a cop wanted one, he had to go out and buy his own. Many different types and makes of vests were on the market, offering differing degrees of protection at differing price levels. Bulletproof vests are expensive; the best ones can cost upwards of $1,000, beyond the reach of most young cops who have families to raise and house payments to make. The vest Hulsey had been wearing consisted only of two rectangular panels covering the center of his chest and back. His shoulders and sides were left unprotected—and the .357 magnum bullet fired by Michael Lee Lockhart had entered Hulsey's unprotected left side and shattered his heart.

Following all this outcry in the press, the citizens of Beaumont reacted as though an alarm had gone off. They had taken their police officers for granted, but now they watched as a one-man patrol car drove by and they watched as they saw their police walking around with nothing but a light-blue shirt between a bullet and a beating heart. The people of Beaumont simply hadn't thought about it before; they'd had no reason to, but they surely thought about it now.

Wayne Sherman, vice-president of Sherman's Lumber

Plus, suggested that all the private citizens and businesses in Beaumont come together for an Adopt-a-Cop program.

"We could compete to see who could raise the most funds to buy the vest," Sherman said. "It would raise pride and morale. And I'd be honored to buy the first vest myself." Wayne and his brother, C. L. "Sonny" Sherman, pledged that their lumber business would be the first in the city to purchase a bulletproof vest for a police officer.

Adopt-a-Cop was born in Beaumont, and now the whole city seemed to come alive and come together in the face of its shared tragedy. The fund for Paul Hulsey's little girls grew to over $19,000 in just two days. People volunteered their time to stand on downtown street corners with buckets labeled "Adopt-a-Cop." Within a matter of months, every police officer, not only in the City of Beaumont, but in all of Jefferson County, was provided with a top-of-the-line wraparound bulletproof vest.

"That whole movement following Paul Hulsey's death changed the face of law enforcement in Beaumont, Texas," said Robert Hobbs. "The whole city came together to show their respect, their concern, their gratitude, and their grief. And the change in attitude wasn't just with the private citizens of Beaumont; the cops, too, started to feel less bitter, less hopeless about their tough jobs, once they began to realize that a whole lot of ordinary, kindhearted, really nice people out there truly cared about what happened to them."

While all these painful issues were being played out in the press, the investigation continued into the circumstances surrounding Paul Hulsey's death and Michael Lee Lockhart's movements leading up to it. Leads were exploding in all directions. Lockhart was wanted in Ohio for the brutal rape of his ex-wife, and now, for the armed robbery of Rick Treadwell, during which he had stolen the red Corvette. Robert Hobbs felt sorry for poor Mr. Treadwell, whose name Lockhart had stolen, too. As the investigation widened, the name Rick Treadwell was cropping up all over, from one state to the next, one crime to the next. Hobbs wondered if the innocent Ohioan would ever be able to recover his reputation, to say nothing of his credit rating.

The Beaumont detectives were busy sending out "information wanted" bulletins throughout the area. One positive connection that came back immediately was about the hundred-dollar bill Lockhart had given "wrong-way Flanagan" for his taxi ride. The serial number of the bill had been prerecorded and was now being reported by the Citizen's Savings and Loan bank in Baton Rouge, Louisiana, as having been taken in an armed robbery on the morning of March 22. So Beaumont would now be investigating Michael Lee Lockhart for bank robbery as well as murder.

The American Express credit card confiscated from Lockhart's motel room, and the gas and motel receipts in his car, were all in the names of George and Debbie Severns of Decatur, Georgia. The card was taken when their home was burglarized in May 1987, along with an expensive camera and a bottle of shampoo. There was also the murder weapon—the police officer's gun stolen in a burglary in Ohio—to check. Texas investigators now found out that the house next door to the police officer's had also been burglarized that same afternoon.

All these leads had to be followed, even while the Beaumont detectives and Robert Hobbs from the D.A.'s office were still putting together the minute-by-minute account of Paul Hulsey's murder and Michael Lee Lockhart's capture. Prosecutor Jim Middleton decided to start a chronology of events. At first, he intended it only as a visual aid of the chaotic, multijurisdictional, hundred-car search for the police officer's killer. But as each new lead, each new crime, came in, Middleton's chronology kept growing. Investigator Hobbs began adding to it all the new information he was developing on a daily basis. Eventually, it would form a logical, readable account of the amazing blaze of destruction caused by one man, Michael Lee Lockhart, who had driven 30,000 miles in nine months, and who would brag that he had committed crimes of violence in every state in the country except the Dakotas and Minnesota.

Once the initial facts leading up to Hulsey's death were known, the Beaumont Police Department issued a "wanted for questioning" bulletin for George McBride, who seemed to have disappeared right after the murder.

Now, on Friday, March 25, McBride came into the station.

"Uh, I can't really say who all told me that you were looking for me," he said to the detectives, "but, uh, I heard it on the street that, uh, somebody had gave BPD my real name, and stuff like that. I didn't see no reason to run, 'cause I haven't did nothing wrong."

Det. Charles Tyler took George's formal statement.

McBride told Det. Tyler that he was standing around at Gladys and Forrest, "shooting some basketball," when he first saw the guy in the red Corvette. He said the 'Vette driver came up to him and asked if he knew where he could "get some weed." He now told Tyler that he didn't know anything about the availability of "weed" in Beaumont, despite his extensive record as a drug dealer.

McBride said that he explained to the driver that he couldn't help him, but then he asked if he could hitch a ride across town with him, and the driver of the Corvette agreed. Drug deals are usually made in a moving car, rather than on the street; it's much less conspicuous. But he said now that wasn't what was happening at all.

"I just needed to uh, uh, visit a, you know, a friend. Across town, like."

As they approached Magnolia and I-10, he saw Officer Hulsey's squad car make a U-turn and come back toward them. The Corvette driver looked in his rearview mirror and then speeded up, blowing right through the stop sign.

"I knew the officer was in our pursuit," McBride said, "because the guy I was with kept speeding up and looking back in the mirror. I said, 'Uh, didn't that cop see you go through those stop signs?' and he says, 'I been stopped before, and they aren't going to stop me again.' So then, we was going like seventy or eighty, and coming to an abrupt-like stop at each corner, where he kept looking back and forth, like to see if we was really getting followed, or what. Which we was."

McBride said that the 'Vette pulled over and dropped him off in front of Salem's Liquors. "And from that point, I went to see about, uh, uh, my friend, you understand me, but my friend wasn't home and all, but that didn't make no difference, 'cause I seen that the cop musta lost the Corvette; in fact, for sure he did, because now there he was, asking questions and all. And he seen me then, and he says, 'Where's your buddy?' and I says 'What buddy?' and all."

Tyler was doing his best to get all this down, and now he asked about the man in the Corvette.

"Can you describe the driver?"

"Uh, a white guy, kinda clean-cut, with, uh, a mustache, frosted blue jeans on, a red and black, and it seemed like maybe a green and white, a sport kind of you know, shirt . . ."

"About how tall?"

"Shit, about five-eleven, maybe . . . shit, maybe five-nine . . ."

"How much do you think he weighed?"

"Shit, comparing with myself and all, shit, about, uh, shit, maybe about a hundred and seventy-five pounds, something like that."

"Anything about his speech or his mannerisms that stood out?"

"Uh, shit, not really. He didn't, I mean he didn't seem

like, uh, like he was just an old ruthless guy or nothing like that."

After he completed this informative interview, Tyler told McBride to stay in town and stay available, in case they needed to talk with him further.

The investigation well under way, Beaumont prepared to bury its first police officer killed in the line of duty in sixty-eight years.

Thirty-six

At 8:30 in the morning, squad cars started lining up along blocked-off Pearl Street. Some had red Mars lights on their roofs, others were blue; still others sported combination-color light bars. There was no sound of sirens, no evidence of haste, no squawk of radios; only the relentless *whirr*-stop, *whirr*-stop of the Mars lights as the squad cars slowly jockeyed, with military precision, into long, straight lines, bumper to bumper. The cars themselves were all different colors; white with a brown stripe; light blue with a broad black stripe; green with large gold-foil emblems on the doors. They were all freshly washed and waxed, spotlessly cleaned and polished right down to the tires.

They had come from all over Texas, and from Louisiana, Arkansas, and Missouri, these men and women in their full-dress uniforms. Some were wearing dark blue; others were in brown pants, tan shirt, and Sam Brown belt crisscrossed across the chest. Many wore light blue shirts and dark blue pants with a gray stripe down each leg. Different city patches adorned their left shoulders—Dallas, Houston, San Antonio, Beaumont, Waco, Baton Rouge, Abilene, Harlingen, Austin, Little Rock, New Orleans, Lake Charles, Orange, Galveston, Kansas City, Corpus Christi. Some patches did not represent cities, but counties: Jefferson, Chambers, Mills, Angelina, Crockett, Washington—the list went on.

They were patrolmen, sergeants, detectives, lieutenants, captains, chiefs, state troopers, sheriff's deputies, federal agents, military police, fire investigators, and game wardens. Eight hundred in all, from over eighty different cities, stretched out into a cortege of squad cars over three miles long. However they were dressed, whatever they drove, they all had three things in common: solemn grief; white gloves; and a black ribbon covering each badge. They were all cops come to lay down one of their own.

The cortege wound its way slowly through the streets of Beaumont. Many private citizens pulled their cars over and stepped out, hand to heart, as the procession passed.

As the procession approached the Cathedral in the Pines christian center, it passed between long rows of two-wheeled escort motorcycles lining the service drive. Each motorcycle had red lights mounted into the windshield, and the words "Dallas Police Department" on the fenders. The motorcycle cops had driven four hundred miles to be there.

Inside the packed 1,400-seat cathedral, the sea of police officers stood at attention while white-gloved Beaumont officers escorted Barbara Hulsey and seven-year-old Ashley; Chief and Mary Jo Hulsey; and Tamara, Steve, and Danny Hulsey up the center aisle to the front pew. Then, as one man, eight hundred police officers quietly sat.

"Paul Hulsey lived life to the fullest," said Pastor Delmar Dabney. "He was more interested in the quality of life than the quantity of years. He was a committed man—a good cop. He knew the price of that commitment, and he paid that price."

The Rev. Lindell Buck was Paul Hulsey's childhood pastor. "Jesus did battle with sin," said Reverend Buck. "Paul Hulsey did battle with drugs. And despite his mischievous grin and kindly disposition, he was serious about the work that kept him away from his home and family for long hours, and eventually, claimed his life."

As the service continued, distraught sobs could be heard from the front rows. But the sea of blue sat rigid and still.

At the conclusion of the service, eight hundred police

officers filed out of the Cathedral in the Pines. They formed into two long lines that stretched from the doors of the church to the limousines waiting at the curbside, so that the Hulsey family could pass between them. All eight hundred held their white-gloved, right-handed salute until the casket, escorted by six Beaumont police officers, was placed into the hearse.

At Magnolia Cemetery, the huge group formed a circle around Paul Hulsey's gravesite, which lay beneath the spring-greening leaves of a draping oak tree. From the rear of the group, police bagpipers sounded the haunting, mournful tones of "Amazing Grace." Then, the seven-man Beaumont rifle team stepped up to the gravesite, lifted their rifles, and fired a twenty-one-gun salute.

"We leave here at the grave only the tent that Paul Hulsey lived in," said Reverend Buck, concluding his address. "When we leave here, we take his spirit and his memories with us."

Two Beaumont police officers stepped forward and removed the American flag from Paul Hulsey's casket. They folded it into a traditional triangle and handed it to Barbara Hulsey, who was able to stand only because police officers at her side supported her arms. Seven-year-old Ashley clung to her mother's skirt.

A second American flag was folded and handed to Chief and Mary Jo Hulsey.

A police trumpeter stepped forward as the group filed away and played a clear, slow rendition of "Taps."

Above the grave, the oak tree would soon burst into full green leaf, welcoming another spring.

Officer Paul Douglas Hulsey, Jr., twenty-nine years old, would never see it.

Thirty-seven

Judge Larry Gist sat all alone in his chambers. It was early evening, and the Jefferson County courthouse was nearly deserted. Only two or three times in the last hour had he heard the muffled echo of footsteps passing along the corridor outside his chambers. Somewhere far down the hall a man coughed, an office door closed, footsteps receded. A woman's light laugh, hollow and far away, drifted up from the lower lobby atrium. And then it was quiet.

The judge scribbled absently at the yellow legal pad that lay on his immaculate cherrywood desk. On the paper, he had written a short list of names; two had been crossed out, and then one of them written back in. Next to several of the names were question marks and the judge's own cryptic notes. Finally, he threw his pen down on the legal pad, and with a heavy sigh, leaned back in his blue leather chair, folding his arms behind his head.

Judge Larry Gist (pronounced with a hard *g*, as in *guest)* would be presiding over the capital murder trial of Michael Lee Lockhart. He and Jefferson County's other sitting criminal court judge, Leonard Giblin, rotated the responsibility whenever a major case came in; all the other, minor cases were distributed evenly between the two judges. The Lockhart case was certainly going to be a major trial, perhaps *the* major trial in the recent memory of Jefferson County, Texas. A uniformed police officer had been gunned down in cold blood right in the center of town; such an outrage

had not happened since the old lawless days near the beginning of the century, and the whole of Southeast Texas
was enraged. Judge Gist knew that the district attorney, Tom
Maness, would be pulling out all stops and throwing all the
considerable legal talent of his office into the prosecution.
The question now before the judge was whom to appoint
as legal counsel for the defense.

Judge Gist had been mulling over this question for several
days now. It was always important to provide competent
defense counsel in a criminal case, but in a capital murder
case the stakes ratcheted upward exponentially—and this
particular capital murder case was like no other in the life-
time of the county. Metaphorically speaking, the D.A. was
going to come out with teeth bared and claws at the ready;
the responsibility to provide him with a worthy opponent
rested squarely on Judge Gist's shoulders, and it was a responsibility that weighed heavily. A defense attorney who
simply wasn't up to all the hammering that the D.A. would
surely initiate might later prove to be the impetus for a
mistrial or an overturning of the lower court's judgment on
appeal. This was going to be an involved, expensive trial
for the people of Jefferson County, and Judge Gist intended
to be as certain as he could that everything in it was going
to be done the right way the first time around.

So now the judge sat alone in his office, weighing his
choices.

Larry Gist had been born in Port Arthur, Texas, on June
7, 1941. Although the family surname is of Dutch origin,
the Gists were American before there was an America, back
when a bunch of ragtag, rabble-rousing colonists on the
East Coast were clamoring for independence from their
European overseers. In 1753 and 1754, frontiersman Christopher Gist acted as guide for a young revolutionary named
George Washington, who had to travel to the Forks of the
Ohio to meet with his fellow seditionists. Along the perilous
journey, Gist twice saved young Washington's life. More

than twenty years later, a newborn United States of America would reap the benefit of Gist's lifesaving heroism and General Washington would become President Washington.

Larry Gist's paternal grandfather settled in Port Arthur, Texas, as a land developer in the late 1800s, and his son, Larry's father, married into a Cajun family from Louisiana bayou country. When Larry graduated from Bishop Byrne Catholic High School, he went on to Notre Dame, where he got his undergraduate degree in accounting, preparatory to entering law school. Young Larry's goal was to be a tax and business attorney. When he returned home to Port Arthur, Texas, he hired on with the D.A.'s office for what he thought would be an obligatory one-year stint before going into private practice. He ended up staying with the D.A.'s office for ten years, and in 1974, at age thirty-three, he was elected the youngest criminal court judge ever to hold the office in the State of Texas.

Judge Gist was a white-haired, white-bearded man with a tremendous mind and an equally tremendous appetite for adventure. A licensed pilot, he would fly his own four-passenger Mooney from Beaumont to the state capital at Austin whenever he had to go there for appellate work. He had also flown his own plane to the Bahamas, Canada, and Venezuela and would even hop-fly over to New Orleans just to have lunch.

Now, Judge Gist looked around his office. His chambers were lined on one wall with floor-to-ceiling leatherbound law books. Highbacked armchairs, padded in bright blue leather with brass stud tacks, faced his desk. On the floor was deeply piled rust-colored carpet, and the wall opposite the bookcases was decorated with various plaques, awards, and personal photo collages. Into one of the collages was stuck a typewritten line that perhaps held a message for those who came before his bench for judgment: "You're going to keep getting what you're getting as long as you keep doing what you're doing."

Judge Gist had practiced law in Jefferson County all his life, he had handled many dozens of capital murder cases both as prosecutor and then as judge, and he knew the history and qualifications of every lawyer in the county. Finally, he made up his mind—he would ask Charles Carver, of the prestigious Port Arthur law firm of Umphrey, Swearingen, Eddins, and Carver, to handle the Michael Lee Lockhart defense.

The Jefferson County grand jury had indicted Lockhart on April 14, three weeks after Officer Hulsey's death. After listening to witnesses in closed session for about an hour, the jury returned its decision: ". . . that Officer Paul Douglas Hulsey, Jr., was a peace officer acting in the lawful discharge of his official duty . . . that Michael Lee Lockhart knew Hulsey to be a peace officer . . . and that Lockhart intentionally and knowingly caused Officer Hulsey's death by shooting him with a deadly weapon."

Judge Gist knew that Charles Carver had acted as defense attorney in more than a dozen Jefferson County capital murder cases; he was a staunch opponent of the death penalty, and he fought hard and skillfully for his clients. Several years earlier, Carver had represented a murderess, Linda May Burnett, in a trial about one of the county's most lurid and heinous atrocities. Linda May was the girlfriend of Ovide Joseph Dugas, a huge, hulking brute of a man whose wife had left him and who was now obsessed with finding her and taking his two children away from her. Burnett and Dugas, dressed in full camouflage, went to the ex-wife's family home in the little town of Winnie, just south of Beaumont. There, they took the ex-wife's mother, father, brother, sister-in-law, and two-year-old niece hostage. The family refused to reveal the whereabouts of their loved one, so Burnett and Dugas took the whole group out into the remote, thickly forested Gilbert woods. Dugas shot them in the head, one after another, dumping them into a mass makeshift grave. When he was done, Burnett held the two-year-old. They shot the child in the head and threw her body on top of the others.

Both Burnett and Dugas received the death sentence, but Burnett was later overturned on appeal and she was sentenced to life in prison. Ovide Joseph Dugas, on death row at Huntsville, was brought back to Jefferson County to give statements implicating Linda May Burnett. On the way back to Huntsville, Dugas, handcuffed and in chains, pulled out a homemade shiv that he had fashioned out of a steel bucket handle and stabbed the D.A.'s investigator in the liver. The investigator was able to pull his gun and shot Ovide Joseph Dugas to death.

Charles Carver had also been the defense attorney in the case of James David Autry, who'd walked into a convenience store, robbed the clerk, and then shot to death both the clerk and a Catholic priest who was in the store at the time. After Autry was sentenced to death, his brother publicly threatened to kill Judge Giblin.

In all, attorney Charles Carver had acted as defense attorney in fifteen capital murder cases, and Judge Gist decided that he would be the best and most logical choice for the Lockhart case, as well—that is, if he would be willing to do it. Carver was a partner in one of the state's wealthiest and most prestigious law firms. In the years to come, Walter Umphrey, founder and senior partner of the firm, would become the state's second largest political contributor, surpassed only by presidential candidate Ross Perot.

His decision made, Judge Gist locked up his desk, turned out the lights in his chambers, and headed home. He would call Charles Carver in the morning.

Thirty-eight

Det. Sgt. Ray Beck and D.A.'s investigator Robert Hobbs glanced out the plane's porthole window and watched as the city of Toledo came into view thousands of feet below. It was a clear blue morning, four weeks after the murder of Paul Hulsey.

The men were heading now into Lockhart's home turf and they were anticipating a busy couple of days. Beck had spent many hours over the last week on the telephone with Ohio detectives, particularly Det. Dan Brimmer, who had handled the rape case filed by Dina Alden, Lockhart's ex-wife. Beck had also contacted Toledo robbery detective Jim Lagger, who'd sent the Corvette robbery reports to Beck in Texas, and who now promised to arrange for Texas investigators to interview Rick Treadwell.

Both Texans were looking forward to learning much during this trip about the real Michael Lee Lockhart. So far, they had only the image that Lockhart had invented, the image of a wealthy, generous, sensitive, slightly mysterious, college-man-about-town who had a way with the ladies. But that entire image had been stolen, bit by bit, from other people, other lives. The Corvette belonged to Treadwell's dealership; the clean-cut college-man persona was similar to Ted Bundy's; the mysterious aura of the worldly traveler who had secrets to keep was right out of James Bond; and the money, at least, that portion of it found on Lockhart when he was captured, belonged to the Citizen's Savings and Loan bank of Baton Rouge, Louisiana.

The bank had confirmed that the hundred-dollar bill Lockhart had given to Marvin Murl Flanagan for the taxi ride to Houston had indeed been taken during an armed robbery of the bank on March 21, 1988, just the day before Officer Hulsey'd been killed in Beaumont. Bank employees had described the armed robber as a tall, slim, "extremely good-looking" white man with light brown hair and mustache. He had been wearing a yellow sweatshirt under a camouflage jacket, a green baseball cap, and faded or stonewashed blue jeans. He had walked up to a teller just before 1 P.M. that Monday afternoon and pulled open his jacket so she could see the gun stuck into his waistband. Putting his right hand on the gun butt, he'd flipped a dark green vinyl zippered bag onto the counter.

"There's the bag," he'd said to the teller, looking steadily into her face. "I want large bills and twenties. Now! I do have a gun!"

The teller said she put her stack of large bills into the bag, and then reached into her cash drawer for a stack of singles.

"Not the ones!" the robber said. He rifled quickly through the stack of bills and pulled out the dye pack, tossing it back on the counter. Then he stuffed the zipper bag into his waist and turned, walking steadily to the door, which he then pushed open with his elbow. And then he was gone, and so was $2,040 of the bank's money.

Obviously, the robber knew about banks using several bills clipped around a packet of indelible dye, which explodes all over the robber when he pulls the bills apart. He had spotted the dye pack immediately and thrown it back to the teller. But what he didn't know, apparently, was that one of the $100 bills he had taken was a "bait bill," whose serial number had been recorded by the bank to be traced later in the event of just such a robbery. It was that bill that Lockhart had given Flanagan.

Ray Beck had traced back the motel receipts found in Lockhart's room at the Best Western. Lockhart had registered at Shone's Inn in Baton Rouge on March 18. He checked out at 1:55 P.M. on March 21, exactly one hour after the robbery of the Citizen's Savings and Loan. A camouflage jacket, yellow sweatshirt, and green baseball cap were recovered from his room at Best Western. Of stonewashed jeans, Lockhart had dozens of pairs.

On the way to the Toledo police station, Robert Hobbs was very interested in looking around the vital blue-collar city.

"Toledo was interesting to me," Hobbs said, "because the only thing I knew about it was from *M*A*S*H;* Corporal Klinger was always wanting to get home to Toledo."

Beck and Hobbs stepped up to the desk sergeant on duty, presented their credentials, and asked for Det. Dan Brimmer. The desk sergeant called over to the detective division.

"You guys are from Texas?" he asked, hanging up the phone. Beck and Hobbs could see the mischief in his eyes. Other policemen around the desk stopped to grin, and to watch.

"Yes, sir, we surely *ore* that," said Ray Beck in his best drawl.

"Uh-huh. I see. So where'd you park your horses?"

"Well now, sir," said Beck, not batting an eye, "since y'all don't *pervide* a hitchin' post out front here for yor visitors, we had to take our horses over and tie 'em up raht in the mayor's front *yord.*"

This got a chuckle around the desk, and a smile and a nod from the desk sergeant. Beck and Hobbs might talk funny, at least to the ears of the midwesterners, but they could take it, and they could dish it out as well. They were immediately accepted.

Dan Brimmer arranged to bring Dina Alden to Beck and Hobbs's hotel, where she would meet with them to talk about her ex-husband. When Brimmer walked in with Dina, Hobbs's first impression of her was that he was looking at a "fragile flower" of a woman. Dina was model slim, very pretty, and quiet in her speech and mannerisms. But she proved to have a solid emotional strength that earned the respect of all the detectives in the room.

Dina said that she had met Michael at a local disco in May 1981.

"Right from the beginning, Michael seemed to be very confident and self-assured, but not at all vain about his looks," Dina told Beck and Hobbs. "I liked that, and I liked *him,* immediately."

The couple spent all their time together, and within a few months, Dina found herself pregnant. She told the detectives that both she and Michael were distressed by this, but she felt strongly that she didn't want him to marry her if he didn't love her. He said he did, and they decided to get married in September.

"Michael didn't have a job," Dina said. "I worked at a bank, and for a while I was supporting both of us. He just couldn't seem to find a job, and later, even when he did, he'd never stay at one job for very long. Something always seemed to happen—somebody would make him mad or do something he didn't like, and he'd quit or get fired. He went from one job to another, but mostly, he just didn't work."

Dina said Michael had earlier enlisted in the Army, and in November, he went for his basic training. She delivered their daughter in April 1982, and in June, Michael received his orders to report to Fort Knox, Kentucky. Michael, Dina, and their baby packed everything up and moved into a little rented house in Elizabethtown, Kentucky, about forty minutes from the army base.

"This was a terrible time for me," Dina said. "I had the baby, and we had no money. We couldn't afford a telephone, and we only had the one car, which Michael took with him to the base every day. So I was stuck out there in that little house, and it seemed like he was never around. I'd make dinner every night, but sometimes he didn't come home until real late, and I never knew where he was or who he was with."

Dina said that Michael hated it when she complained about his never being home, or questioned him about where he was going and who with. He began telling her that she had "forced" him to marry her, and that being "stuck" with a wife and a baby was ruining his life. Dina said that Michael would deliberately ogle other young women right in front of her, and then berate her and sneer at her looks and clothes.

"That's where I should be," he would say, looking at some attractive young woman. "Going out with someone like that, partying and being free and having the time of my life." He would look Dina up and down with contempt. "Instead, here I am, stuck with *you.*"

That winter, Michael got his orders—he was shipping out for Korea. He was very afraid about having to go to Korea, very worried that he "wouldn't come back alive," and he talked and fretted about it constantly. Finally, he shipped out. Dina and the baby went back to Toledo and moved in with Michael's oldest sister.

While he was in Korea, Michael would call his parents collect, telling his father that they'd really sent him to Guam, where conditions were absolutely frightful. It was a war zone, he said. There were bodies lying all over the streets, everybody shooting at everybody and sick with dysentery and malaria and who knew what else.

Within a month, Michael was sent back to the States with a general discharge. Robert Hobbs would later obtain Lockhart's military record, which ended with the cryptic notation: "This soldier simply refuses to soldier." He had, in Hobbs's estimation, "whined his way out of the Army."

When he came home, Michael blamed Dina for his having left the Army. He told her that he was so worried she would be going out on him, he simply couldn't concentrate on his duties. He said that he had spoken with the chaplain and explained that his wife and baby girl needed him at home. By this time, Dina was attaining a healthy skepticism about her husband's self-serving versions of events, and she continued to press him about what really had happened in Korea. Finally, Michael admitted that he was heavily into using cocaine over there, and besides, he was so depressed about having to be there at all that his attitude was bringing down everybody around him, so he just left.

Dina, Michael, and the baby moved into a little apartment, but the same old routine started all over again. Michael would stay out until all hours, and he simply couldn't, or wouldn't, keep a job.

"I was getting so thin," Dina said, "because there just wasn't enough money on my salary to pay the rent and take care of the baby and buy food, too. I managed to cook something every night, but I would wait until Michael and the baby had eaten, to see if there was enough for me to eat. If there wasn't, I just didn't eat."

During this time, Dina said, Michael was gone constantly, partying with his friends all night, sleeping all day. At one point, he managed to pick up a minimum-wage job, and Dina was pleased that finally some money would be coming in. But after a few days, when Michael would get dressed and say he was heading for work, she checked and found out that he had been fired after the first day for sitting around smoking marijuana on the job. At home, he had been getting up and heading off every day since then, to who knows where.

Michael kept at Dina constantly throughout this period that she was the cause of everything that was wrong with his life. It was her fault he was "stuck" with a wife and baby; it was her fault he couldn't hold a job; it was her fault they were always broke; it was even her fault he wasn't able to make it in the Army.

"Pretty soon," Dina told the detectives, "he just started taking off. I'd come home and he would be gone. Then he would call, days or weeks later, and ask me for money to come home on. He called once from Wyoming, another time from Kentucky, and a couple of times from Chicago. He was always very apologetic when he came back and promised he wouldn't take off and disappear again. But he always did."

Finally, in the fall of 1983, Dina couldn't take it anymore. She told her husband either to stay or to go, but to make up his mind once and for all. They had a huge argument, and Dina ran into the bedroom and threw all Michael's clothes in a heap on the living room floor.

"Okay, okay," he said, "I'll go. But you don't have to mess up my stuff." He smoothed out and neatly refolded all his clothes. Then he left. Dina filed for a divorce, which was final in March 1984.

Michael was gone for some time after that. Then, he suddenly reappeared in town, staying sometimes with his parents, sometimes with his new girlfriend, Betty.

It was during this time that Michael Lee Lockhart stepped into a pattern that he would continue to follow until his capture at the Old and Lost Rivers Bridge in March 1988. Michael liked to dress well; he liked to have a wad of cash in his pocket; he liked to go out partying and styling with his friends, flashing money and impressing the girls, and generally living the life of a good-looking, free-wheeling high-roller. The only downside was putting together the money to support his lifestyle—the one thing Michael definitely did *not* like was having to work for a living. His entire employment history consists of menial, five-dollar-an-hour unskilled labor jobs that he simply couldn't keep. One of his employers said that for nearly two weeks, Lockhart had been coming to work only sporadically, calling in most days to say that his mother was gravely ill and he had to be with her. Finally, one of Lockhart's sisters happened to call the job and the employer found out there was nothing at all wrong with Mrs. Lockhart. Michael was fired from that job, too, just like all the others.

In early October of 1987, Lockhart took off for Wyoming with his parents' car, after stealing some of his father's tools and $90 from his mother's purse. While he was in Wyoming, Lockhart walked into a gas station and convenience store in Cheyenne, stuck his hand in his pocket, and told the girl behind the counter he had a gun. She handed him the money out of the till, and Lockhart took off running across the parking lot. Within minutes, squad cars converged. Lockhart tried running and dodging, but then, seeing they had him surrounded, he threw his hands into the air and gave up. He was charged with robbery, and the $107 he'd gotten was returned to the gas station. At first, Lockhart tried to plead insanity, but evaluation at the Southeast Mental Health Center nixed that ploy, and he changed his plea to guilty. On January 25, 1985, he was sentenced to three years' felony probation, with the stipulation that he return home to Toledo and not leave that state for the term of the probation. The judge handed down such a lenient sentence because Lockhart pleaded that his wife had problems and his little girl desperately needed him at home.

Back in Toledo, Lockhart got a job working at a Union 76 truckstop. That job lasted six weeks. Dina said that Michael would come over at odd times to see his daughter, never calling first or setting up visits ahead of time; but she said that he was always good with the child.

"He would sit with her and play, teach her ABC's. She loved him, loved having him come over to visit."

But Michael's behavior was so erratic that Dina was always watchful when he was there. He would say that his life was so messed up, he was going to commit suicide. A couple of times, he said he was thinking of killing her and the baby, and then shooting himself so he wouldn't have to go to jail for it. He wasn't paying any child support, telling Dina that he couldn't because he had to pay his mother rent. Dina talked to Michael's mother and found out that Michael had told her he couldn't pay rent because he had to pay child support. He always seemed to have enough money to dress nicely and to party night after night with his bar buddies and girlfriends, but never enough for rent or child support for his family. He was working only sporadically, but when Dina said she was going to seek a wage-assignment for child support, Michael told her if she tried it, he would simply quit his job.

Dina said Michael was heavily into drugs and alcohol during this time. His suicide threats and erratic behavior were getting more serious, and she finally talked him into checking himself into a hospital for treatment. He did, but within a few days, he checked himself back out again and went right back to his usual habits.

Finally, Dina told him he couldn't just come around any time he pleased; it was too disrupting to her life, and too traumatic for their little girl, who never knew if he would be there when he promised or not.

"Then, that's when it got really frightening," Dina told Hobbs and Beck. "He started breaking into my apartment. I'd come home and he would jump out of the closet at me. Or, I'd be in bed sleeping, and all of a sudden, there he was, crawling into bed with me. It was all so nutty, I was terrified, for myself and for my daughter."

One day, Dina got a notice from her bank that her checking account was overdrawn. She knew she'd had sufficient funds in the account for the checks she'd written, but she looked into her withdrawal record, just to be sure. Five checks had been taken out of her checkbook, which she kept in her bedroom, and one for $250, supposedly bearing her signature, had been cashed. She confronted Michael with it, and he finally admitted he'd stolen the checks and forged her name. Dina filed a case report for forgery, and also complained to Michael's probation officer about his sneaking into her apartment. The probation officer said that he would warn Lockhart that his actions were bringing him closer to violating his felony probation, and that he was risking being sent to the penitentiary in Wyoming.

Then, in January, Michael suddenly disappeared again. Dina would later learn that he had taken off for Florida, where he'd gotten arrested for filling up the gas tank of a friend's car he had "borrowed" without permission and driving off without paying for the gas. This was the last straw for his probation officer. On February 11, 1986, Michael Lee Lockhart was taken back to Wyoming, where Judge Meier sentenced him to two-to-four years for the armed robbery of the gas station. But the Wyoming penitentiary system was severely overcrowded, and Lockhart was again released on December 10, after serving only ten months of his sentence. He immediately returned to Toledo.

Dina said that in early October of 1987, Michael called her on the phone. He was sobbing and told her that he had just found out he was dying. Could he come over? He needed someone to talk to. Dina said he could.

When he got to her place, Michael was still beside himself, weeping and sobbing. He told Dina that he had AIDS. She was stunned, of course, and sorry for him, but she didn't doubt his story. She knew that he slept around a great deal. Michael told her a long story about a young woman he had been with in Berkeley, California, who'd given him the virus. He repeated several times that he'd gotten AIDS from a woman, not a man. It seemed quite important to him that she know that. Then, Michael told his five-year-old daughter that her daddy was sick and was going to die. The little girl was grief-stricken, of course, and now the whole little family wept for Michael. Finally, exhausted, he asked

Dina if he could spend the night. At first, she said he could, but then she changed her mind. She was too afraid to go to sleep with him in the apartment. She told him he couldn't stay, and he left, to all appearances a broken and dying man.

Later that month, Michael called Dina and said that he would like to take their little girl out trick-or-treating for Halloween. He said it might well be the last time he would be healthy enough to spend time with his beloved daughter. Dina was too kindhearted to refuse. Michael showed up in a new-looking silver-blue Toyota, which he told Dina was a stolen car. She was in the passenger seat and noticed a Delta Airlines identification sticker on the windshield. But she didn't ask Michael about the car—she didn't want to know.

Detectives would later learn that months earlier, Lockhart had met and then spent the night at a motel in Georgia with a beautiful black Delta Airlines stewardess. When she woke up in the morning, she found that her companion was gone, along with her jewelry, $300 in cash, and her 1986 silver-blue Toyota.

Now, when they came back from trick-or-treating and Michael had left, Dina's little girl started to cry. She told her mother that she didn't want to see her father anymore. She wouldn't say why, only that she didn't want to have to be with him. She said she was afraid to tell him herself and asked that Dina tell him for her.

Michael called, and Dina explained that their little girl didn't want anything further to do with him. He was furious. The next day, a Saturday, he called again and said that he had some toys and gifts for his daughter, including a Barbie doll. Could he just come by to drop them off? Dina said he could, but only after their little girl was asleep. Dina didn't want the baby to be upset any more than she already had been.

When Michael got there that night, he didn't have a Barbie doll, but he handed Dina a proof silver dollar, still shiny-new and encased in plastic. He also gave her a small pearl ring and told her to keep it for their daughter. Then, he asked if he could lie down on the couch for a few minutes, as he was feeling weak and dizzy. After a bit, he excused himself to go to the bathroom. Coming back from the bathroom, he stepped behind Dina and put a big knife to her throat, telling her to keep quiet or he would kill both her and their sleeping daughter.

Michael took Dina into the living room. He pulled torn strips of bedsheet material out of his pocket and tied Dina's hands behind her back, all the while telling her to do exactly as he ordered if she didn't want their daughter to die. He led her into the bedroom and forced her down on the bed. Then, he used the knife, which Dina would later describe as a large, folding-type knife, to cut off her sweater, bra, and pants.

After he repeatedly raped her, Michael told Dina that he was going to hold her captive until Monday morning, when she was to call her mother and get $7,000 for him. Dina tried to explain that her mother didn't have that kind of money, but Michael wouldn't listen. She kept trying to talk to him, to talk him out of what he was doing, but finally, he told her to shut up or he would rape her again. Dina lay quietly on the bed.

As the night wore on, Dina had to risk talking again. She told Michael that she had to go to their daughter's bedroom to turn the electric blanket down; it wasn't safe to leave it on all night. Michael said she could, but then he got up and pulled a big silver gun out of his jacket.

"I'm going in there with you," he said, pointing the gun at her. "If you try anything, I'll kill you and the baby."

After she saw to her daughter, Dina lay back down quietly on the bed. Michael lay down beside her. Toward dawn, she dozed off, and then the alarm clock rang at 6 A.M. Michael got up, shut off the alarm, and started taking off his pants.

"No, why?" Dina wept. "I was quiet, like you said. I did everything you told me to! Why?"

"Because," Michael said, lowering himself on top of her, "it gets me going in the morning."

When they came out of the bedroom, their little girl was up. She had expected never to see her father again, and now she was upset and confused. Dina had promised to take her daughter shopping for a new jacket this morning, and now the little girl kept at her mother about it. She wanted to go shopping, just her and her mother. She wanted to be away from here, away from her father. Dina kept telling her daughter that they couldn't go. Michael sat and watched her, his gun tucked into his waistband. Finally, he stood up and looked at his daughter. Then he left.

And Dina began her long, agonizing months of worry that her ex-husband had given her AIDS, and she would never live to see her daughter grow up. She filed a rape case with Det. Dan Brimmer, and over the next weeks, went to rape-counseling sessions. She had a blood test for AIDS, which proved negative, but she was told that she should have another test every three months; the deadly virus could lie undetected in her bloodstream for a long time. The horror that she had been infected during the rape was with her twenty-four hours a day. It filled her with terror and seemed to hang over her head like a guillotine, until she couldn't sleep without nightmares, couldn't force herself to eat, couldn't think what was to happen to her little girl without her.

Michael Lee Lockhart's entire AIDS story had been a fabrication.

Ray Beck and Robert Hobbs were able to reassure Dina that Michael's blood had been tested, and that he did not have the AIDS virus. The brutality of the rape, the cruelty of the AIDS lie, stood in stark contrast now to Dina's quiet dignity.

"It's hard to explain to someone else," Dina told them now, in her soft voice. "Michael can lie so believably that no one can tell what is the truth and what isn't. Not even him."

The Texas detectives' next interview in Toledo was at the car dealership where Lockhart had stolen the red Corvette.

"When Rick Treadwell described for us that moment in the Corvette, all of us could feel our spines stiffening up," said Robert Hobbs. The Texas detectives had met with the unfortunate Toledo auto finance dealer, whose car, identity, and peace of mind had been stolen at the point of a gun—by Michael Lee Lockhart. Treadwell had described being ordered out of the car alongside the highway. He said he turned away from the driver, opened the passenger-side door, and, as he was stepping out onto the shoulder of the road, with that big silver gun still pointing at the base of his back, held his breath waiting for that bullet to smash into his spine. He said that expecting violent death within moments, all he could think of was that he would never see his wife and kids again.

Treadwell was obviously still extremely shaken up over what he had been through five months before, but he was a dignified, intelligent man. Hobbs made a note to himself at the end of the interview to tell Paul McWilliams and Jim Middleton, the Jefferson County prosecutors, that Treadwell was going to make an excellent witness at Lockhart's trial. Hobbs had deliberately kept the interview with Treadwell short. The man's description of his ordeal, his fear, had been so compelling that Hobbs didn't want to dilute the force of it by having Treadwell repeat it over and over.

On the night before Robert Hobbs and Ray Beck were to leave Ohio and fly back to Texas, the Toledo detectives hosted them to a "policeman's night out." They all went to the F.O.P. club for some drinks and shop talk. In honor of their Texas guests, the Ohio policemen insisted on playing the jukebox's few country-and-western tunes over and over.

Thirty-nine

"Sergeant Beck, my name is Detective Fay Wilber, from Pasco County, Florida. I'm calling because of a profile you put into the ROCIC journal. The guy who killed one of your police officers?"

"Michael Lee Lockhart."

"Right. You've got him listed as driving a stolen 1986 red Corvette. Well, this may be a long shot, but we're looking for a guy here in Florida who butchered a little girl back in January, and who *may* have been driving a red 'Vette. We've turned the state upside down looking for it, but no luck so far. Then we ran across this profile and I figured, hey, it's worth a phone call, right?"

It was the first week in June, 1988, and this telephone call was to turn what was already a storm of investigative activity for Ray Beck, Robert Hobbs, and Bill Gates into a veritable hurricane.

In the two and a half months since Paul Hulsey's death, the three Texas detectives had been working sixty, seventy, and even eighty hours a week, backtracking Lockhart's fifteen-month cross-country crime spree—and it had indeed been a spree, like none they'd ever seen before.

Driving first the silver-blue stolen Toyota and then the red Corvette, Lockhart had traveled nearly 30,000 miles. On just the 'Vette alone he had clocked nearly 14,000 miles in four months. And during all that time, he had lived well, spending his nights in motels, dining in restaurants, nightclubbing with attractive women he met and charmed along the way. Where did all the money come from? Lockhart would eventually admit to pulling off "thousands" of home burglaries as well as armed robberies.

As Hobbs and the Beaumont detectives retraced Lockhart's movements across the country, using hotel and gas station receipts, phone records, and girlfriends' statements, they were able to verify that he had spent the spring and early summer of 1987 traveling to Atlanta, where he stole the blue Toyota from the stewardess while she slept in their motel room. While in Georgia, he burglarized George and Debbie Severns's home, and their next-door neighbor's house at the same time. The proof silver dollar the detectives later recovered from Lockhart's ex-wife in Ohio was part of a large cache of silver coins taken from the Severns's next-door neighbor. In the little town of Locust Grove, Georgia, Lockhart had gotten caught prowling a car in a restaurant parking lot. He had a small amount of marijuana on him, and he spent the next two weeks in jail. When the female Locust Grove police officer took "Mike Locke" into custody, she said he very calmly told her to do what she had to do, but to know that he was going to come back to Locust Grove later and kill her.

Next, the detectives tracked him to Tampa, Miami, Clearwater, Panama City, and Jacksonville, Florida, this last where his armed robbery of a Payless shoestore was captured on a security video camera. Lockhart was carrying the IDs and credit cards of the Payless manager when he was captured at the Old and Lost Rivers Bridge.

Tired of Florida, and probably feeling that his many girlfriends were getting too close to knowing the real man behind the mask, Lockhart, now using the name and credit cards of George Severns, next headed west on I-10, toward California. He left a trail of credit card charges across Florida, Alabama, Mississippi, Louisiana, Texas, New Mexico, Nevada, Arizona, and finally, California.

The Texas detectives tracked Lockhart's movements through California and were able to establish his stayovers in Los Angeles, San Francisco, Berkeley, Oakland, Sacramento, and San Jose. While he was in Berkeley, Lockhart met the chef and owner of a local vegetarian restaurant. The two men hit it off and Lockhart went to work at the restaurant, where his charm and friendliness instantly made him a most valued employee. Lockhart, now using the name Michael B. Locke, began an immediate affair with a young woman, Elaine, who lived above the restaurant. Within two weeks, Lockhart was throwing temper tantrums at the restaurant—he wasn't being treated right, he didn't get the proper respect, he wanted more money. Finally, he stormed out. When the owner got home that night, he found that his apartment had been burglarized. Gone was his Nikon camera, $500 in cash, and some photos he had taken of the restaurant employees, Lockhart's among them.

As soon as she heard about the burglary, Elaine called the police. She told them that she was afraid of "Mike Locke," that he had a violent and volatile temper and was always mumbling threats about what he was going to do with that big silver gun. Elaine said that her boyfriend had shown inordinate interest in her family's personal possessions, asking about the worth of this or that. This had become so obvious that at one point, she and her family had just stood and looked at him as he'd picked up and admired a particular figurine. He looked around, then, and apparently realized how suspicious all his questions were. He never asked about the value of their furnishings again, but now, with this burglary, they were afraid they were next on his list. Elaine asked that the police put a special watch on her apartment, which they did. She never saw Mike Locke again. Lockhart would later brag that he had found "easy pickings" in California, and that if authorities had done their job right, they would have found a string of armed robberies all across the state.

After the burglary in Berkeley, Lockhart headed east on I-80, probably traveling through Nevada, Wyoming, Utah, Colorado, Nebraska, Missouri, Illinois, Indiana, and back into Ohio, where he stayed only a short time with his family in Toledo, before heading out again—eastward this time.

Texas detectives were able to place Lockhart definitely in New York City, Providence, Pittsburgh, Boston, Washington, D.C., Baltimore, and Chicago, with several side trips into Canada.

In Boston, he spent a few nights with a couple of guys he met in a bar. He introduced himself as Officer Richard Armstrong, from Elyria, Ohio. He stayed a few nights at their apartment, showing off his .357 magnum and talking about all his girlfriends, and when he left, he gave them "his" police coat badge, saying he could easily get another one from his department. Officer Armstrong's badge was later recovered by Ohio authorities.

Lockhart would later recount to Robert Hobbs a chilling scenario that had played out just outside Boston. He pulled over onto the shoulder of the expressway, got out of his car, and stood looking down into a subdivision, deciding which home he wanted to break into. He saw a house with its rear sliding glass doors open, only the screen closed. He left the expressway and headed for that house. In the back yard, he called out, but no one came to the door, and Lockhart assumed the house was empty. He cut the screen and went in. While he was in the dining room, stuffing the family silver into his pockets, he looked up—and there was a little boy, about four years old, standing in the doorway, staring at him. Lockhart said he put his finger to his lips; the little boy nodded and stood there quietly. When Lockhart was finished with his haul, he patted the boy on the head, waved goodbye, and went back out through the cut screen door. The child's parents, presumably asleep in another room, never knew who had been in their dining room alone with their little boy.

While he was in New York State, Lockhart committed at least one armed robbery of a branch bank, and was probably responsible in half a dozen more.

In Chicago, Lockhart spent several months, on and off, staying at a flophouse hotel on Broadway, while he did business with a drug-dealing girl named Betty and her drug-dealing mother. Betty told the detectives that "Mike Locke," as she knew him, always carried a big silver gun. At first, he was driving a shiny blue Toyota, but then, in November, he suddenly showed up with a red Corvette, which Betty said he was "paranoid" about, always parking it in the alley or hidden away on a side street.

Betty said that Mike was heavy into dealing drugs with her and her mother, mostly using connections on Chicago's South Side. But, she said, he always talked about wanting to go back to Florida. Betty said Mike and her brother talked about it constantly, and that the two of them seemed to have gotten so close that Betty began to wonder if Mike and her brother "had something going together," and if they were going to take off for Florida together, leaving her behind. She said that she and Mike had only "made it" about five or six times, but that sex wasn't any good with him "because half the time, he couldn't even get it up."

The last time Betty saw "Mike Locke" in Chicago was toward the end of November. By Thanksgiving, the detectives knew he was living with one woman in Miami, meeting another in the weight room of the University of Miami, and romancing a third, all under the guise of the Harvard-bound law student, "Rick Treadwell." In a six-week period from January through mid-February 1988, Lockhart robbed a branch bank just off I-95 in Hollywood, Florida, the First Federated Savings Bank in Fort Lauderdale, and the Barnett Bank on South Dixie Highway in Miami. In each instance, bank video cameras recorded the gun-toting robber as cool, sporty, good-looking, and perfectly in control of himself, calmly pulling out the dye packs in each stack of money and tossing them back on the counter before turning to walk out of the bank. In each case, employees and guards rushed to the windows after the robber left, but no one reported seeing any kind of getaway vehicle.

Putting this trail together, week by week, city by city, crime by crime, while still preparing for their upcoming murder trial, took up all the Texas detectives' time and effort. But even while they were adding crime after crime to Jim Middleton's chronology—which by now had become invaluable—they knew there was still much more to learn about the man behind the pretty face, the pretty car, and the stolen identities.

When Lockhart pulled in to Beaumont, Texas, on March 21, just hours after robbing the savings and loan in Baton Rouge, two weeks after robbing a bank in New Orleans, and one day before killing Officer Paul Hulsey, he checked into the Best Western Motel, and then went shopping—for women. At a local department store, he stood around the counter, flirting with a pretty twenty-one-year-old. Finally, he said he would like to ask her out for dinner, but that he knew she would want to be careful not to leave herself vulnerable to someone she didn't really know. Lockhart said he approved of this caution, that "there's a lot of maniacs out there" who would take advantage of a pretty girl. She agreed, and the talk turned to "maniacs." The girl said that two famous serial killers, Henry Lee Lucas and Christopher Wilder, had, in their time, come through Beaumont. At this, Lockhart asked her about Ted Bundy, who was at that time being tried for murder in Florida. Had Bundy ever been in Beaumont? How many women did she think Bundy had really killed? Did she think Bundy was as good-looking as he was said to be? Lockhart said he had recently been in Florida, where authorities were trying to enforce an unpopular seat-belt law. People had taken to putting bumper stickers on their cars that said: "I'll Buckle Up When Bundy Does." The girl said later that this conversation was "definitely getting weird," and she couldn't quite figure out how she and this handsome stranger had gotten so deeply into a discussion of Ted Bundy.

Even without Lockhart's evident interest in Bundy, the comparisons between him and the notorious serial killer were obvious—the personable, cocky charm; the sexy, collegiate warmth that masked a cold-hearted, pouting, narcissistic child hiding behind a man's face and body. The whole image that Lockhart had built for himself and used so effectively with women was a take-off on that created by his mentor. A man who gained the trust and affection of his girlfriends only to use them, steal from them, and then abandon them; a man who supported his flashy cross-country lifestyle by sticking a loaded gun into people's faces—that man will kill, whenever it suits his desires of the moment, and whenever he thinks he can get away with it.

The Texas detectives drew up a profile of Lockhart, including a broad sketch of his known travels, the cars he was known to have been driving, and his method of approaching women, and had it published in the Regional Organized Crime Information Center bulletin. The ROCIC is an information-sharing network for law enforcement authorities based in Nashville, Tennessee. Since they'd published the bulletin, Hobbs, Beck, and Gates had been inundated with calls from police officers around the country. Robert Hobbs, especially, as the investigative arm of the D.A.'s office, was responsible for fielding the hundreds of calls that were pouring in and following up any that seemed likely. He relied heavily on the chronology they had put together of Lockhart's movements, which by now had stretched into twenty single-spaced legal-sized sheets of paper. The chronology, bulky as it was becoming with each new discovery of Lockhart's multistate crimes, shrank in comparison with the total load of paperwork the cases were generating. Hobbs started out carrying around first one large briefcase, then two, then three. Finally, all the information coming in about Lockhart's activities filled several cardboard boxes, then half a dozen, and eventually, a storeroomful.

During these hectic weeks, the Texas detectives were flying all over the country, interviewing witnesses and police officers, and bringing back paperwork to add to the burgeoning files. The Jefferson County D.A.'s office filed a new criminal complaint against Michael Lee Lockhart as sufficient evidence of each new crime was developed by Robert Hobbs and the Beaumont detectives. There was a certain grim satisfaction in piling on charge after charge: should anything happen to their murder case against Lockhart, unthinkable as that might be, they now had enough felony-level evidence to send him to trial around the country a dozen times over. And that was even before the shattering call from Fay Wilber in Florida.

As the weeks passed and the trial drew closer, Lockhart continued to find great enjoyment in all the publicity that surrounded him. The jailers reported that he spent his days reading about himself and discussing himself, reciting passages from newspapers out loud to the guards and other prisoners, exploding into childish temper tantrums at news articles that were less than flattering. One day, he said he wasn't feeling well and demanded to see a doctor.

The doctor found that Lockhart was in perfect physical shape and refused his demand for a Valium for his "nerves." But this was a man who had spent his entire life determined to get his own way. The next night, he took apart his disposable razor and cut himself on the left forearm. The cut bled and was quite nasty-looking, but the guards saw immediately that it was shallow and not at all life-threatening. They immediately suspected an escape attempt.

"We believe he may have wanted to create a one-on-one situation with a jailer," said Chief Deputy Sheriff Calise

Blanchard. "But because the cut was not severe, we were able to wait until the morning before taking him to have the wound sutured."

The guards bandaged Lockhart's arm right inside the jail infirmary, and then returned him to his closely supervised cell. The next morning, once they were able to make the proper arrangements, they took him to an immediate-care center for stitches.

"We treated him like we would any other capital murder suspect," Blanchard said. "We shackled him with leg irons and body restraints. He wasn't too happy about that," added Blanchard dryly.

Lockhart told his jailers that he had not been attempting suicide, but only cutting himself to "protest my medical treatment," by which he meant the doctor's refusal to issue Valium for his "nerves."

"I told him we can't overrule the doctor," Blanchard said, "and that if he wants to continue to hurt himself, we'll continue to bandage him up."

Lockhart did not cut himself again, but that didn't mean he was yet through with his histrionics. Now, he had another demand—he wanted to see Det. Sgts. Ray Beck and Bill Gates.

Beck sent word to the jail that if Lockhart wanted to talk about the murder, he should do so in the presence of an attorney, but Lockhart said it wasn't about the case, so the detectives agreed to go to the jail.

"You guys aren't dumb," Lockhart began, after Beck again reminded him of his rights. "You know I wasn't alone in that motel room when the officer came in."

Lockhart then spun for the detectives an obviously well-thought-out tale. He hinted that he'd been heavily involved in an international drug conspiracy that he called the "Jamaican Connection," and that one of the "Connection's" enforcers had been in the room with him at the Best Western when Officer Hulsey had come to the door, and it was he who'd shot the cop.

"Even if my prints are on the gun," Lockhart said, "that doesn't mean that I pulled the trigger." He told the detectives that he had been silent until now "to protect my family," but that he wasn't going to "take the rap for some other asshole."

No, Mr. Lockhart, thought the detectives, as they left after hearing this absurd tale, you're not going to take the rap for some *other* asshole, you're going to take it all for your own self.

While the D.A.'s office was busy preparing its murder case and putting together a shopping list of charges against Lockhart, and Lockhart himself was busy preening over all the publicity, Charles Carver was busy being one very unhappy defense attorney.

Forty

"I'm being forced to defend a crime a day," complained Lockhart's defense attorney. And Carver had a point. When Judge Gist asked him to represent Michael Lee Lockhart, their understanding was that Carver would be acting on Lockhart's behalf in the state's murder case against him. Carver had taken the case reluctantly, and only after meeting with and getting the okay of his partners at Umphrey, Swearingen. Carver would be paid to act as public defender, but the state's rate of $750 per day plus expenses amounted to "minimum wage" rates for an attorney of his standing, and the law firm itself would not have the use of his services during the duration of the trial. After much deliberation, Carver, a sincere opponent of the death penalty, agreed to take on Lockhart's defense. But he had barely accepted the appointment before all hell broke loose and what had begun as a single charge of capital murder against his client now expanded exponentially to include multiple bank robberies, auto thefts, rape, forgery, credit card thefts, several armed robberies, and finally, with the call from Fay Wilber in Florida, another murder charge.

The very day after Wilber's initial call to Ray Beck, Wilber's partner, Gary Fairbanks, flew to Beaumont, and the investigators from both states began burning up their office Xerox machines, trading case files back and forth. Since the only hard evidence recovered from Jennifer Colhouer's murder was the semen stain, Florida now needed samplars from Michael Lee Lockhart to compare his DNA against the semen they had preserved in their lab. Robert Hobbs helped obtain the appropriate court order, and they went to see Lockhart at the Jefferson County Jail.

"We've got a court order, so there's two ways we can go about this," Hobbs said to Lockhart. "Either I'm going to pull the hairs out of your groin and your eyelashes, or you can do it yourself."

Hobbs later said that Lockhart handled this whole process stoically and with a shrug, as though he was somehow disconnected, or not personally involved, in what was happening to him.

"He chose to pull out his own body hairs," Hobbs said dryly, "a decision for which I was extremely grateful." The detectives stood watch, wincing, while Lockhart plucked out several groin hairs. But it was watching him try over and over to pull out his eyelashes that made everyone's eyes sting and start to water with empathic pain.

The hairs came from the groin and eyelashes because they would be less likely than head hairs to be contaminated with years-long accumulations of dyes, gels, hairsprays, and other chemicals. And the body hairs had to be plucked out by the root rather than cut because it is in the living tissue of the root, or "bulb," that the individual's genetic code exists. Lockhart's body hairs were flown to Cellmark Diagnostics in Germantown, Maryland, but the genetic-match tests would take six to eight weeks to complete.

Florida was certain they had finally found Jennifer Colhouer's murderer, but they wouldn't formally seek extradition from Texas until they had the DNA results. Meanwhile, the detectives would bring their case before a Pasco County grand jury for a Florida murder indictment. Wilber and Fairbanks told the Texas investigators about Lt. John Mowery and the Indiana detectives' search for the killer of Windy Gallagher.

* * *

Det. Karl Grimmer and his wife Becky had just dropped their sons off at the daycare center and now stopped by the police station so Karl could pick up some paperwork he had been waiting for. They stood amazed in the lobby of the station and watched a smiling, excited Lt. John Mowery rush toward them.

"It looks like Florida's found their man!" Mowery said. "Texas has a guy in custody for the murder of a police officer. He was driving a red Corvette, and Wilber says their composite drawing matches this guy like it's his own photograph!"

"Anything to connect him to our case?" Grimmer asked. The Gallagher case was now seven months old and boxes stacked upon boxes in the detective squad room overflowed with vehicle registrations on hundreds of silver-blue Datsuns, and mug shots and Polaroids of hundreds of young men with dirty blond or light brown hair parted in the middle.

Mowery shook his head. "I'm waiting for a call from Texas, but I'm afraid to hope. Their guy's driving a red 'Vette. Nothing at all about the car we're looking for."

"Lieutenant Mowery?" called out the dispatcher. "Phone call for you. Long distance from . . . where is that again? Long distance from Beaumont, Texas." Mowery rushed to his office, Karl and Becky Grimmer right behind him.

"The Florida detectives gave us a brief rundown on your case," Robert Hobbs said from Texas. "How about if I fax you a clear likeness of Lockhart's prints, and you can have your fingerprint techs do a comparison?"

"No, no," Mowery shook his head.

"What?" whispered Karl Grimmer. "What's going on?"

"I couldn't settle for a fax comparison," Mowery said into the phone. "I've got to see the actual print cards."

Hobbs tried to explain that he could get a clear fax sent

to Griffith, Indiana, within minutes, but Mowery was adamant. He had waited too long, hoped and been disappointed too many times with too many suspects. Hobbs agreed to have Lockhart reprinted, but said it would be the next day before he could FedEx the prints to Indiana. Mowery gave him the address of the county lab in Crown Point and said he would be there, waiting, when the prints arrived.

"The only problem I have," Mowery said, "is that your guy was using a red Corvette and the guy we're looking for had a silver-blue Datsun."

"Hold on to your hat," Hobbs said into the phone. "Would you settle for a silver-blue Toyota?" He explained that Lockhart had stolen such a car from the stewardess at the Georgia motel, abandoning it only after taking the Corvette, at gunpoint, from an Ohio expressway. Mowery agreed that Joyce Wilson in Chicago could have mistaken a Datsun for a Toyota, the cars were so similar. But, he said, he wasn't going to let himself have even a twinge of hope until his own fingerprint techs compared Lockhart's fingerprints against those recovered from the water glass and the wall in the Gallagher apartment.

Hobbs said that he would call Mowery the minute the new fingerprints were turned over to FedEx, and Mowery agreed to call Texas from the lab in Crown Point the minute the package arrived.

He made that call at 3 P.M. the next day.

"Jim Fedorchek has the cards spread out now," Mowery said into the telephone.

A thousand miles away, Robert Hobbs sat at his desk, his eyes closed, the telephone receiver pressed against his ear. Long moments passed. He could hear Mowery breathing into the phone and other muffled noises and voices in the background.

"It's him!" shouted a voice.

"No, no, look again!" Mowery shouted back, oblivious

now to Hobbs on the other end of the line. "Check again. Be careful! Be *sure!*"

"I *am* careful! I *am* sure! I'm telling you, we got a perfect match! It's him!"

"God Almighty," Mowery sighed, "it's finally over."

And then, into the phone: "I'll be there on the next plane."

Forty-one

"Michael Lee Lockhart," intoned Judge Larry Gist, on the morning of June 17, 1988, "this court has received a warrant against you from the State of Indiana, charging you with the murder of Windy Patricia Gallagher."

Robert Hobbs was standing with John Mowery before the judge's bench, and as Judge Gist spoke these words, Hobbs turned to watch Lockhart's reaction.

As soon as he heard the name "Windy Patricia Gallagher," Lockhart's head snapped back and his spine stiffened, as though he'd been struck in the face. He inhaled audibly and looked up at the ceiling. Hobbs was astonished to see that Lockhart was blinking back tears.

As he was led out of the courtroom following the brief hearing, Lockhart turned to Hobbs.

"It was the water glass, wasn't it?"

"Yes, Michael," Robert Hobbs said, "it was the water glass."

"I *knew* it! *Damn!*" Lockhart shook his head in apparent disgust at his own carelessness.

"PORTRAIT OF A KILLER," read the Toledo newspapers, and, accompanied by a high school wrestling team photo of Michael Lee Lockhart in gym shorts: "DID ALL-AMERICAN BOY GO BAD?" And in Indiana: "WINDY'S KILLER CAUGHT?" And in Florida: "PASCO SUSPECT MAY BE SE-

RIAL KILLER." Newspapers and television reporters in Texas, Florida, Indiana, and Ohio headlined the new murder charges, and over the following weeks, story after story in all four states described Michael Lee Lockhart's cross-country trail of terror and murder. Reporters hounded the Lockhart family, dug through court records, and gleaned quotes from neighbors, schoolteachers, and former classmates. They were searching, as the public does every time another serial killer is brought to bay, for a reason, an understanding, a set of circumstances that might give some explanation to the creation of a human pathological aberration like Michael Lee Lockhart. It is always more palatable and less frightening to believe that a human becomes a monster through somebody else's fault, than it is to accept, as Ted Bundy would admit on his deathbed, that he did what he did simply because "I liked it."

Michael Lee Lockhart was born in Wallbridge, Ohio, a little town of 4,000 just outside Toledo, on September 30, 1960. He was the ninth of ten children born to Noble and Betty Jean Lockhart. Both of Michael's parents were originally from the little coalmining town of Kenvir, Kentucky. Betty Jean's father had worked all his life in the coalmines and was killed in a mining accident when Betty Jean was just two years old. She and her sister went to live with their grandparents and watched over the years as their grandfather slowly died of that insidious coalminers' scourge— black lung disease.

In 1946, when Betty Jean was seventeen, she met Noble Lockhart, also a coalmining "townie" who had just returned from service in World War II. Noble and Betty Jean were married in July 1946, and Noble liked to tell folks he had to travel the whole world before "coming down home to find me a little hillbilly girl to marry." Noble went to work in the mines, and Betty Jean began to have children. Judy was born in 1947, followed by Bob in 1949, Sue in 1951, Jim in 1953, and Don in 1954. There was never enough money, and Betty Jean told her husband she wanted to stop having babies. She went to a doctor who gave her a birth control device, telling her it was meant to be used, not to be kept on a shelf. But Noble felt that God would decide when they had had enough children, and refused to let his wife use protection. "I don't know what God has to do with this," Betty Jean said. "Seems to me this is something between the two of us." But the device stayed on the shelf, and Betty Jean and Noble went on to have five more children over the next seven years. The family was devoutly religious, beginning and ending each day with readings from the Bible.

When the coalmining business began to fail, Noble Lockhart took the train up to Ohio, found a job on the railroad head in Wallbridge, and brought his young family to their new home. Noble refused to let his wife work, believing that her place was at home with their children. Michael's father was not an educated or sophisticated man, but he worked grueling hours year after year to support his household, leaving at 5 A.M. for the railroad job, rushing home in the evening for a quick dinner, and then going on to a plumbing job. He would often get home at 1 A.M. and then be back up and out to work again at 5 A.M.

Little Michael was a beautiful child, gifted with a natural sense of charm and flattery, and his sisters adored and petted him. But his big, rough-talking, hard-playing brothers were not so impressed. Michael learned early that when he turned on the sweetness, he was able to get his own way in almost anything. But when he didn't get his way, he would often break down in tears and temper tantrums, and his brothers were appalled—calling him a "sissy" and a "wimp" and taunting him for his cutesy, feminine mannerisms. This ability to talk his way into whatever he wanted, and talk his way *out* of ever having to take the consequences of his behavior, continued into Michael's teen years. He was never a good student, but he had the looks and the charm to be a popular one, and he put more time and energy into sports than he did schoolwork. Even in sports, though, Michael's self-centeredness was always a problem. If he couldn't be the star, he didn't want to play. Once, when he was fifteen, Michael got into an argument on the baseball field with his coach, who had refused to let him make a certain play. To the astonishment of his teammates, Michael threw the baseball bat to the ground in a pouting rage and stomped off the field, crying.

"If you had two dollars in your pocket and Michael wanted it, he could talk you out of it and leave you smiling," was a common assessment among his high school girl-friends. This inborn gift of a schemer's silver tongue contributed to his older brothers' contempt for Michael—they felt that real men get what they want by working for it, earning it, or even fighting for it, but *not* by wheedling, cajoling, lying, flattering, and generally sucking up to women. But Noble Lockhart was awestruck by his youngest son's beauty and grace. "With his looks and that mouth of his, that boy is going to make something of himself," Mr. Lockhart would brag. "Why, when he gets going, Michael can talk your pants right off!"

When Michael met and was getting ready to marry Dina Alden, his future mother-in-law stood to one side at a family gathering and listened as Michael strutted and dazzled the group with his future plans—he was going to drive a luxury car, he would travel the world and live in a mansion and be a millionaire before he was forty years old.

"He's just a bigmouth blowhard," said Dina's mother. "He doesn't even have a job."

When he was arrested for murder in Beaumont, Texas, Michael's parents were naturally devastated. Noble Lockhart had had a heart attack several years earlier, and everyone feared now that he was going to have another, perhaps the final one. Michael's parents and his sisters scraped the money together to fly to Texas, where Noble Lockhart would fight like a tiger for his youngest boy. But Michael's brothers were less sanguine. "He makes me sick," said one of the older Lockhart boys. "Our parents worked hard and did everything they could for all of us while we were growing up, and all Michael ever did was leech off of them. If he really killed those people like everybody's saying he did, I hope he fries."

"So many people in Beaumont have already formed an opinion about this case," said Charles Carver, "that my client cannot receive a fair trial in this jurisdiction."

Judge Larry Gist agreed with Carver's motion for a change of venue, and so did Jefferson County D.A. Tom Maness.

"As in all cases, the state is concerned that the defendant's due process rights are protected," said Mr. Maness. "This falls within both the constitutional and statutory duties of the criminal district attorney's office. If there is a denial, or a deprivation of some sort, of a defendant's due process rights, an appealable error is presented. And we only want to put the Hulsey family and this community through one trial.

"As the events unfolded," said Mr. Maness, "it became obvious to all people in our community that we not only had family, friends, and co-workers grieving over the death of Paul Douglas Hulsey, Jr., we had an entire community touched very deeply and grieving. And the state would be hard pressed to deny that the sheer volume of the publicity has been unseen in recent memory in a local criminal case."

Judge Gist granted the defense motion for change of venue to Corpus Christi. Over two hundred miles away from Beaumont, the Nueces County Courthouse at Corpus volunteered one of its courtrooms for approximately a month. Maness sent Robert Hobbs to find suitable lodgings for everyone in Corpus Christi, but it was quickly becoming apparent that with the defense team busy hiring out-of-state experts and investigators, and with all the witnesses and evidence coming in from Florida and Indiana, this trial was going to take longer than a month. Finally, after many phone calls, Judge Gist was able to borrow a courtroom at the Bexar County Courthouse in San Antonio, nearly three hundred miles away, for the trial to begin on August 1, 1988. However, Gist would continue to hear pretrial motions in Beaumont, among which was Lockhart's demand that he be allowed to act as his own cocounsel, and the first of Charles Carver's many demands for a delay.

In addressing Lockhart's Bundy-like demand to act as one of his own lawyers, Judge Gist issued an immediate denial, stating that "while you have a constitutional right to represent yourself, *and* the right to an attorney, the law does not permit you to do both at the same time." Lockhart shrugged off this ruling, but he would not easily give up such a golden opportunity to strut his stuff in front of a packed courtroom.

"I am asking that this trial be delayed until January," Charles Carver petitioned the court. "I had no earthly idea when I was appointed to represent Mr. Lockhart that I'd be called on to defend him on *three* capital murder charges. I have grave concerns about being able to provide an adequate defense in the time allowed."

D.A. Maness argued vehemently against any delay. "If you reset this case, we will be harmed," Maness told Judge Gist. "Witnesses forget, they die, or we may lose them. We have some witnesses who have been hard to keep tabs on in this case." Maness also argued that Carver would have plenty of time to prepare his case, since jury selection alone would probably take three weeks or longer, and the prosecution would likely not finish presenting its side of the case until sometime in mid-September. Maness also told the court that Lockhart had bragged to his cellmate in the Jefferson County Jail, relating the exact details of his murder of Officer Hulsey.

Carver told Judge Gist that he wanted to withdraw from the case rather than proceed to trial on August 1 and risk not being able to properly defend Lockhart. "What you've done," he said, "is to back me into a corner and put my law license on the line. I feel incompetent now to proceed and I request to be withdrawn from this case."

Judge Gist denied Carver's request for a delay and denied also his request to withdraw from the case. He cited Carver's qualifications as a defense attorney and reminded him that the court had authorized the defense to hire investigators to help with their preparation. The trial would begin in San Antonio on August 1, as scheduled.

All this was too much for Michael Lee Lockhart. The judge had denied his request to act as his own lawyer, and now he was denying a delay, as well. Lockhart reacted exactly as he always did when he didn't get his own way, exactly as he had when he was fifteen years old and didn't get his way with the baseball coach.

"This is a bunch of fucking bullshit!" Lockhart suddenly slammed his notepad down on the table and leaped out of his chair. Hands manacled in front of him, he whirled around and headed for the door, trying to push his way out of the room. "I want to get out of here!" he screamed. Judge Gist's bailiff and two police officers grabbed him and tried to push him back into his chair. Lockhart fought and kicked out at them and skidded his feet as they tried to drag him forward.

"Fuck you!" he screamed. "I want to get *out* of here! *I want out!*"

From the bench, Judge Gist pointed down at Lockhart.

"Remove that man from my courtroom," the judge said quietly.

As the court officers were pulling a screaming Lockhart

out of the room, he turned to face the open-mouthed spectators seated behind a bulletproof glass shield.

"I have a statement for the press!" Lockhart shouted. "There is a *conspiracy* going on between this judge and the fucking district attorney!"

Everyone in the hushed room could hear his shouting all the way down the hall. "This is bullshit! It's a fucking conspiracy! I want *out* of here!"

"This hearing is concluded," said Judge Gist. "Trial will proceed on August 1."

Forty-two

"It would be highly prejudicial to allow them to remain in the courtroom," said Charles Carver. The trial had begun in San Antonio and Lockhart's defense attorney was arguing that Paul Hulsey's widow, Barbara, and his parents should be excluded from the courtroom.

"The jury would be able to see the emotional trauma going through them. It will be difficult for Barbara to maintain her composure throughout the trial," Mr. Carver argued. "The state has shown no need for them to be here. They will inflame the minds of the jurors and create bias and prejudice on the part of the jury."

Judge Gist pointed out that Texas law allows citizens to attend trials in which they are victims, and Paul Hulsey's family members were certainly victims in this matter.

"But we're talking about victims who are also witnesses in this case," Carver argued.

Judge Gist said he would review recent case rulings on the issue and come back the next morning with his decision. But the D.A.'s office, knowing how much it meant to Barbara Hulsey and to Chief and Mrs. Hulsey that they be able to sit through the trial of their son's murderer, simply excused them as potential witnesses. This effectively altered their status to spectator; and as such, the defense team could not keep them out of the courtroom.

Judge Gist did grant Carver's demand that police officers not be permitted to appear in uniform, with or without the black ribbon of mourning covering their badges. D.A. Maness objected, pointing to Debra Stewart, a' juror consultant hired by Carver.

"That lady sitting next to the defendant," Maness said, "she is touching him and making him human in front of the jurors—that's no different than officers wearing their uniforms in court."

"No, Mr. Maness," said Judge Gist. "I am ordering that police officers, on duty or off duty, not wear their uniforms in court. I am going to make sure that this man gets a fair trial."

Gist also ordered that each side restrict its questioning of prospective jurors to thirty minutes. Assistant D.A. Paul McWilliams, in his slow-talking West Texas drawl, jokingly objected, saying that the thirty-minute rule put him at a disadvantage since he couldn't speak as many words in thirty minutes as Carver could. Everyone, including the judge, chuckled at this. But, "Thirty minutes, Mr. McWilliams," said Judge Gist.

Robert Hobbs and Det. Sgts. Ray Beck and Bill Gates were working around the clock now. Just coordinating all the witnesses and evidence to be presented by the prosecutors was a logistical nightmare. Travel and lodging had to be arranged for more than a hundred witnesses from all over the country who were scheduled to testify; they were robbery victims, police officers, detectives, and FBI ballistics examiners, the families and investigators from Indiana and Florida, and for the first time in Texas history, DNA experts. DNA as a positive identifier was just being admitted into courtrooms in various states, and the Lockhart trial would be its first court test in Texas.

Even though Lockhart was on trial for the murder of Officer Hulsey, D.A. Tom Maness was determined to bring in all the evidence of his previous crimes, including the residential burglaries, the bank robberies, and the murders of Windy Gallagher and Jennifer Colhouer. One of the criteria in the State of Texas for imposition of the death penalty is establishing that the defendant "poses a continuing threat to society." That criterion had been instituted for just such a man as Michael Lee Lockhart, and Maness intended to prove it beyond any doubt.

"We would be remiss if we didn't show the jury every bit of legal proof we have to demonstrate his previous acts of misconduct and violence," Maness said. "If he's found guilty, the death penalty is the only proper punishment, due to the facts of the case and his background. But we have no idea what the court of criminal appeals will require down the road in order to uphold that death penalty."

Jefferson County had not only to bear responsibility for the staggeringly complicated traveling, scheduling, and lodging arrangements for the prosecution and defense teams, their investigators, the judge and his bailiff, the court investigator and court reporter, and all of the outside experts and witnesses to be brought to San Antonio by either side during the trial, but also for the staggering costs involved in this trial that was to be like no other before it. Jefferson County was not by any standard a wealthy county, and criminal district court administrator Randy Kitchen told reporters the only case he could compare it to was that of Linda May Burnett, who had also been tried in San Antonio at defense attorney Charles Carver's request. But the Burnett case had lasted only three weeks, and the Lockhart trial was expected to take three or four times that long and would involve many dozens of out-of-state witnesses.

At the conclusion of the Burnett case, Charles Carver had submitted to the county his bill for $117,500; Judge Gist, always conscious of his position as "keeper of the king's purse," had granted Carver only $47,155. Now, county auditor Jerry Ware said he couldn't put a price tag on the Lockhart trial because "there really has never been anything here to compare to this," but he said estimates ranged as high as a half-million dollars, all to ensure that Lockhart received a fair trial.

As the jury selection ground through its second week, Michael Lee Lockhart, nattily attired in a suit and tie, smiled cordially at potential jurors and flashed smiles as well to reporters clustered around the courtroom doors.

"What do you think of the proceedings so far, Michael?" called out one reporter.

Lockhart shook his head and sighed as he walked past the reporters. Rolling his eyes, he answered, "Ridiculous."

Lockhart seemed inordinately bored by the whole courtroom process, absentmindedly doodling on a steno pad as he sat next to his lawyers and investigators, or leaning back in his chair and looking around the room.

Robert Hobbs, who had by now spent every waking hour of the last five months studying, tracing, and reconstructing the *real* Michael Lee Lockhart, worried that this ho-hum attitude was yet another mask, and he wondered what was really going on inside Lockhart's head. Hobbs stood to the side and watched every move that Lockhart made, and every so often, he would see Lockhart's eyes flick to a window at the rear of the courtroom, and then away again, his face perfectly expressionless.

During a break in the proceedings, Hobbs walked back to the window and looked out through the heavy wooden-louvered blinds. They were on the third floor of the old granite courthouse. Fifteen feet below the courtroom window was the tar-papered roof of the second-floor building extension. It was a long drop, but Lockhart's carefully disguised interest in this window made Robert Hobbs very nervous, and he warned the court bailiffs to keep a close eye on their prisoner.

On Thursday, August 18, the jury selection procedure continued throughout the morning hours. Judge Gist called a lunch recess at noon and ordered that the jury selection would resume at 1:30.

At 1:15, two bailiffs escorted Lockhart from his cell back into the nearly empty courtroom. Judge Gist had just taken his seat at the bench, and the attorneys were beginning to file in. Robert Hobbs, who was still being inundated with calls from other jurisdictions about Lockhart's activities, was at the far end of the building, copying files.

The bailiffs led Lockhart to his seat at the defense table. Already at the table, defense jury consultant Debra Stewart was reading a book. The bailiffs, as they did every time they brought Lockhart into the courtroom, removed his handcuffs and ankle chains. Defense attorney Carver had requested this concession, and Judge Gist had granted it so as to prevent prospective jurors from developing a bias against the defendant.

Lockhart sat in his chair and leaned toward Ms. Stewart, asking her what book she was reading. She looked up from her book, but before she could answer, Lockhart suddenly sprang from his chair, raced through the courtroom, and dived headfirst out the third-floor window.

Shattering glass exploded. Everyone screamed and shouted. The bailiffs pulled their guns and raced for the window. Judge Gist pulled a .38 from his desk drawer and joined them. People were running into the courtroom, and several bailiffs rushed out and down the fire escape. Other bailiffs on the second floor were already running out onto the roof.

Robert Hobbs was at the other end of the building, but he ran out into the corridor when all the commotion started. Everyone was running toward the courtroom, and he knew instantly what had happened. "Damn it! Damn it! I *knew* it!" He, too, ran.

Lockhart lay on his back, moaning, surrounded by a dozen guns aimed down at him. Paramedics were there within minutes. As they put a neck brace on Lockhart and lifted him onto a stretcher, defense consultant Debra Stewart held his hand. "He said that his back hurt. He asked me to say a prayer with him, which I did," she said later. "And he asked me to tell his parents that he loved them."

Outside, spectators who had gathered to watch the excitement had a slightly different attitude. "Just shoot him!" yelled one man.

"Put him out of his misery!" yelled another. "Save everybody a lot of time and expense!"

Lockhart's defense team immediately began to paint the leap from the third-floor window as a suicide attempt. Charles Carver would again ask for a delay and then demand a mistrial. The prosecution called it an escape attempt. Lockhart himself later admitted that his plan was to "tuck and roll" onto the second-floor roof, take the fire escape to the ground, and hide out until the heat died down. He would then make his way the 175 miles to the Mexican border and from there down to Argentina. It was the height of the crowded tourist season in downtown San Antonio, and had the heavy wooden blinds not thrown off Lockhart's tuck and roll, he might have been able to carry out that plan.

As it was, Bexar County Sheriff Harlan Copeland sniffed at all the heated debate about the real intent behind Lockhart's dive from the third-floor window. "It don't really matter whether it was a suicide try or an escape try," Copeland said to the press. "He screwed 'em both up."

"Too bad he wasn't hurt worse," said Cheryl Colhouer in Florida, when she heard of the escape attempt. "I don't mind one bit if he suffers, after what he's done to this family."

Dina Alden, Lockhart's ex-wife in Ohio, also received the news with less than overwhelming concern for the man who had brutally and repeatedly raped her at knifepoint. "Did he land on his head, I hope?"

At the Bexar County Medical Center Hospital, Michael Lee Lockhart immediately began complaining loudly about his treatment. He kept demanding pain medication, and orthopedic surgeon Dr. Michael Dean kept refusing, telling his patient that narcotics could mask the vital-sign responses he was monitoring. But here again, Lockhart had thrust himself into his favorite of all positions—center stage—and he was not to be denied when he wanted his own way.

"I'll sue you, and everybody else here!" he shouted. "I have my constitutional rights, and I won't be treated this way! Before I'm through with you, I'll *own* this place!"

"It's your own fault you're in pain," responded Dr. Dean, mildly going about his business. "So just lie still and be quiet."

"If I was a paying customer, you wouldn't be denying me my rights!" Lockhart continued to rail on. "I'll be rich, my *kids'll* be rich by the time I get done suing this hospital!"

"Oh, for heaven's sakes," said Dr. Dean, "will you just lie still and be quiet?"

Robert Hobbs had come to the hospital to take statements from the courtroom guards who bore the responsibility for Lockhart's escape attempt, and who were now gathered around his doorway, guarding him against any further attempts. All of the guards happened to be tall, proud Hispanic men. They were embarrassed, enraged, and humiliated that this had happened during their watch, and now, as they stood in the hallway waiting for lab test results, they talked among themselves and pointedly ignored Lockhart.

While they waited, the men began to discuss the upcoming presidential elections. Lockhart, always oblivious to the unspoken dynamics that said he was not wanted, that said, in fact, he was *despised,* kept joining their conversations. He propped himself up on his gurney and chattered on and on, offering his political opinions with assurance and confidence, never seeming to notice that his comments and questions fell into the chilly, rigid silence of hatred.

At one point, when he had again interjected an unasked,

unwanted opinion, captain of the guards Dan Vella turned and looked at him.

At the look in Capt. Vella's eyes, Lockhart stopped chattering. Then he seemed to switch gears, smiling coyly, for all the world like a naughty child who will be forgiven anything because he's so *cute*.

"Aw, what's the matter, boss?" Lockhart smirked at Captain Vella. "Did I make your day worse?"

When he saw Robert Hobbs standing with the guards and taking notes, Lockhart called out to him, asking if Hobbs was going to write down everything he was saying. Hobbs said he most certainly was, and reminded Lockhart again that he had the right to remain silent, and that anything he did say could be used against him.

"Hey, don't get excited," Lockhart sneered, "I'm not going to say anything to discriminate against myself." Hobbs had noticed before that whenever Lockhart found himself in a vulnerable and weakened social position, he would try to talk beyond the competence of his vocabulary, as he did now with the use of the word "discriminate" instead of "incriminate."

Several hours had passed at the hospital by this time, and test results showed that Lockhart's only serious injury was a chipped bone in his pelvis. But the hospital still had other tests to run, to make certain there were no hidden internal or spinal injuries. Meanwhile, everyone stood around and waited.

Sensing, perhaps, that Robert Hobbs did not radiate the overt hatred of him that everyone else seemed to, Lockhart kept up a running, one-sided conversation with the D.A.'s investigator, even though Hobbs repeatedly warned him that his own words could only cause him further damage. This driving need to flirt with danger, to repeatedly pit oneself against a powerful adversary at nearly impossible odds, is an absolute component of the narcissistic sociopathic personality. It is akin to standing alongside the road and darting out in front of traffic, over and over again, just for the rush of getting away with it yet one more time. It pumps up the sense of superiority, which in the end is all that a sociopath, who feels no other true emotion, has to look forward to in life—to be smarter than, tougher than, scarier than, wittier than, or prettier than somebody else. It is ironic that this most empty of all human beings is at the same time the most needful of other people. Only with an audience to play off of is he able to glitter and swell. Alone, he is simply hollow and drab, and he knows it. It is usually after he has exhausted, used up, and discarded all possible audiences that a sociopath will commonly turn to suicide, which is infinitely preferable to being alone with his little nobody self. The audience is everything.

Robert Hobbs would be asked many times what he thought of Lockhart's innate intelligence level.

"Michael wasn't stupid," Hobbs would answer. "But he wasn't nearly as smart as *he* thought he was."

"So," Lockhart now asked Robert Hobbs, "are you going to write a book about me?"

"I don't think you've achieved enough notoriety to be worth a book," Hobbs said. "There will be some interest in you in Indiana and Florida, and here in Texas, of course. And maybe Ohio, because you're from there. But that's about it, I think."

Lockhart bristled. Then he laughed.

"You don't know a fraction of the crimes I've committed," he said.

Lockhart told Hobbs that he had committed crimes in every state in the country, with the exception of the Dakotas, Minnesota, Alaska, and Hawaii. He said he had burglarized homes "by the hundreds" and pulled an armed robbery, usually of a quick-stop convenience store, whenever he'd run short of money.

Hobbs remained unimpressed.

"When do you think I actually started killing people?" Lockhart asked.

"I wouldn't know," said Hobbs, being very careful that any comment he made did not take the form of a question. He had warned Lockhart over and over that anything he said could be used against him, and Hobbs wasn't going to take the ghost of a chance that any defense lawyer could later claim this conversation was actually an interrogation.

"How many people do you think Ted Bundy really killed?" Lockhart now asked. "I've heard it's somewhere in the three figures."

Hobbs said that he thought "three figures" was probably too high, and that he thought the actual number was somewhere between 40 and 50.

"That's not that many," Lockhart shrugged. "I've killed between 20 and 30 myself."

Lockhart would later resent it that people often compared him to Bundy and found him "lacking" in the number of murders he had committed.

"I've robbed banks all over the country," Lockhart would brag. "Did Bundy do that? Bundy didn't do that—Michael Lee Lockhart did it."

Hobbs assured Lockhart that even after the trial was over, he would continue looking for other murders, other victims.

"Well, don't be stupid and look for the same patterns every time," Lockhart advised Hobbs. "You guys aren't the only ones who read all the books, you know."

"Thank you," Robert Hobbs said. "We'll try our best not to be stupid."

Forty-three

"Society has no defense against the intelligent serial killer," prosecutor Paul McWilliams told the jury.

Following Lockhart's failed escape attempt, his attorney had tried every means within his power to have the trial delayed. First, Carver had requested a delay, asking Judge Gist for permission to hire an orthopedic specialist to examine Lockhart. The judge said he would neither grant nor deny that request until Carver had shown justification for such further expense. Next, Carver resubmitted a previous motion for delay, claiming that he had not received all of the state's evidence, and saying that if the trial proceeded, Lockhart's constitutional right to effective representation would be violated. Judge Gist denied that motion, and Carver then asked for a mistrial, claiming that all the publicity surrounding Lockhart's dramatic leap from the window had contaminated the jury panel.

D.A. Maness voiced his strenuous objection. "We can't be sure of that, Your Honor," Maness said. "The jurors have not been questioned as to whether, from hearsay or otherwise, they have preconceived notions about this case. Additionally, there is case law that says a defendant cannot profit from his own wrongdoing."

Judge Gist agreed that the jurors should be repolled, while Carver threatened to ask for yet another change of venue, which would have entailed picking up the entire trial and all its participants and moving to yet another city.

After the jurors were repolled and reseated, Judge Gist agreed with the D.A. that Lockhart should not benefit from his own misconduct and ruled that the trial would proceed. But, he ordered, Lockhart would now come to court handcuffed and chained in leg irons. Carver was furious. "Under our laws," Carver said, "a person is presumed innocent until proven guilty by legal and competent evidence. Allowing the jury to see him in shackles greatly damages our case."

While all these machinations were proceeding, Michael Lee Lockhart reveled in the spotlight that his swan-dive had focused on him. Each day, the bailiffs wheeled him into court in a wheelchair and then transferred him to a cushioned seat at the defense table. Lockhart grimaced and sighed and bit at his lower lip during these transfers. At one point, he pulled out a tissue and dabbed at his eyes.

"I am physically, mentally, and painfully really hurting right now," Lockhart said, his voice breaking. Again he dabbed at the corners of his eyes. "I am trying to block out my pain, but it's difficult. It's very difficult . . ."

Judge Gist ruled that the murder trial would proceed.

The prosecution began its long list of witnesses with Elyria, Ohio, police officer Richard Armstrong, who described the burglary of his home and the theft of his service revolver. An FBI ballistics expert then verified that the bullet that had pierced Officer Hulsey's side and shattered his heart had come from the stolen service revolver. Next, Rick Treadwell took the stand and recounted his frightful ordeal as Lockhart had pulled the red Corvette to the side of the highway and put a gun into his face.

Witness after witness narrated the sequence of events that began at the Best Western Motel on the night of March 22, moved along at over 100 miles per hour into downtown Orange, and then ended at the Old and Lost Rivers Bridge outside Houston. Marvin Murl Flanagan told how he had picked up Lockhart at Bennigan's Restaurant and agreed to drive him to Houston. A bank teller from Baton Rouge then

identified the hundred-dollar bill Lockhart had used to pay
the taxi driver as one of the marked bills taken during the
bank robbery.

While this portion of the trial was in progress, the courtroom doors opened and thirty-seven uniformed San Antonio
police cadets who had been touring the courthouse walked
in and took seats.

Carver was on his feet immediately. Judge Gist called for
a recess and listened as Carver objected to the presence of
the police recruits. "It's highly prejudicial," Carver argued.
"I turned around and all of a sudden, all I saw was a sea
of blue."

The defense attorney again demanded a mistrial, saying
that the police recruits showing up in a large group like
that had been "inflammatory." Judge Gist agreed to order
the rookies to leave the courtroom, but he again denied
Carver's request for a mistrial. Newspapers, both in San
Antonio and in Beaumont, had seen every nuance in the
trial. "'SEA OF BLUE' . . . BOOTED FROM LOCKHART
MURDER TRIAL," read the next day's headlines.

Each day, as the prosecution prepared for the next step
of the trial, Robert Hobbs would lay out the state's evidence
against Michael Lee Lockhart. A large U.S. map stood on
an easel, dotted with blue stickers to show Lockhart's movements across the country. The stickers highlighted Wyoming, Chicago, Indiana, Toledo, New York, Atlanta,
Jacksonville, Miami, Tampa, Baton Rouge, and Beaumont.
A large scale model of room 157 sat on the floor next to
a table, on which were spread out an envelope of stolen
credit cards, a videotape of the Payless shoestore robbery,
the Georgia Bulldogs baseball cap Lockhart had been wearing during that robbery, and the fingerprint cards that
matched the prints taken from the water glass and the wall
of Windy Gallagher's bedroom. Also on the table were two
black three-ring binders that were kept closed: the binders
contained page after page of color crime-scene photos taken

of the murders of Windy Patricia Gallagher and of Jennifer Lynn Colhouer.

Beaumont crime-scene tech Bill Tatum testified as to his identification and testing of Lockhart's personal possessions taken from room 157, among which was a small 1987-1988 calendar book. The police dispatch tapes from those few pivotal minutes surrounding Officer Hulsey's death were then played to a hushed courtroom. Hulsey's terrified voice, shouting for help, echoed again and again through the cavernous room. Then, Sgt. Tatum quietly identified Officer Hulsey's torn and bloody uniform.

In the spectator section, tears streamed down the cheeks of a stony-faced Chief Paul Hulsey, Sr. Next to him, his wife Mary Jo and daughter-in-law Barbara held one another's hands and sobbed quietly, handkerchiefs cupped over their mouths.

"Your Honor, I object," said Mr. Carver. "I appreciate and understand why they have become emotional, but it distracts the jury from hearing testimony and creates sympathy. If they continue to be emotional, I ask that they be removed."

Judge Gist looked out at the Hulsey family, sitting together quietly as they had every minute of every day of the trial.

"They are causing no disruption, Mr. Carver," said the judge quietly. "Overruled."

Next, out of the jury's hearing, Charles Carver argued fervently against admitting Lockhart's calendar book into evidence, saying that Lockhart's scribbled notations were irrelevant to the case against him, and that admitting the book into evidence would "confuse, mislead, and prejudice" the jurors against his client.

Lockhart had apparently used his little calendar book to record the "high points" of his travels. January 20, 1988, was circled, with the initials "T.B.F." scribbled on the back of the page. Jennifer Colhouer was murdered on January 20, 1988, just outside Tampa Bay, Florida.

"That is not relevant to this case," argued Lockhart's defense attorney. "To subject this jury to that now would be highly prejudicial."

In another notation, Lockhart had scrawled at the top of a page, "Money Is Everything," and the word "Corvette" was scribbled several times on the circled date page of November 9, 1987. The February 22 date listed the figures $14,000 and $2,100, and on February 27, Lockhart had written in $3,600 and $7,500.

"The state has indicated it intends to show that this was the result of robberies or burglaries on those dates," Mr. Carver said. "Again, that is not relevant to deciding whether the defendant killed Officer Hulsey without justification or excuse."

Judge Gist heard all the arguments and then ruled that the calendar book would be admitted into evidence. As he listened to the discussions, Robert Hobbs wondered again, as he had many times before this day, about another of Michael Lee Lockhart's calendar books.

When Hobbs had made his fact-finding trip to Chicago several months earlier, he interviewed tenants of the Uptown Hotel, where Lockhart had been staying during the fall of 1987. One young woman, a tall, strikingly beautiful redhead, said that she had met "Mike Locke" at the hotel and gone out to dinner with him once. She told Hobbs that something about "Locke" made her extremely uneasy, and she didn't date him again. But she distinctly remembered a thick, rubberband-bound calendar book that he carried everywhere with him. She said the book was so stuffed with papers that it was several inches thick. "Locke" wouldn't let anyone look at or touch the book, and he kept it with him at all times.

Not only the redhead, but also Betty, Lockhart's Chicago-based girlfriend, had remembered and commented on the thick, stuffed calendar book. Betty had told Hobbs that while they sat at her mother's kitchen table discussing their drug business, Lockhart would frequently open his book and scribble notations in it. But he wouldn't let her, or anyone, see into the book.

Hobbs had originally theorized that Lockhart had hidden the book: given his obsessiveness about it, chances were he would not have destroyed it, and Lockhart had bragged to at least one of his girlfriends along the way that he had a secret safe-deposit box. But back in April, when Lockhart had asked to meet with Sgts. Ray Beck and Bill Gates to tell them his ludicrous story about not having been alone in room 157, he had hinted then about a book of names. He said he had hidden the book out in the woods somewhere.

Police officers had searched the woods around the apartment complex in Orange where Lockhart had bailed out of the Corvette after the high-speed chase. They'd also searched the area adjacent to the Old and Lost Rivers Bridge, but many miles of dense woodland lie between Beaumont and Houston, and the book was never found.

Robert Hobbs did not doubt that wherever Lockhart's book was hidden, Windy Gallagher's stolen photo was in it—and Jennifer Colhouer's—and Joyce Wilson's. How many more photos were in that book? And where was it? Haunting as the idea is, authorities may never know the answer.

Charles Carver's whole defense of Michael Lee Lockhart was based on the premise that Lockhart was forced to shoot Officer Hulsey in self-defense.

"Paul Hulsey fired first and attempted to kill Michael Lee Lockhart," Carver told the jury. "The evidence will show that Michael Lee Lockhart acted in self-defense."

In contrast to the fifty-six witnesses and over two hundred pieces of evidence presented by the prosecution, Carver called only seven witnesses, the last being Lockhart himself. But first, Mr. Carver put his hired psychologist on the stand.

Dr. Rashni Skadegaard, whom the defense had flown in from New Jersey, told the jury that Michael Lee Lockhart was haunted by anxiety, sexual dysfunction, and anger toward women as a result of incidents of molestation when he was a child. While he had initially told authorities he had never been mistreated as a child, Lockhart later claimed that an adult friend of his parents' had sexually molested him as a youngster. Dr. Skadegaard described Lockhart as "a person whose anger toward women is totally out of control. It's not the behavior of a sane person who is in his right mind."

The New Jersey psychologist also said that because Lockhart blamed women for his sexual problems, he would not be a threat to men "unless cornered" and would not be a danger in a structured prison setting, where he could receive treatment.

In the audience, the Hulsey family held hands and hoped the jury would remember the testimony several weeks earlier of Lockhart's Beaumont jailers.

Jefferson County sheriff's deputy Charles Wiggins had testified that while he was in custody in Beaumont, Lockhart had complained so loudly and so often about jail conditions that Wiggins had asked Capt. Nora Webb to meet with the prisoner. Capt. Webb had agreed, and Wiggins had instructed his control officer to key in the intercom to Lockhart's cell and inform the prisoner that the captain was on the way.

Over the intercom, the jailers heard Lockhart in conversation with another prisoner. Lockhart was bragging about having had ten years of martial arts training and said that he would soon be back out on the street, where "I'm going to kill a few more motherfuckers." He also said that if he

had a gun, he would shoot all the jailers, and if any of the
Jefferson County officers "try to lay a hand on me, I'm
going to fuck them up real bad."

A very different Michael Lee Lockhart than that one now
took the stand in his own defense. Before he did, his defense
team handed him a card in a lavender envelope. It was September
30, Lockhart's twenty-eighth birthday.

Immaculately groomed and very subdued in manner,
Lockhart admitted on the stand that he had been living a
"make-believe life" based on lies and deceit.

"But I didn't want to shoot that police officer," Lockhart
said. "I tried everything not to. But I thought he was going
to kill me."

Lockhart said that he had locked himself out of his room
at the Best Western, and when he went to the front office
to get another key, he encountered Officer Hulsey. He said
that he and Hulsey said "hello" to each other, and then he
returned to his room.

Lockhart said that moments later, there was a knock on
his door, and Officer Hulsey was standing there.

"He asked me for some identification, and I said why,
and he said because he wanted to see it." Lockhart said he
asked the police officer if he had a search warrant, and the
officer said he didn't, but that he still wanted to see some
identification. "He was very insistent, so I said my identification
was on the dresser and that I'd get it. I shut the
door, took two or three steps, and then heard a big bang. I
turned around, the door was wide open, and the police officer
was in my room. I asked him what he was doing in
my room. Within seconds, he had his gun out and he told
me to get against the wall. He told me to put my hands up
against the wall or he was going to blow my head off."

Lockhart said that he put his hands against the wall, "and
then I hit him."

"Why?" asked Carver.

"I was scared he would harm me," Lockhart said. "He wasn't acting like a police officer. I didn't understand why he would come into my room like that and then pull a gun on me."

Lockhart said that he and Officer Hulsey fought across the small room, and that he repeatedly asked the police officer to drop his gun. In the struggle, Hulsey bit Lockhart's finger, and Lockhart grabbed a pen and stabbed Hulsey in the forehead with it.

"Somehow," Lockhart said, "he threw me, and my gun went off. I told him not to touch his gun, but he went for it. He picked it up and I fired my gun."

Then, according to Lockhart, the already twice-struck officer begged him not to shoot again.

"I said 'okay,' and I didn't shoot him again. Then I got in my car and left."

Paul McWilliams tore into this story, probing for the obvious inconsistencies. He had Lockhart repeat his entire scenario about Officer Hulsey coming into the room, this time without Carver's prompting. In Lockhart's version, which he now repeated, he had closed the motel room door, and then "heard a big bang" as Officer Hulsey had come bursting into the room.

"Those doors have a self-locking mechanism," McWilliams said. "If you had closed the door, Officer Hulsey could not have come busting in because the door would have locked itself."

"Well, I shut the door, but I don't think I shut it all the way," Lockhart said now.

McWilliams strode back and forth, flipping through the pages of women's names in Lockhart's calendar book, ticking off all those who thought the man they knew was an undercover investigator.

"You played pretend police officer with girls all up and down the Gulf Coast, didn't you?" McWilliams asked.

"Yes, sir," Lockhart replied.

Then McWilliams repeated Lockhart's comments to Sgt. Bill Gates on the night of Hulsey's murder.

"That was taken out of context," Lockhart protested. "When I told him the officer fucked up that night, I meant by the way he barged into my room without a warrant."

"When did you first tell this story about what happened in the room being self-defense?"

"I said it from the beginning," Lockhart answered, "but the word I used back then was 'accident.' "

Finally, the grueling two-month case wound down. Charles Carver asked Judge Gist for a directed verdict of acquittal, saying that Officer Paul Hulsey had not followed proper police procedure on the night of his murder.

"The evidence has shown that Officer Hulsey had no warrant for the arrest of Mr. Lockhart and no warrant to search his premises," Carver said. "Officer Hulsey was in Mr. Lockhart's room unlawfully and therefore could not have been acting in the lawful discharge of his official duties."

Judge Gist denied the motion and gave each side ninety minutes for closing arguments. During his summation, Carver repeated his client's right to defend himself against the "unlawful conduct" of Officer Hulsey.

"They want you to find Mr. Lockhart guilty and later kill him because they want to show this community that we are good law-abiding citizens," Carver told the jury. "They want you to sacrifice this man so the appetites of the police officers in Beaumont can be satisfied because they lost a friend."

Paul McWilliams, as he always did in capital murder cases, warned the Hulsey family that they might not want to stay in the courtroom during his summation. He would be detailing their loved one's death in the most graphic possible manner, and he feared leaving them with this last ugly memory. But neither Chief Hulsey, his wife Mary Jo, nor

Officer Hulsey's widow, Barbara, hesitated for even a moment. They would all stay.

Throughout his summation, McWilliams spoke of Officer Hulsey's dedication to his family and his job. McWilliams likened Michael Lee Lockhart to Ted Bundy, who was to face execution in Florida in three months' time. He pointed out that everything Lockhart had presented, or invented, about himself was a mimicry of Bundy, from his claims of being a law student bound for Harvard to his mysterious hints about undercover police missions to his flashy ladies' man image, and even to his daring, Bundy-imitation escape attempt.

It was a rousing summation, and McWilliams's voice was raw by the time he told the jury that "society has no defense against the intelligent serial killer."

McWilliams's fifteen-year-old son, Dee, had asked if he could sit in the courtroom for the final closing arguments, and now the boy, overcome with pride, jumped from his seat and ran to hug his father. Paul McWilliams fought back tears.

"This was the most difficult case of my life," he would say later. "Paul Hulsey was not only a police officer. He was my friend."

After instructions from Judge Gist, the eight-woman, four-man jury retired to deliberate.

"Preliminary arrangements for sequestering the jury have been made at a local downtown hotel should jurors not reach a verdict today," Ken Dollinger, the Jefferson County witness coordinator, told the waiting press.

But ninety minutes later, the jury filed back in.

"Michael Lee Lockhart, we find you guilty of the capital murder of Officer Paul D. Hulsey, Jr."

The Hulseys leaped to their feet, crying and hugging one another. Chief Hulsey was struck by the fact that the date was October 4. "10-4" in police lingo signals "message received and understood," and the Hulseys, strong in their deeply Christian faith, felt that more than coincidence was at work.

"My son started an investigation, and as a result he lost his life," Chief Hulsey said to waiting reporters. "This jury today finished his job for him. Like him, they didn't want this beast, this monster, like a roving lion out in society, devouring whoever he wants."

Coprosecutor Jim Middleton reminded everyone that "our job isn't over yet. We intend to seek the death penalty for this murderer." Middleton estimated that the penalty phase of the trial could last another two weeks.

Tom and Cheryl Colhouer had flown to Texas to testify about Jennifer's murder. April, Tom, and Chrissy Gallagher were there, too, along with Lt. John Mowery, Det. Karl Grimmer, and Thomas Vanes, the prosecutor from Crown Point, Indiana. Both Indiana and Florida had obtained governor's warrants for Lockhart's extradition. Indiana was next in line after Texas, and Vanes was there to take a good look at Lockhart's demeanor and personality.

As the jury announced its verdict, Lockhart only shrugged, telling reporters as he was led past them that the verdict would be overturned on appeal.

"Why?" asked a reporter.

"Because of corruption," Lockhart answered. "Corruption in the Jefferson County district attorney's office."

By the next morning, Michael Lee Lockhart was on the phone for a two-hour discussion with a reporter from the *Toledo Blade*.

Lockhart told the reporter that until his arrest in Texas, he had been a firm believer in the death penalty.

"But now, I have totally different views about it," Lockhart told the reporter. "After hearing some of the views of our vice-president [Bush], I don't know if I want that guy in office anymore. He wants to kill every drug pusher and every murderer around! We might as well start lining people up against the wall like the Commies did in Russia. I don't believe anymore that the death penalty is a deterrent."

The reporter refrained from pointing out the obvious—that given the Texas jury's likely decision within the next few weeks, Lockhart might be considered to have very subjective reasons for changing his mind about the death penalty. Instead, he asked about Lockhart's own case.

"I don't think Michael should do any time," Lockhart said. "I think Michael Lockhart is totally innocent. I don't think there should be any punishment for Michael. What kind of punishment would there have been if Hulsey had gotten me? None! He would have gotten patted on the back!"

Lockhart had high praise for Charles Carver, saying that he and his defense attorney were very comfortable that the verdict in San Antonio would be overturned.

"I'm sure I'll get a retrial and everything," Lockhart told the *Blade* reporter. "If the state did anything for Michael, it's given me a decent lawyer. Mr. Carver felt how I felt. He's the type of man who can really relate to you."

When the reporter asked about the upcoming cases in Indiana and Florida, Lockhart got angry.

"Michael did not do it," he said. "Michael's not an angel, but he wouldn't have done nothing like that. Those are the allegations that hurt me the most, because Michael did not do it. No matter what evidence they think they have, Michael Lockhart did not do it. He did not do it. Period."

Forty-four

"Who is the President of the United States?"

"Mickey Mouse."

"Which is the longest river in the world?"

"What's a river?"

"Do you know what a defense attorney's job is?"

"Yeah, to be a puppet for the prosecutors."

"And what's a prosecutor's job?"

"To find people guilty whether they are or not."

Thus Michael Lee Lockhart showed his displeasure at being examined for competency by the court-appointed psychiatrist in Crown Point, Indiana.

Going into his trial for the murder of Windy Gallagher, Lockhart insisted that only one doctor, Dr. Rashni Skadegaard, from New Jersey, could give an accurate assessment of his mental condition. His request for his own favorite doctor was merely one in a long series of obstructionary tactics on Lockhart's part.

From the time he arrived in Crown Point in February 1989, Lockhart complained and objected to every phase of the Indiana procedures. He didn't like his court-appointed lawyer, so superior court judge James E. Letsinger appointed a second attorney as cocounsel. Lockhart didn't like that lawyer, either, and the judge allowed the additional expense to the county of having a third attorney appointed to the defense team.

Lockhart complained that the two court-appointed investigators weren't good enough—he wanted Patty Wolter, who had done previous investigative work for Texas defense attorney Charles Carver. When Judge Letsinger refused this demand, Lockhart refused to leave his cell for any further court proceedings, telling his attorneys he was "boycotting until my demands for new attorneys and other matters are properly satisfied."

Judge Letsinger called Lockhart into the courtroom and asked him why he wouldn't cooperate with the court psychiatrists.

"Because I don't feel comfortable with them," Lockhart answered.

"I see. Do you feel *comfortable* with anyone in the State of Indiana?"

"No, I don't."

The judge ruled that Lockhart's presence in the courtroom wasn't necessary, and that the judicial proceedings would continue without him.

Indiana rules require that a jury be sequestered for a capital murder trial, and since the extradition warrant allowing the state to bring Lockhart to Indiana was good for only 120 days, Judge Letsinger decided that the trial would proceed seven days a week, under the tightest security ever imposed in Lake County. The county had hired a private plane, and Robert Hobbs, Ray Beck, John Mowery, Karl Grimmer, and two Lake County sheriff's detectives accompanied Lockhart on the flight from Huntsville, Texas, to Crown Point, Indiana. Lockhart had been sentenced to death in Texas, and Hobbs and Beck were going to make absolutely certain that Officer Hulsey's killer never traveled without them. Additionally, Judge Letsinger ordered that all cameras and other recording equipment be barred from the entire second floor of Government Center, where the courtroom was. Such restrictions had never before been put into effect in the history of the courthouse.

"There will be no commotion, there will be no circus

atmosphere, there will be no escape attempts," said Judge Letsinger.

Lockhart's Indiana murder trial lasted for eleven days. Like the Hulseys before them, the entire Gallagher family now sat holding hands, listening as Lt. Mowery and the other Griffith police officers recounted processing the Gallagher apartment on the night of Windy's murder and finding the fingerprints on the water glass and on the wall in the murder room. Chrissy Gallagher spoke from the stand about "hoping I was crazy and that I didn't see what I saw" when she found her sister's body.

Robert Hobbs testified that on the night of Lockhart's escape attempt, the defendant had told him that they all knew "only a fraction" of the crimes he had committed, and that he had murdered between twenty and thirty people.

Defense attorney Robert Lewis tried to have Hobbs's testimony suppressed on the grounds that Lockhart had made the statements without a lawyer being present. But Judge Letsinger overruled the objection.

"All this man did," the judge said, pointing to Investigator Hobbs, "is sit there and listen to Lockhart's own worst enemy—himself."

The defense team had finally been able to get Dr. Rashni Skadegaard appointed to testify, at Lockhart's insistent request. On the stand, Dr. Skadegaard spoke for nearly four hours in a discourse that the newspapers later called "rambling."

"It was a very volatile and aggressive atmosphere that Mr. Lockhart grew up in," said Dr. Skadegaard. "Familial problems included sexual abuse, aggressive behavior, lack of communication, and sibling rivalries."

The doctor said that Lockhart adopted different personas because he was unhappy with his true identity, and she described him as a psychosexually, emotionally disturbed individual.

"But," said Dr. Skadegaard, "Mr. Lockhart would benefit

from long-term treatment in a highly structured setting such as jail. He has the type of personality that makes him conducive to receiving treatment."

"Dr. Skadegaard," asked prosecutor Thomas Vanes, "you say that Mr. Lockhart, a person who has killed three people, responds well to treatment? Exactly how many triple-murderers have you treated before this?"

Vanes also brushed aside Lockhart's claims of sexual abuse. "If the information going in, on which you make your judgment, is not true, then the opinion itself has no validity." Vanes had Dr. Skadegaard read from a report that had been prepared by Charles Carver's investigators. In it, one of Lockhart's sisters is quoted as saying: "Mom got to the point that she could not believe anything that Michael said."

It took the jury one hour to find Michael Lee Lockhart guilty of the murder of Windy Patricia Gallagher.

In asking for the death penalty, prosecutor Thomas Vanes told the jury that since Lockhart had adopted Ted Bundy as his idol, "then let's do to him what was done to Bundy."

In opposing the defense request for a sixty-year sentence, Vanes read from Windy Gallagher's datebook, in which the teenager had written, "My no stress day!" on the Tuesday she was killed. "There are no more dates in this girl's calendar," Vanes exhorted the jury. "And frankly, the idea of sixty more years of dates for this man, alive and breathing, is absolutely nauseating."

Mr. Vanes concluded, "Someday, someone somewhere must put the final date in Mr. Lockhart's calendar."

The jury took six hours before returning its recommendation—the death penalty. Before he imposed sentence, Judge Letsinger asked Lockhart if he had anything to say.

Michael Lee Lockhart spoke for half an hour, telling jurors that "I suffer every day behind bars" and wondering again why he should be singled out for the death penalty when "a lot of people have done a lot worse things than I did."

"Mr. Lockhart, you are not fit to live," said Judge Letsinger. "You tortured and tormented that little girl. You *carved* her to death. This court sentences you to death."

When reporters later asked Judge Letsinger whether he thought Lockhart's death penalty would be appealed, he replied, "Oh, hell, yes. There's practically a whole national industry in this country that does nothing but file appeals in murder cases. I won't be a bit surprised to be sitting in my living room ten years from now, reading about still another appeal being filed on behalf of Mr. Lockhart."

In the months between the end of the Indiana trial and the beginning of the Florida trial, Robert Hobbs continued uncovering more of Lockhart's crimes, including the very strong probability of at least two more murders of young girls.

Chief Paul Hulsey had been watching *Unsolved Mysteries* in his Dallas home on October 23, 1989. The TV program outlined the murder of a sixteen-year-old Las Vegas girl on August 11, 1987. The desiccated body of Katherine Marie Hobbs (no relation to Robert Hobbs) had been found in the desert several days after she'd disappeared while walking to a store to buy a book.

"Something just happened to me when I saw that program," said Chief Hulsey. "I looked at it and I knew it was Lockhart."

Chief Hulsey called Robert Hobbs, who contacted the Las Vegas detectives. The only physical evidence they had were several blue carpet fibers. Both Robert Hobbs and Lieutenant John Mowery had taken and inventoried carpet fibers from the stolen silver-blue 1986 Toyota Celica that Lockhart had been using, and they now compared them to the evidence in Vegas. The fibers were produced by DuPont, who told investigators that they had sold a huge lot of carpet to the Toyota Corporation for use in its 1986 Celica cars. Investigators were able to trace the fibers to the identical model of car Lockhart had been driving, but not to *the* car. The chronology of Lockhart's movements put together by the Texas investigators showed that Lockhart was in and around Las Vegas in the days immediately surrounding the murder of Katherine Marie Hobbs.

Other murders of young women, in Bowling Green, Ohio, and in Fort Knox, Kentucky, in Indiana, and in Missouri and California, seemed to point to Lockhart, but Hobbs and other investigators have never been able to pull together enough conclusive physical evidence to charge him. As Hobbs would say during a television interview, "Michael got better as he went along. He left fingerprints at the Gallagher scene. By the time he got to Florida, he didn't leave prints again."

In October 1989, Det. Fay Wilber and FTO Bobby Lightfoot flew Lockhart in a small rented plane from Huntsville, Texas, to Dade City, Florida, where he would stand trial for the murder of Jennifer Lynn Colhouer. They had to stop and refuel in Gulfport, Mississippi, and Wilber was amazed to watch as Lockhart, in chains, leg irons, and shackles, began a flirtation with the young lady behind the counter. When they were ready to take off again and Wilber told her what he was in custody for, she said, "Oh no, he's much too nice. You must have the wrong man!"

On the plane, Lockhart suddenly asked Wilber, "Wasn't Ted Bundy executed here in Florida?" Wilber said yes, that Bundy had been executed ten months earlier, on January 24.

"I know I'm going to die in the electric chair," Lockhart

said, "but I don't want to go back to Texas. I want to die here, just like Ted Bundy did."

With Lockhart safely installed in the Dade City Jail, Assistant D.A. Allen Allweiss prepared to gear up the whole judicial mechanism to put Lockhart on trial. When a reporter asked why Florida was going to the expense of trying a man who had already been twice sentenced to death, Allweiss responded: "He's not dead yet, is he? If they call and tell us he died, okay then, we'll have nothing to worry about. Until then, we're going to trial."

But Lockhart was tired now of all the long, boring days in court. He suddenly pleaded guilty to the murder of Jennifer Colhouer and asked that the court immediately impose sentence. When Judge Maynard Swanson explained that a jury would have to be empaneled to pass sentence, Lockhart demanded to act as his own attorney.

Striding up and down before his prospective jurors, Lockhart teased and flirted with them, telling one older woman he thought her dress was really pretty, and commiserating with several others about how cold it was up north, and how much nicer Florida was. Once he had his jury, Lockhart confronted them with his now-familiar diatribe against capital punishment.

"There are 36,000 people in prison for murder," he told the jury. "How come they get to live, but I get to die?" He then lectured the jury about crime, telling them to "stand up to criminals."

They did—they sentenced him to death. One seventy-four-year-old juror said she was not impressed with Lockhart's stage show. "To me, it just showed what a smooth talker he is—he showed me how easy it was for him to get into those little girls' homes."

Cheryl and Tom Colhouer were not impressed, either. "He was just enjoying himself up there," said Tom Colhouer. "He got a big kick out of it, putting on his big show."

During her turn to speak at the sentencing hearing, Cheryl Colhouer confronted Lockhart directly.

"You think you're so big," said Jennifer's mother. "Why didn't you come after me? Why go after little girls? Because you have no *balls,* that's why!"

After the sentencing, Lockhart agreed to see Cheryl Colhouer, who had since Lockhart's capture been asking Fay Wilber to arrange such a meeting. She had to ask him why. Why her town? Why her house? Why her little girl? Lockhart could only tell Mrs. Colhouer that he didn't know why "Michael does what Michael does." But he pointed out to her that her daughter "messed up" because she let him into the house to use the phone when he posed as a real estate agent. Cheryl Colhouer said she didn't believe him, that Jennifer was far too security conscious to let a stranger into the house. Lockhart shrugged at this, telling her: "You believe whatever you want, Mrs. Colhouer."

Today Michael Lee Lockhart is still alive and well at the Texas State Prison in Huntsville. Appeals of all three death sentences from all three states are still continuing. At each step of the appeals process over the years, the trial courts in Texas, Indiana, and Florida have all been upheld, but that has not slowed down what Judge Letsinger referred to as "practically a national industry," since all the appellate defense attorneys have to do if they lose an appeal—is simply file another one, and then another one.

Michael Lee Lockhart granted the following interview to the *San Antonio Express News* on March 29, 1990: "While I was in prison in Wyoming in the mid-1980s, I read a magazine article that labeled Texas prisons as the toughest in the nation, and I vowed to myself that I would never go to Texas—never, never, never. But here I am. And now that I'm here, it's a laugh. It's not that bad. I pictured there would be these big guys covered with tattoos. It's not like that at all. I've got a roof over my head, I eat three times a day, I get to watch HBO and Showtime and ESPN. I got it better than half the people in this world. The only thing is, they're going to kill me."

The Hulsey family in Texas, the Gallagher family in Indiana, and the Colhouer family in Florida have just one question: When?

Forty-five

The Honorable Larry Gist, senior criminal district judge, Jefferson County, Texas, has consented to write the last chapter of this book.

The Honorable Larry Gist:

"Michael Lee Lockhart was convicted October 25, 1988, of capital murder for the killing of Beaumont police officer Paul Hulsey, Jr. Based on a jury finding that there was a probability he would continue to commit criminal acts of violence in the future and therefore constituted a continuing threat to society, he was sentenced to death.

"During the trial, two significant things occurred. Lockhart unsuccessfully tried to escape by diving through a third-floor window. And the state introduced evidence of several other crimes he had committed, including the murders of young girls in Indiana and Florida.

"Texas law requires that an automatic appeal must be taken from any capital murder conviction. That's exactly what happened in the Lockhart case. On December 2, 1992, the Texas Court of Criminal Appeals affirmed Lockhart's conviction and death sentence. He asked for a rehearing, and on February 24, 1993, the highest criminal court in Texas again found that Lockhart had received a fair trial and that his conviction was legally valid.

"Since the U.S. Supreme Court allowed states to resume capital murder prosecutions, Texas has by far been more active than anyone else. Just recently, Texas executed its one-hundredth offender, and over four hundred inmates are presently confined on death row.

"Lockhart's trip through the appellate system is moving at an expected slow speed. But at some point, what was originally intended as reasonable review turns into folly.

"Some offenders have stayed on death row for fifteen or twenty years after their trial conviction. That disgraceful situation may be improving, however, and Lockhart might well become a part of the procedural reformation now in progress.

"After his Texas conviction, Lockhart was taken to Indiana, where he was convicted of capital murder and sentenced to death. He was then taken from Texas custody to Florida, where he entered a plea of guilty to capital murder and received the death penalty. Three states—three death sentences. Appeals are pending in those states as well as in Texas, and the inefficiency of their systems appears to parallel ours. Lockhart will be executed in the first state in which all avenues of appeal are exhausted. And that state may very well be Texas.

"After the Texas Court of Criminal Appeals denied his appeal and rehearing, he went directly to the U.S. Supreme Court and filed a petition for relief with them. The highest court in our nation affirmed his conviction on October 4, 1993.

"Upon learning of the Supreme Court decision, the trial court scheduled Lockhart's execution to be carried out before sunrise on November 23, 1993. Literally hours before the execution was to take place, Lockhart filed a motion with the trial court asking that his execution be stopped so he could file an application for habeas corpus.

"In layman's terms, habeas corpus amounts to a second appeal—or in some cases, a third appeal, or a fourth one. In his motion to delay his execution, Lockhart alleged that he had no attorney representing him, but that he had been assisted in presenting the motion by the Texas Resource Center.

"The Texas Resource Center is a federally funded organization that has been active in capital murder appellate matters for years. Their stated mission is 'to recruit and assist counsel for death row inmates in state court.' And they have been inordinately successful in having appellate courts delay executions by appearing only hours before a scheduled execution and urging claims that seldom were ultimately found to be accurate. Their strategy of waiting until the eve of execution was successful because it put enormous pressure on judges. Would an innocent man be executed? Many judges felt it a moral necessity to stop the execution to give them time to fully explore the merits of the inmate's claim. And it is exactly that successful manipulation that motivated the Texas Resource Center to use that tactic over and over again.

"In Lockhart's twelfth-hour claim, the Resource Center indicated that 'the imminent execution date makes it virtually impossible to recruit qualified counsel. Few attorneys will consider taking a case without some assurance that they can become familiar with the case and provide adequate representation before being faced with an execution date.'

"The issue thus squarely presented to the court was 'whether the defendant has justified his request for a stay to enable counsel to be found to represent him or whether his current status is the result of a deliberate and calculated manipulation of the Texas criminal justice system.'

"Lockhart was represented on his direct appeal by Mr. Doug Barlow, who was appointed by the trial court in accordance with Texas law. After the Court of Criminal Appeals ruled against Lockhart, Mr. Barlow notified the Texas Resource Center on December 17, 1992, that he would not file a motion for rehearing.

"That very date, an attorney for the Resource Center filed a request with the Court of Criminal Appeals to permit a forty-five-day extension of the time in which to seek a re-hearing. An extension was granted by that court, and the Resource Center was given until February 1, 1993, to seek a rehearing.

"Resource Center attorneys filed their motion on February 2, 1993, and the court denied relief on February 24, 1993. During that period, Resource Center attorneys corresponded with Lockhart on several occasions and regularly visited him on death row. During each visit, they obtained permission to see him by signing a form that provided: 'I affirm that my visit with this inmate is for the purpose of assisting me in matters relating to the attorney-client relationship and no other purpose.'

"Correspondence and visits between Lockhart and Resource Center attorneys continued on a regular basis. On July 2, 1993, the trial court set the execution date for November 23, 1993, specifically providing Lockhart almost five months to file any additional claims he may have. Death row received the execution order on July 13, and the very next day he was visited by a Resource Center attorney.

"During the next five months, Lockhart and Resource Center attorneys continued to visit and correspond.

"On November 19, 1993, the Resource Center notified the trial court that they had found an attorney in Washington, D.C., who would agree to represent Lockhart, but only if (1) he was to be paid $50 per hour with no limitation on the number of hours charged; (2) he was to receive expenses for 7 to 10 trips to Texas for himself and either his cocounsel or paralegal; (3) that cocounsel be appointed at the same rate of pay; (4) that a full-time paralegal be appointed; (5) that he be paid monthly; and (6) that he receive an execution delay of six months to permit him to prepare and file motions on Lockhart's behalf.

"The trial court denied that request and found that the Texas Resource Center had deliberately and intentionally manipulated the system as a matter of strategy and not as the result of some legitimate misfortune.

"Specifically, the court found: 'By waiting until shortly before execution to request counsel and a stay, both the defendant and the Texas Resource Center are dangling his life in a perilous maneuver deliberately contrived to pressure the legal system to delay his execution. The defendant is in an emergency he and the Texas Resource Center created, and this type of manipulation should not be permitted to prevail in any Texas or Federal Court.'

"The court concluded: 'The status of the Texas Resource Center cannot, like the tide, roll in and roll out when it suits their purpose. They either represent someone or they don't. If they don't, then they should not be heard on any issue, as they have no standing. If they do, then they should be held to the same "effective representation" standards they so often use against others. And effective representation certainly requires that legal issues be addressed in a timely and orderly manner.

" 'Their deliberate strategic plans have resulted in many other defendants receiving a stay [of execution]. In fact, a stay under these circumstances has become virtually automatic and the expectations of defendants and the Texas Resource Center have been fulfilled. As long as courts continue to permit defendants and the Texas Resource Center to manipulate the orderly administration of justice, they will continue to successfully do so.

"This court does not and will not approve of such dilatory actions that cause the disruption of the judicial system. The motion for stay is hereby denied, and the court strongly urges that the Court of Criminal Appeals and the Federal Courts do likewise. To do otherwise will permit this type of sham to perpetuate, proliferate, and continue to bring discredit and disrespect to our legal system.'

"The same day the trial court entered its order, the Texas Court of Criminal Appeals refused to stay Lockhart's execution. Resource Center attorneys went immediately to a federal district court in San Antonio, which immediately entered an order stopping Lockhart's execution. The federal court also appointed the Washington attorney to represent Lockhart on the same conditions mentioned previously, giving the attorney six months to review the facts of the case and six more months to file an application for habeas corpus.

"As of now, that's where Lockhart's Texas case remains. Under federal law, the federal district judge may grant Lockhart a new trial or order that another execution date be set. The losing side can then appeal to the Federal Fifth Circuit Court of Appeals. And whichever side loses there can then take the case again to the U.S. Supreme Court.

"If Lockhart loses at every stage, his execution may still be a legally distant event. That's because he can start all over again by seeking a stay of execution and habeas corpus relief from the trial court under the identical procedures that have already occurred—all the way back to the U.S. Supreme Court. Some defendants have made this legal trip as many as five times because the process can be used over and over again.

"However, there is some relief in sight. Texas has adopted new habeas corpus procedures in capital cases that are intended to significantly reduce the time involved. Congress is considering doing something similar in the federal court procedures.

"The Texas Board of Criminal Justice just adopted an amendment to their rules which will now permit up to five relatives of the capital crime victim to view the execution. For years Texas law has given the inmate the right to invite five people to watch the execution, but friends and relatives of the victim have been excluded. That disparity has now been officially corrected.

"Texas law has also been changed to now reflect that an execution shall occur at 'any time after 6 P.M. on the day set for execution by intravenous injection of a substance or substances in a lethal quantity sufficient to cause death and until such convict is dead.'

"After death, 'if the body is not delivered to a relative, bona fide friend, or the Anatomical Board of the State of Texas, the Director of the Department of Corrections shall cause the body to be decently buried and the fee not to exceed $25 for embalming shall be paid by the county in which the indictment which resulted in conviction was found.'

"That's a fee Jefferson County would gladly pay if the legal system will only provide the opportunity.

"The cost of prosecuting and defending Lockhart, prosecuting and defending his direct appeal, and addressing his current legal attacks will ultimately probably exceed $1 million. It costs Texas about $35,000 a year to keep him on death row. But all that pales when compared to the cost paid by Officer Paul Hulsey and his family.

"So far, the legal system has given Lockhart, and the Hulseys, a verdict. But only time and the state and federal appellate systems can ensure that the trial court death sentence is carried into effect. Then and only then will there be closure. Then and only then will there be justice."

Judge Larry Gist
15 November 1995

Author's Afterword

No one who was involved with the case has any doubt that Lockhart committed many more armed robberies and murdered more people than those detailed in this book. Lockhart himself has admitted it, promising both Robert Hobbs and Cheryl Colhouer that only when he "is strapped to the gurney" will he tell authorities the names of his other murder victims. Will he keep his word? Who can say? I personally believe that he dangles this incentive to keep these dedicated people hovering around him, and perhaps to try gaining yet another delay if and when he ever is finally "strapped to the gurney." The game is everything to Michael Lee Lockhart, and I cannot imagine any situation more pleasing to him than to be holding a trump card which he knows someone else desperately wants.

But you can help to spoil Lockhart's neverending games with other people's lives, other people's hearts. Robert Hobbs, who knows more about Lockhart's movements and motivations than probably anyone else on earth, has agreed that I can put this request in my book:

If you recognize Michael Lee Lockhart as having been in your town between 1983 and March 1988, and if you now realize that there is an unsolved murder, particularly of a girl or young woman, while he was there—contact your local police agency. Police officers who feel that Lockhart may be a viable suspect are invited to contact Cdr.

Robert Hobbs, in care of the Jefferson County Narcotics Task Force (409-722-7763) in Beaumont, Texas.

In closing, I feel I have gained many new, and hopefully lifelong, friends through my experiences with the writing of this book. To the Hulseys in Texas, the Gallaghers in Indiana, and the Colhouers in Florida, I grieve your losses and I hope I have given your loved ones the memorial and respect they deserve. To all the prosecutors in all three states who worked so long and so hard to put Lockhart away, you have my thanks and the thanks of everyone out here who has a family. And to all the police officers, I can only say this—as one cop to another, I salute you.

JSF

FROM BEST-SELLING AUTHOR
NOEL HYND!

A ROOM FOR THE DEAD
                    (Hardcover, 0-8217-4583-2, $18.95)
                    (Paperback, 0-7860-0089-9, $5.99)

Detective Sgt. Frank O'Hara should have seen it all in his twenty years as a state cop. But then he must deal with a grisly murder spree marked with the personal signature of a killer he sent to the electric chair years ago. If it isn't Gary Ledbetter commiting these murders, then who can it be? Is it someone beyond the grave—a demon from Hell come to exact a chilling retribution against his executioners? Or is Frank losing his mind, his sanity slipping beneath grueling pressure and the burden of guilt and rage carried by every good cop . . .

GHOSTS   (0-8217-4359-7, $4.99)

For Academy Award-winning actress Annette Carlson, Nantucket Island is the perfect refuge from a demanding career. For brilliant, burnt-out cop Tim Brooks, it's a chance to get away from the crime-ridden streets of the big city. And for Reverend George Osaro, ghost hunter, it is about to become a place of unspeakable terror . . .

WHETHER IT'S A CRIME OF PASSION
OR
A COLD-BLOODED MURDER—
PINNACLE'S GOT THE TRUE STORY!

CRUEL SACRIFICE   (884, $4.99)
by Aphrodite Jones

This is a tragic tale of twisted love and insane jealousy, occultism and sadistic ritual killing in small-town America . . . and of the young innocent who paid the ultimate price. One freezing night five teenage girls crowded into a car. By the end of the night, only four of them were alive. One of the most savage crimes in the history of Indiana, the four accused murderers were all girls under the age of eighteen!

BLOOD MONEY   (773, $4.99)
by Clifford L. Linedecker

One winter day in Trail Creek, Indiana, seventy-four-year-old Elaine Witte left a Christmas party—and was never heard from again. Local authorities became suspicious when her widowed daughter-in-law, Hilma, and Hilma's two sons gave conflicting stories about her disappearance . . . then fled town. Driven by her insane greed for Witte's social security checks, Hilma had convinced her teenage son to kill his own grandmother with a crossbow, and then he fed her body parts to their dogs!

CONTRACT KILLER   (788, $4.99)
by William Hoffman and Lake Headley

He knows where Jimmy Hoffa is buried—and who killed him. He knows who pulled the trigger on Joey Gallo. And now, Donald "Tony the Greek" Frankos—pimp, heroin dealer, loan shark and hit man for the mob—breaks his thirty year oath of silence and tells all. His incredible story reads like a who's who of the Mafia in America. Frankos has killed dozens of people in cold blood for thousands of dollars!

X-RATED   (780, $4.99)
by David McCumber

Brothers Jim and Artie Mitchell were the undisputed porn kings of America. Multi-millionaires after such mega-hit flicks as BEHIND THE GREEN DOOR, theirs was a blood bond that survived battles with the mob and the Meese Commission, bitter divorces, and mind-numbing addictions. But their world exploded in tragedy when seemingly mild-mannered Jim gunned down his younger brother in cold blood. This is a riveting tale of a modern day Cain and Abel!

Available wherever paperbacks are sold, or order direct from the Publisher. Send cover price plus 50¢ per copy for mailing and handling to Penguin USA, P.O. Box 999, c/o Dept. 17109, Bergenfield, NJ 07621. Residents of New York and Tennessee must include sales tax. DO NOT SEND CASH.